D0994497

EDUCATION STUDIES

stu
ivc
d P.

ren

ne
123

ne

EDUCATION STUDIES

Essential Issues

Edited by
Steve Bartlett and Diana Burton

SAGE Publications
London ● Thousand Oaks ● New Delhi

Editorial Material © Steve Bartlett and Diana Burton 2003

Chapter 1 © Steve Bartlett and Diana Burton 2003

Chapter 2 © Helen Moylett 2003

Chapter 3 © Diana Burton 2003

Chapter 4 © Peter Clough and Philip Garner 2003

Chapter 5 © Dean Garratt 2003

Chapter 6 © Steve Bartlett and Diana Burton 2003

Chapter 7 © James Avis 2003

Chapter 8 © Anne-Marie Bathmaker 2003

Chapter 9 © Steve Bartlett 2003

Chapter 10 © Tim Wright 2003

Chapter 11 © John Robinson 2003

First published 2003

Apart from any fair dealing for the purposes of research
or private study, or criticism or review, as permitted
under the Copyright, Designs and Patents Act, 1988, this
publication may be reproduced, stored or transmitted
in any form, or by any means, only with the prior
permission in writing of the publishers, or in the case of
reprographic reproduction, in accordance with the terms
of licences issued by the Copyright Licensing Agency.
Inquiries concerning reproduction outside those terms
should be sent to the publishers.

 SAGE Publications Ltd
6 Bonhill Street
London EC2A 4PU

SAGE Publications Inc
2455 Teller Road
Thousand Oaks, California 91320

SAGE Publications India Pvt Ltd
32, M-Block Market
Greater Kailash - I
New Delhi 110 048

Library of Congress Control Number: 2002109968

A catalogue record for this book is available from the
British Library

ISBN 0 7619 4049 9
ISBN 0 7619 4050 2 (pbk)

Typeset by Pantek Arts Ltd, Maidstone, Kent
Printed in Great Britain by Athenaeum Press, Gateshead

Contents

Contents

List of Contributors

James Avis taught sociology in further education before moving to Oxford Brookes University where he taught educational studies. He has since moved to the University of Wolverhampton where he is Professor of Education Studies. His research interests are focused around post-compulsory education and training, its policy contextualization as well as its political economy. He co-authored *Education Limited* and *Knowledge and Nationhood* (Cassell, 1996). His work has been published in journals such as the *Journal of Educational Policy* and *British Journal of Educational Studies*.

Steve Bartlett was a social studies teacher and head of department in a large comprehensive school before becoming an area co-ordinator for the Technical Vocational Educational Initiative in the late 1980s. He has since worked as senior lecturer at Wolverhampton University where he became subject leader for education studies. He is currently Reader in Education at Chester College of Higher Education. His areas of research and publication include the professional development of teachers, action research, teacher appraisal and education studies. His work has been published in such journals as the *British Journal of Educational Studies* and the *Journal of In-Service Education*. He has conducted several small-scale evaluation projects within education Action Zones and is co-author of *Introduction to Education Studies* (Paul Chapman, 2001) which introduces many of the issues that are developed further in this book.

Ann-Marie Bathmaker is a lecturer at the University of Sheffield. She started her career in education as an English as a second language teacher, later becoming a local authority co-ordinator for the Technical and Vocational Education Initiative. She worked at the University of Wolverhampton for six years, becoming Principal Lecturer with responsibility for teaching and learning. Her areas of research and publication include policy and practice in post-compulsory education and training, teacher and learner identity, young people's transitions, and qualifications and training for teaching and learning professionals.

Diana Burton was a humanities teacher and head of year in a large comprehensive school until the late 1980s. She has since worked in teacher education at Manchester Metropolitan University where she was Head of Education Programmes. Now Dean of the Faculty of Education, Community and Leisure at Liverpool John Moores University, her areas of research and publication include differentiation and cognitive style, identity issues within teacher education and the professional development of teachers. She has published in journals such as the *Journal of Education for Teaching* and the *British Journal of Educational Psychology*. She has contributed to books on teacher education and is co-author of *Introduction to Education Studies* (Paul Chapman, 2001).

Peter Clough taught for many years in mainstream and special schools before moving to the School of Education at the University of Sheffield, where he is Director of Continuing Professional Development and a core member of the Inclusion and Equality Research Centre. He has authored and edited a number of books on special and inclusive education and is particularly occupied with the dissemination of research findings through biographical and fictional forms of ethnographic inquiry; some of this work appears in his recent *Narratives and Fictions in Educational Research* (Open University Press, 2002).

Philip Garner has taught in mainstream and special schools in Coventry, Lancashire and London for 17 years. He was formerly Reader and Director of research at Brunel University and is now Research Professor (Special Educational Needs) at Nottingham Trent University. He has published widely in the fields of SEN, inclusion, children's behaviour and teacher education. He is currently Chair of a DfES Regional Partnership task group and was awarded a British Academy Fellowship in 2002. He is a co-author of a forthcoming international handbook on children who experience emotional and behavioural difficulties (Sage, 2004).

Dean Garrett is a research fellow in the Research and Graduate School of the Institute of Education at the Manchester Metropolitan University. Since completing his doctoral thesis five years ago, he has written about issues concerning qualitative research methodology, curriculum and citizenship. He is currently a member of a team working on an empirical project funded by the Joint Information Systems Committee (JISC), exploring issues of professional development within the context of ICT.

Helen Moylett was a junior, infant, nursery and home–school liaison teacher in primary schools in Manchester. She was then a senior advisory teacher and, more recently, a senior lecturer in education studies and early years at Manchester Metropolitan University. She was Chair of Stockport Early Years Development and Childcare Partnership from 1998 to 2000. Since 2000 she has been Head of Tamworth early Years Centre in Staffordshire. Her areas of research and publication include provision for the under-threes, leadership and management in the early years and working with parents and carers.

John Robinson taught sociology in a sixth form college in north-west England. He has worked in teacher education since the mid-1980s. He is now Head of Research Programmes, Institute of Education, Manchester Metropolitan University. His main research areas include education for sustainable futures and evaluation research. He is the co-editor (with Tony Shallcross) of *Global Citizenship and Environmental Ethics: Probing the Boundaries/At the Interface* (Rodopi, 2002) and editor of *Diversity and Difference: Paradigms of Educational Research* (Ashgate, 2003).

Tim Wright is currently Senior Lecturer in the School of Education at Chester College of Higher Education. Following an initial career as a dentist, he began primary teaching in 1975, held posts as head-teacher of two primary schools and entered teacher education in the early 1990s. He has held a variety of positions in higher education, including Associate Dean of the School of Education at Chester College of Higher Education. Tim's research is in the area of education and development.

1

The Study of Education

Steve Bartlett and Diana Burton

This chapter outlines the development of education as an area of study. Key theoretical issues and areas for investigation are raised and the development of a critical approach is emphasized.

What is education studies?

This is a difficult question to answer in any precise manner. In the editors' experience, education studies is made up of a variety of components. In what proportion and with what particular emphasis depends upon the perspective of the definer (see Bartlett et al., 2001, for a discussion of such issues). Education studies, as with all areas of knowledge, is contested by various interested parties. It is worth noting that the Quality Assurance Agency (QAA) has developed benchmarks for education studies in higher education. These cannot be considered in any way definitive. They are another viewpoint amongst many, and QAA itself had difficulty in deciding exactly what the benchmarks should include and how they should be written. What the development of these benchmarks does indicate is that education is now such an important area of study that it warrants attention by the national body that monitors standards of subject teaching in higher education (HE).

Whilst accepting that there can be no single definition of education studies, let us consider what it should, could and often does contain. There is a need to question the nature and purposes of education, to engage in continuing dialogue about what education is, what an educational experience should involve, why education is so often considered a 'good' thing, what its purposes are for individuals and for society.

Some analyses of education focus upon the education of the individual and involve such notions as the development of the mind, reasoning and the mental processes involved in cognitive development. Others focus upon content and what should be learnt as part of the educative process. These consider knowledge, its organization and appropriateness to learners. Both these approaches lead us to a further focus which is the relationship of education to society. One view here, for example, is that we are educated by society to play our part in that society. This approach emphasizes the notion of education being important for the inculcation of values and the maintenance of social stability. Without it – what might at times be construed as a certain level of higher control or at others as a degree of social consensus – society would collapse into lawlessness and chaos. Of course, a Marxist view sees education systems operating primarily as agencies of the state. They are there to inculcate the values of the capitalist system, legitimate inequality and ensure a passive workforce.

A liberal educationalist takes a more central position and argues that the purposes of education are to promote individual development whilst also developing a respect for others. This fits well with a social democratic ideology which holds that a combination of individual rights and responsibilities is a central tenet of a liberal democracy. There are many ideological standpoints on the purposes of education (see Bartlett et al., 2001) and these have implications for all aspects of the education process, such as how learning should be organized, what counts as appropriate content and how progress and achievement should be assessed.

What becomes apparent to the student of education at an early stage is the political nature of the process. Education plays a significant part in the development of the young and therefore in future generations of our society. Even though everyone in the system, from the prime minister to the classroom teacher, claims to be interested in the good of the pupils/students and wishes to keep politics out of the classroom, this is, of course, not possible given the ideologically vested nature of the whole education process. There are always significant arguments concerning what should be taught (curriculum content), how it should be taught (for instance, whether individualized through online learning packages, in mixed or setted groups or through lecture or activity methods) and to whom it should be taught (considering equality of opportunity issues, access to different forms of education, the legitimacy of excluding pupils/students). There are political decisions to be made at all levels, from what happens in the individual classroom in a small rural school, to the formation of national policy in the seats of power, to international aid programmes involving education. It is interesting to consider the various groups who take part in the making of these decisions and the power wielded at different points. Politicians, teachers, parents, employers and even the pupils/students themselves are all involved and have differing degrees of influence over the process.

Who studies education?

The study of education was undertaken by large numbers of students between the 1950s and 1970s largely as part of their three-year teacher training courses. When teaching became an all-graduate profession courses were lengthened to four years and became Bachelor of Education degrees. In this way they were able to incorporate degree-level study, of which education studies was a significant component. At this time Bachelor of Science and Arts degrees were not usually modularized and students took one or sometimes two subjects over a three-year course. Education was not a widely offered degree subject and it was generally confined to a component of a major discipline area such as philosophy, sociology, psychology or history (see McCulloch, 2002, for a discussion of the disciplines contributing to the study of education). Within the BEd courses the study of education was usually broken down into the separate areas of philosophy of education, sociology of education, history of education and educational psychology, each of which was studied separately from pedagogy.

From the 1970s onwards, often with the aid of in-service funding for practising teachers, education came to be studied more widely at Masters level. This added to the size and status of schools of education at universities and polytechnics. At the same time, as a consequence of the reorganization and rationalization of HE provision, the old colleges of education found themselves shut down, became free-standing colleges of HE or were subsumed into the poly-technics. Thus schools or departments of education assumed greater stature within many HE institutions. The study of education was at this point considered to be primarily about teacher training and concerned exclusively with schooling (i.e. compulsory education).

From the mid-1970s onwards, when Labour Prime Minister, James Callaghan, made the landmark Ruskin speech, publicly funded education came under increasing criticism, and pressure for reform and calls for greater accountability of the teaching profession grew. The curriculum and standards of teaching were increasingly placed under the spotlight. There was concern about what was being taught to pupils, the teaching methods employed, which were seen as too progressive, and the increasing indiscipline which was apparently occurring in schools (see Bartlett et al., 2001). The curriculum issue was 'solved' by removing control of what was taught away from the teachers through the introduction of a National Curriculum from 1988 onwards. Teaching methods became greatly influenced by the need to ensure that pupils achieved good results in the National Curriculum assessments, especially since league tables of school performance were published. The introduction of regular school inspections through the 1993 Education Act increased the external constraints on teachers and schools. The preparation of teachers for the classroom was also examined and 'reformed' (Furlong, 2001). Emphasis was now placed upon the training of how to teach rather than on the discrete study of education. The previous 'academic' approach was alleged to have failed to prepare trainee teachers for their future role adequately. Sociology and psychology were seen as subversive influences and philosophy as an irrelevance to classroom teaching. In this way old teacher training courses and the academics teaching on them could be blamed for contributing to the crisis of low standards of achievement and even for the declining standards of behaviour in society generally (Cox and Dyson, 1969).

In the 1980s and 1990s great changes were made in initial teacher training (ITT). The academic study of education was marginalized in what Crook (2002) characterizes as a sustained attack upon the theoretical aspects of educational studies. Sets of competencies which students had to achieve were developed. These itemized skills were rooted in classroom practice with students spending a great deal more time in schools. Regular inspection of initial teacher training (ITT) provision ensured 'compliance' with the competencies, later known as standards (DfEE, 1998). Partnerships between schools and HE were developed which enhanced the integration of theory and practice. However, many would argue that this was at the expense of deeper questioning and analysis of education.

Since the 1990s there has been a growing demand by students to study education. However these are not teacher training students. Education studies has become increasingly important as an area of study within the modular degree programmes of the 'new universities' and colleges of HE. Students are now able to study modules in education as part of their first degree. Education studies may make up a large enough portion of their studies to be a named subject in their award or they may just take several education modules in their first or second year as subsidiaries to their main subjects. These 'new' students of education wish to study the system in which they have been involved as a learner and, though a number may wish to become teachers later, many do not. Their aim is to develop an analytical understanding of what education means rather than to be trained in the mechanics of classroom control. It is worth noting that a high proportion of students of education studies are expecting to pursue careers in a range of areas, such as industrial management, personnel, social services and marketing, and see their study of education as applicable to employment in these areas.

A number of other study areas such as early childhood studies, special needs and inclusion, and youth studies have also been developing rapidly alongside education studies within HE departments of education. These reflect the academic expertise that exists in these departments and also how degree-level study is broadening to consider newly developing professional groups and expanding areas of employment.

The aims of this volume

Education studies programmes often begin with more general modules that introduce the student to the major concerns or purposes of education, theories of learning, sociological aspects of educational achievement and some historical consideration of the change and development of education systems. Students then go on to choose specialist modules that look in more depth at particular areas. The difficulty for any student is in relating the fundamental issues learnt in the introductory modules to the specialist modules. Modules can often be treated as separate units of study with their own assessment rather than stressing the overarching and inter-related issues within the study of education. This is not to advocate some kind of neat functionalist view where all parts of an education system dovetail neatly together. On the contrary, the conflicting views around aspects of education, such as content, assessment, opportunity and pedagogy, are well known. However, it is helpful to avoid the tendency to think only within modules. Students need to explore education at what Ball (1987) identified as the macro, meso and micro levels and to be aware of interaction between the levels. The very partitioning of the curriculum into neat packages, which has facilitated the development of education studies, encourages an approach whereby students often consider only the immediate assignment. They can become overly concerned with the knowledge required for the assignment, avoiding anything that does not at first appear to be directly linked to the module title. What we wish to nurture through this text is an approach that is broad and explores theoretical links whilst still looking at particular areas in depth.

In this volume we have deliberately chosen to look at areas that are the most popular in education studies programmes – what could be termed the 'hot spots'. Each of these has its own particular issues, developments and debates as each inevitably relates to political and social concerns. The chapters deal with their own areas of interest in a self-contained way, outlining key themes and arguments. In reading the whole book, readers can see and make the connections between the chapters, thus developing both their overall understanding of education as well as of the individual topic areas.

By its nature the study of education is influenced by, and provides commentary on, the issues and concerns which characterize policy and practice at the time of study. This allows the authors to do two things. First, they can analyse past issues within their topic area with the benefit of both hindsight and the knowledge of how these issues have impacted on current trends. Thus they are able to comment upon developments in a systematic way that is imbued with both their own perspectives and those of the analysts and researchers they refer to. Secondly, the authors are able to inform readers of this book of the very latest developments in their areas of discussion. This might be events, policy, practices, legislation, but all are contextualized within contemporary socio-political frames of reference and are analysed through the particular lens and discourse used by commentators on the subject or selected by the author. To this extent, books of this type have a degree of in-built redundancy for their purpose in building arguments and analyses is for others to review, amend and develop them in the light of new events or perspectives. As student readers it is your job to synthesize information from the chapters with that from other sources, adding your own voice to the analysis of the issues.

It is possible to organize the approach to the study of education in any number of ways. We could start with the young child and follow the pupil through the system chronologically. Alternatively we could look at the individual, then the organizational, the national and then beyond into the global. Or the book could be divided into compulsory and post-compulsory education. Some important areas of study, such as citizenship, differentiation, special needs and inclusion, the nature of teaching and lifelong learning, straddle the aforementioned categories.

Constructing education studies, then, is a controversial process and though we, the editors, have done it ourselves in organizing this text, it is debatable to what extent the contributing authors would agree with our creation. To exemplify, if one looks closely at the government discourse around its major legislative proposals, the 'story' that it creates to support its plans is, according to the Centre for Public Policy Research (2002), an exercise in the obfuscation of fundamental questions about the purposes of education. Their commentary was in relation specifically to the government white paper *Schools Achieving Success* (DfES, 2001). It is argued that the white paper's discourse creates hegemonic status for the 'truth' that it conveys about the successes that previous Labour government reforms have achieved (p. 24). In using phrases such as 'successful schools' and polarizing these with 'failing' ones the paper creates an image that schools either succeed or fail with no shades of grey, ambiguities or alternative explanations (p.16). Thus we see that in creating texts and discourses as authors and editors we are similarly developing and directing meanings.

It is expected that, in a reader such as this, students will pick and choose chapters as appropriate. In reading several chapters, readers will discover that, although the chapters are written by different authors analysing their specialist areas, certain significant issues seem persistently to rise to the surface, such as the significance of market forces, equal opportunities and individual choice, the role of the state in controlling and monitoring education, a preoccupation with cost effectiveness and standards, and increasing global movements which operate beyond the scope of individual state boundaries.

Key issues in education studies

We begin this volume with Helen Moylett's consideration of early childhood education. There is currently a rapid expansion of provision for the very young and concomitantly the development of associated employment opportunities. This has resulted in the development of courses to prepare new employees and the publishing of relevant new texts. Whilst frequently neglected in the past there is now more interest in the whole nature of early childhood, how children develop and appropriate forms of education for young children. This growing interest in the content and nature of early childhood education is reflected in increased political involvement. Provision has become more formal at an earlier age and there is pressure to use the early years to prepare for the strictures of the National Curriculum. Experience in literacy, numeracy and basic formal learning is increasingly being presented as a way of helping young children prepare to engage with the National Curriculum and its assessment. Thus the education of even the youngest children is subsumed within the drive to raise standards, modernize education and, ultimately, develop the labour force.

This contrasts with other approaches which hold play and the development of the individual child to be central. The aim here is to keep education for the young child informal and for it to be based upon freedom of expression and experimentation for as long as possible. Chapter 2 shows how even in these initial stages education can involve tensions between this self-development of the individual and external direction or control.

The following three chapters on differentiation of schooling and pedagogy, special needs and education, and citizenship for social justice apply with equal relevance to all sectors of education. Chapter 3 explores both the growth of differentiated instructional and assessment practices and the structural features of schooling policy which serve to create differentiated systems for pupils and students. Taking developments in the UK over the past decade, the emergence of differentiation as a discrete set of pedagogic strategies is analysed. Diana Burton discusses a range of research conducted during the 1990s into the educational achievement of pupils when calls for differentiated classroom approaches were at their height. This is contextualized within the changes taking place to the content and assessment of the National Curriculum and the publishing of league tables of examination results. Current legislative developments and proposals are outlined, including the creation of specialist schools, the establishment of an academy for the gifted and talented and changes to the 14–19 curriculum. These issues are set against the backcloth of competition for places in education and, later, for employment. The chapter highlights the conflict between viewing differentiation as a means of catering equally for every individual student's needs and as a means of preparing pupils for their future place in a stratified society.

Looking at special needs in education, Peter Clough and Philip Garner examine what is meant by the term special needs and how our understanding of the concept has altered over time. Chapter 4 considers learning, physical, emotional and behavioural difficulties in particular. Changes in the type and status of educational provision for those with special needs are evaluated alongside the policies of inclusion which form a central part of current government policy. These encourage the participation of all regardless of difference. The chapter reveals, however, that changes in provision may, whilst using the rhetoric of inclusion, be continuing to reinforce former divisions.

Citizenship is very topical at present, with the current government committed to it becoming a compulsory National Curriculum subject from September 2002. In Chapter 5 we see that citizenship is a complex social construct that can be interpreted in different ways. It may stress the active involvement of individuals in the development of their society and encourage constructive criticism. However, on the other hand, to be a good citizen may be seen to involve obedience, unquestioning loyalty to the state and being prepared to play one's part in ensuring the continuation of the social 'consensus'. Thus education systems may be considered to promote individual freedom and responsibility or they may be regarded as an apparatus of state control. Due to the myriad of interpretations and uses to which the concept of citizenship can be put, Dean Garratt emphasizes in this chapter that too simplistic an analysis of citizenship is always likely to be inadequate.

All sectors of education underwent substantial change in the second half of the twentieth century. The development of market forces in education, the introduction of new teaching and learning technologies and the call for more accountability in the public sector significantly affected the work of teachers. The changing nature of teacher professionalism and the development of new management cultures in schools is examined in Chapter 6. Here, Steve Bartlett and Diana Burton explore how the professional status of teachers is currently being promoted by politicians. However, it is contended that the focus on achieving classroom targets based upon pupil performance has led to a more technicist approach to teaching and a more restricted form of professionalism than existed previously. Certainly the work of teachers is now focused in, rather than beyond, the classroom.

Chapter 7 considers associated issues within the curriculum for 16–18-year-olds. James Avis analyses the rapid increase in demand for post-16 education, the nature of an academic/vocational divide in the sector resulting from high-status A-levels and low-status vocational qualifications, and developments which have taken place in order to resolve these issues. Rather than being primarily concerned with the detail of changes to systems, the chapter analyses the political rhetoric that emphasizes the need to develop a highly skilled, adaptable workforce in order to remain competitive in world markets against the reality of low-skills training for a low-skills economy. A model comprising Fordism, post-Fordism and neo-Fordism is used to evaluate developments in post-compulsory education. It is at this point that world economic developments appear to be a useful means of justification for policy by national governments.

Pursuing the perceived political necessity to educate more of the population to higher levels for economic reasons, Anne-Marie Bathmaker (in Chapter 8) considers the expansion of higher education, reviewing the change in philosophy in England from Robbins to Dearing. Alongside the need to open up higher education (HE) to a greater proportion of the population there is the question of who pays for it. This was not such a problem when comparatively small numbers of students could be supported by state grants in their studies as undergraduates. It is much more of an issue in a mass system where the majority of young people are expected to partake of some form of HE. The problem for the politicians has been how to expand student numbers whilst keeping costs as low as possible yet not compromising the quality of the education received. The political solution to this issue has resulted in massive change in the nature of the student experience and academic life. The chapter charts the rapid expansion in student numbers that has been achieved largely by the increasing control of successive governments over HE through funding of universities and colleges, the development of competition between increasingly diverse providers of HE and the introduction of student loans and fees. Once again we are left considering if such change heralds the opening up of opportunity for all sections of society or if the same old divisions remain largely unaltered.

Following on from the analyses of post-compulsory and higher education, Steve Bartlett (in Chapter 9) considers the process of lifelong learning, which is rapidly increasing in importance, at least in terms of political rhetoric. The concept of lifelong learning, and its development as an educational construct, draws together many of the issues discussed in previous chapters. A highly skilled, adaptable workforce is said to be needed to maintain and develop our competitive edge in world markets. Indeed, it is assumed that we now operate in a 'knowledge economy' in which continuous learning is of increasing value as changes in technology mean that there is a constant need for all to update skills. To fall behind in technological development would result in a low-skills, low-wage economy such as operates in the third world. Thus lifelong learning is a crucial part of Labour's modernization project. These vocational applications of lifelong learning link it closely to developments in post-compulsory education, HE and training. It is important, though, to realize that the term 'lifelong' means that it is relevant to all sectors of education and to learners of any age. The critical question is whether we are seeing the development of true lifelong learning for its own sake or if the whole policy is merely a sophisticated means of enforcing training and retraining on different sections of the population. Perhaps this is an example of how governments use the rhetoric of globalization, international capitalism and competition to develop their own education and training policies.

Up to this point we have considered educational developments as they relate to England, in particular, though, many of these can be applied more widely to other western industrial societies. In Chapter 10 education is examined as a positive force for development in third-world countries. However, Tim Wright also presents an alternative perspective showing that the 'exporting' of education from the 'developed' west leads to the domination of particular forms of knowledge and ideologies. From this second viewpoint education and knowledge are seen as a means by which colonial powers are able to maintain their hold over colonies or newly independent nations.

Having looked at a range of key areas of development in education it is clear that there were great changes in the last quarter of the twentieth century. What is apparent is the growing awareness of international transference of educational ideas and policies. Certainly the development of world markets and global competition has had considerable impact upon the lives of us all and on the policies of individual governments, particularly from the 1970s. In the final chapter (Chapter 11) John Robinson considers globalization and its impact upon education. He examines the meaning of the term globalization and how it is reflected in worldwide developments in education. Globalization is seen as a positive development for some groups signalling improved standards of living and increased wealth. For other sections of the world population, however, the impact of globalization has been more negative, bringing increased poverty and domination by international corporations.

In this volume we have examined a number of key issues in education studies. Though each chapter is looking at very different aspects of education there are a number of common threads that run through the book which students can analyse at different levels. In recognizing that we need to examine individual, organizational, national and global dimensions in our search for greater understanding, readers of this book can apply aspects of the authors' analyses to other educational settings, issues and developments. For instance, students may be interested in some of the issues which we have not been able to explore in this volume:

• The political drive within UK higher education for universities to select their mission as either teaching or research.

- The increasingly divisive effect on UK students of differential living costs between the north and south and the associated impact of the likely differential fee levels between old and new universities.
- The university in the community – links with local industry and regional economic development.
- The range of school-level initiatives designed to raise standards in areas of urban deprivation – e.g. Excellence in Cities (which have evolved from Education Action Zones), dissemination of best practice via advanced skills teachers and teacher sabbaticals for those working in challenging schools.
- The effect of integrationist policies within a pluralist society on ethnic and religious minorities' educational goals – for instance, the growth of single-faith schools and competing discourses around educational research (e.g. the emphasis on classroom-based research underpinned by a received view of 'effective' classroom practices competes with a problematizing approach wherein policy is critiqued rather than justified).
- The development of new thinking about how people learn, how brains function or how emotional intelligence impacts on educational performance.

References

Ball, S. (1987) *The Micro-politics of the School*. London: Routledge.

Bartlett, S., Burton, D. and Peim, N. (2001) *Introduction to Education Studies*. London: Paul Chapman.

Centre for Public Policy Research (2002) Achieving success? Discursive strategies and policy tensions in New Labour's white paper for schools. *Education and Social Justice*, 4(1): 15–25.

Cox, C.B. and Dyson, A.E. (eds) (1969) *Fight for Education: A Black Paper*. Manchester: Critical Quarterly Society.

Crook, D. (2002) Educational studies and teacher education. *British Journal of Educational Studies*, 50(1): 57–75.

DfEE (1998) *Teaching: High Status, High Standards, Requirements for Courses of Initial Teacher Training*. London: DFEE.

DfES (2001) *Schools Achieving Success*. Nottingham: DfES Publications.

Furlong, J. (2001) Reforming teacher education, re-forming teachers: accountability, professionalism and competence. In R. Philips and J. Furlong (eds) *Education, Reform and the State. Twenty–five Years of Politics, Policy and Practice*. London: RoutledgeFalmer.

McCulloch, G. (2002) Disciplines contributing to education? Education studies and the disciplines. *British Journal of Educational Studies*, 50(1): pp. 100–19.

2

Early Years Education and Care

Helen Moylett

A society can be judged by its attitude to its youngest children, not only in what is said about them but how this attitude is expressed in what is offered to them as they grow up (Goldschmied and Jackson, 1994: 1).

If we look at what is offered to young children in England[1] today we see a history of patchy provision, a huge investment by the present Labour government and some deeply ambivalent attitudes. This chapter outlines some of the recent history of education and care in the early years, explains what is happening now and explores some of the cultural attitudes to young children which underpin current provision. It investigates the way in which the curriculum may be subject to competing agendas, describes some of the key aspects of good early years practice and concludes by looking briefly at training issues.

Background and recent history – the politics of early years

In the past, 'early years' has been used to describe the ages 3–8 years. More recently it has been used in relation to the stages of learning and development from birth to 5 years old. This is how it is used here. In some of the literature provision for 3–5 years-olds is described as education, and provision for the under-threes as care, but here 'education' or 'education and care' are used in relation to provision for all children from birth to 5 years. Most early years practitioners would agree that education and care are inseparable in the early years and, indeed, the terms 'educare' and 'educarer' are sometimes used to indicate this. For readers who find themselves becoming confused by any other descriptors and acronyms used, a glossary of terms can be found at the end of the chapter.

Children between the ages of birth and 5 years learn more during these years than they ever will again. They may be found in many types of out-of-home provision – for example, a childminder's house, nursery school, family centre, community nursery, play-group, nursery class, reception class, pre-reception class, early years centre, private day nursery or crèche. Many children and their parents access more than one of these, often during the same day. It is not until children enter statutory compulsory education, officially the term during which they are 5 years, that they are all entitled to free provision every weekday during school hours.

McCalla et al. (2001: 6) group early years provision into three broad categories: first, education provision which employs qualified teachers and is a free entitlement; secondly, care for children in need which employs care or social workers and is also free; and, thirdly, childcare for working parents which is chosen and bought mainly from the private sector. This last category includes child-minding and private day nurseries. Central government has blurred distinctions between both provision and practitioners in ways which make it impossible to include only local education authority nurseries and schools in any consideration of early years education.

The Nursery Education Voucher scheme was introduced in 1996 by the then Conservative government. It sanctioned the idea of a market-led economy in the early years with the aim of giving parents purchasing power – a voucher worth up to £1,100. This could buy up to three terms of nursery education in validated provision. The scheme's most significant effect was the way in which it led to a redefinition of the term 'nursery education' in that it enabled all forms of preschool provision to be included in the scheme. This was consistent with the Conservative ideology of including the private and voluntary sector in meeting market demand. However this backfired to some extent as many small private and voluntary providers gave a less than warm welcome to the scheme because it enabled schools to admit children at the age of 4 years in order to benefit from the vouchers. When this duly happened, in many local authorities significant numbers of small playgroups and day nurseries had to close or provide more places for younger children in order to stay viable (places for younger children are more expensive because of higher staff:child ratios required and space and equipment needed).

The Labour government, which came to power in 1997, scrapped the unpopular nursery education voucher scheme but remained true to the ideology of including all providers under the funded early years umbrella. It also did nothing to prevent schools taking children into reception classes at the age of 4 years. So what was essentially an attempt to include private enterprise in mainstream early years provision led to a lowering of the school starting age and children entering the 'formal' school system even earlier.

Since 1997 the government has tried to ensure that eventually all parents will have access to affordable, flexible and wraparound (i.e. more than just nursery or school session time) childcare and education. All local authorities now have Early Years Development and Childcare Partnerships (EYDCP) that include representatives from all sectors and have responsibility for delivering the National Childcare Strategy. The partnership, whose lead officer works for the local authority, is responsible for drawing up and monitoring the local authority's early years development and childcare plan. The funding allocation for nursery education entitlement may be awarded to the maintained or private and voluntary sector. Providers have to be validated by the partnership to provide free places for 3 and 4-year-olds.

Clearly, deciding that a small playgroup that meets in a church hall may have equal educational status with a large nursery school whose environment, resources, staffing and levels of staff qualification are much better has all sorts of implications for children, parents and practitioners. How can parents be sure there is any real equality of provision? The government has sought to ensure some standardization of provision by the following measures:

- All forms of provision catering for 3–5-year-olds must deliver the Foundation Stage curriculum in accordance with the DfEE/QCA (2000) *Curriculum Guidance for the Foundation Stage* document.
- A qualified teacher must be 'involved' in all early years settings. (The precise level of involvement varies considerably – from being on site teaching every day to occasional visits.)
- All providers registered with the EYDCP are inspected by the new specialist early years directorate of the Office for Standards in Education (Ofsted).

(However, reception classes and nursery schools and classes are subject to Section 10 inspections – the same as primary and secondary schools.)

- All forms of provision must have at least 50 per cent of staff qualified to NVQ Level 2 or above. (This is much lower than the maintained sector where all staff are usually qualified to at least NVQ 3.)
- Each EYDCP is responsible for providing appropriate training for local staff.

It can therefore be seen that in many ways it is easier for the maintained sector – nursery schools, and nursery and reception classes in primary schools – to provide consistently high standards of education. Indeed, the fact that this is generally the case is borne out by recent reports from the longitudinal study being carried out by the Effective Provision of Preschool Education (EPPE) project (Sylva et al., 1999). However, the maintained sector caters mainly for 3–5-year-olds and there are thousands of children who are under 3 years of age being educated in the private and voluntary sector and it is not realistic to expect a huge expansion in maintained provision. The only huge expansion that has happened recently is in the private nursery sector with much of the growth being in large nursery chains. England has never opted for a standard form of local provision for every child unlike many other European countries. Although there is great diversity of provision the choices available are largely still dictated by parental income. As McCalla et al. (2001: 7) point out: 'The higher the income, the more options are available to a family, including transport to and from the service and nannies to bridge any gaps.' However it has been shown that even relatively advantaged middle-class parents may have difficulties (Vincent and Ball, 2001). Working Families Tax Credit and the Childcare Tax Credit, which can be seen as successors to the voucher scheme, go only a little way in already poor families.

These tax credit schemes are part of the government's strategy for fighting social exclusion which exists alongside its commitment to a marketplace in childcare and education for working parents. One way of providing affordable, flexible childcare and education and including even the most socially deprived is to provide a range of services for families under one roof. Since the early 1970s some local education authorities have financed early years centres which provide nursery education for 3–5-year-olds as well as social care and family support and a range of other services (see, for example, Makins, 1997). All these centres differ but typically have a staff team of headteacher with other teachers and nursery nurses employed in working with 3–5-year-olds and nursery nurses employed by social services working on family support programmes of various kinds (e.g. education and care for children under 3 years, parenting programmes, supervised contact). The centre will also be used by parents and carers and other members of the community for a range of courses and groups and may have health profession-als such as health visitors and community paediatricians running informal sessions. The underpinning philosophy is that the services provided are integrated and non-stigmatized and easily accessible to local people. Most of these centres are in areas of high social dep-rivation. Since 1997 the Labour government has given status to these centres by designating some of them 'Early Excellence Centres'. The aim is that there will be 100 of these by 2004. The idea is that they will be spread around England and will have a role in working with all local providers to ensure good-quality childcare and education.

Another very important element in the government's fight against social exclusion is the Sure Start initiative. This is targeted at the poorest areas and, like early years centres, brings profession-als together to work with local parents of children from before birth to 4 years. The 500 Sure Start programmes that are planned by 2006 aim to improve young children's life chances by concentrating on community needs, maternal health, emotional and social develop-ment and access to play and learning. Many early years providers are involved in Sure Start programmes.

These initiatives recognize the interconnectedness of various dif-ferent aspects of children's lives – for instance, that children who are hungry or abused when they come to nursery will not find it easy to learn – as well as the importance of a multi-professional approach. However, one might question how much the govern-ment is able, or wishes, to avoid the constraints of the British class system. Polly Toynbee, a New Labour supporter, questioned the meaning attributed to 'family' in 1998: 'Family for the Tories was anti-sex and moral control. For Labour it's a code for poor families failing to survive, a language for helping families without stigmatis-ing them. "Family" and "parenting" sounds like everyone – but Labour really means "them" not "us"' (*Guardian*, 24 July 1998). One might claim that there is nothing wrong with wanting to help those less fortunate than oneself – many great human advances have happened as a result but so has much disastrous missionary work. A deficit model implies that the disadvantaged have to change because they need to know better while the middle-class establishment has no need for self-examination. If we take this sentence and substitute 'children' for 'the disadvantaged' and 'adults' for 'the middle-class establishment' it may facilitate understanding of how, in spite of much research and evidence to the contrary, we persist in maintaining a deficit model of children and their care and education.

Thinking about children

One has only to glance at some common assumptions about childhood to see what underpins many taken-for-granted ways of relating to children and how these assumptions also inform the provision that is made for them. From the moment a baby is born he or she is being socially and culturally constructed. As James and Prout (1990: 7) point out: 'The immaturity of children is a biological fact of life but the ways in which this immaturity is understood and made meaningful is a fact of culture.' Parents receive cards congratulating them on their new arrival. Some of these cards will be colour coded – pink for a girl, blue for a boy. These gender-specific cards often include hearts and flowers and appropriately saccharine sentiments to accompany them – welcome to your baby boy, a bundle of unending joy. On the mantelpiece alongside these rose-tinted views will be the cartoon cards depicting the new arrival as a screeching sleep depriver into whose hungry maw the parents will be pouring money, food and effort for at least the next 18 years. Even at this early stage contradictory stereotypes begin to be established.

The first question new parents are often asked is 'is/he or she good?' Can babies be good – or bad? This is not the place to investigate the moral theology of this question but the idea of original sin still underpins much taken-for-granted thinking. One does not have to look far to see that British culture is full of notions of the inherent wickedness of children. We even call them 'little devils'. I have seen a day nursery with this title and others like Scallywags and Cheeky Monkeys. Alongside this there are plenty more with titles like Little Cherubs and Honeybuns – again reflecting the polarized nice or naughty views of the birth congratulations cards!

Of course that question 'is he or she good?' is really shorthand
for 'does he or she let you get any sleep and is he or she quiet?' and
establishes early on the notion that a quiet child equals a good
child. The Victorian notion that children should be seen and not
heard is not dead! This denial of the voice of the child and his or
her power to change the way adults might think and act as a result
of being able to interact and empathize with him or her is seen in
all sorts of ways, both in family life and in the education system. In
its most extreme form it sanctions abusive behaviour. Smacking is
OK because young children are not yet reasonable and must be
brought into line by treatment that would be deeply offensive to
another adult – and of course they cannot retaliate. Nursery staff
can talk about children literally over their heads because 'they
don't understand' – perhaps they do not know the meaning of the
words, but even very young babies are sensitive to tone of voice
and atmosphere.

We know from much recent research that the ideas prevalent
during most of the last century about the absolute egocentricity of
young children are flawed. Which means that one deficit model –
that children are empty vessels waiting to be filled with knowledge
and rationality by adults – is looking ever more unsound. Piaget's
famous experiments have been challenged by Donaldson (1981)
and others for being decontextualized and for concentrating on
what children cannot do (the deficit model again) rather than what
they can do. When Donaldson replicated some of his experiments
using contexts with meaning to the children they were seen to be
more competent than Piaget had allowed. Trevarthen (1992) has
investigated the ways in which babies seem to be 'programmed' to
make sense of the world in which they find themselves. These and
other ideas such as those of Kessen (1979) and Morss (1996) challenge received ideas 'that children have certain characteristics, that
adults have others, and that it is natural to grow from one to the
other' (Morss, 1996: 29). Gopnik et al.'s (1999) fascinating studies
show children developing a theory of mind (i.e. understanding that
another person may have different likes and dislikes from themselves by the age of 18 months). They also talk about babies and
young children using the same strategies as scientists – observing,
formulating theories, making predictions and doing experiments.
As David (1999: 87) says: 'It would appear that young children
have dispositions to learn different things, that they are not

simply bundles of biological urges slowly being transformed, as they pass through universal pre-set stages of development, until they become fully formed humans as adults.'

We are finally beginning to realize that the years before 3 are where the real foundations of healthy dispositions to learning are developed and that very young children are neither deeply deficient nor dependent. Although as David (ibid.) goes on to claim: 'The idea of babies and young children as people with the capacity to learn and the need to relate to others in meaningful ways, not as objects or possessions who should be mainly restricted to their own homes with only their own mothers for company, remains largely unrecognised.' David's claim would seem to be borne out by the fact that the curriculum guidance for 3–5-year-olds introduced in 2000 is called guidance for the Foundation Stage! The period from birth to 3 years old must surely be the real foundation stage. What happens in the womb and during those first three years lays the foundations for all other learning and development.

Alongside the research there has been a recent growth in the number of books and training materials directly targeted at those who work with the under-threes (Goldschmied and Jackson, 1994; Abbott and Moylett, 1997a; 1997b; Lindon, 1999; Manning-Morton and Thorpe, 2000; Bruce, 2001) All these texts urge practitioners to see children's development holistically (i.e. not to compartmentalize children's learning into either developmental milestone or curriculum subject boxes).

Developmental milestones are found in charts telling parents and practitioners when they can expect certain events to take place, one of the most well-known being Sheridan. Such charts divide development into areas and emphasize biological aspects such as gross and fine motor skills, sensory development, cognitive and language development. These may be very useful when checking that all is well, celebrating progress and planning special help but tend to ignore the idea of what is now termed the 'contextualized' child. As Meggitt and Sutherland (2000) explain in the introduction to their book which takes Sheridan's normative approach and sets it in a more holistic context: 'The different areas of development are inter-related. The ideas, language, communication, feelings, relationships and other cultural elements among which each child is brought up influence his or her development profoundly.' Again these approaches challenge the idea of the child as passive and irrational.

Children are whole people from the start who live in different socio-cultural contexts. It can be helpful to focus on one area of development but it is not useful to isolate thinking about this from other areas and from other knowledge about the child. Children seem to go through the same stages of development but will vary in the ways in which they do so and milestones can be very misleading for this reason.

The basis of the early years curriculum

It was only in 2001 that the DfES recognized the need for an official 'framework of effective practice for supporting children from birth to three years'. 'Birth to Three Matters' was published in the autumn of 2002. It is based on extensive consultation with practitioners and other experts in the field.

It has built upon what is being said in all the recent research and standard textbooks (e.g. Bruce and Meggitt, 2000) about the necessity of seeing young children as powerful and competent communicators and learners and their right to sensitive, responsive care and education. The framework focuses on four overarching aspects of the learning and developing child. Each aspect will, in turn, be subdivided into four themes. The aspects are:

1 A strong child
2 A skilful communicator
3 A competent learner
4 A healthy child

One extremely interesting issue here is that it is hard to recognize a 'subject' in this proposed list for the under-threes. In Britain we introduce subjects very early on and begin to make judgements on children's abilities in the so-called 'core' subjects of English, maths and science in reception class at the age of 4 years. Other countries in Europe and elsewhere do not emphasize formal skills until children reach the age of 6 or 7 years. Before that they are engaged in a lot of play, social and emotional development and language and communication (not literacy).

The areas of learning laid out for 3–5-year-olds in the DfES/QCA (2000) curriculum guidance for the Foundation Stage are Personal, Social and Emotional Development, Communication, Language and Literacy, Mathematical Development, Creative Development, Knowledge and Understanding of the World and Physical Development. It does not take much imagination to see this as an early years version of an essentially secondary subject-orientated curriculum. However, that would be to ignore some important principles which are written into the Foundation stage guidance and at the same time to gloss over the two major and competing agendas informing all early years planning and assessment.

These two competing agendas are illustrated in various ways in the Foundation Stage guidance. The Foreword by Margaret Hodge MP, then the parliamentary under secretary of state responsible for employment and equal opportunities as well as early years, emphasizes the government's aim to provide a high-quality, integrated early education and childcare service for all who want it and the importance of the early years for children's development. She then mentions the two agendas:

> The foundation stage is about developing key learning skills such as listening, speaking, concentration, persistence and learning to work together and cooperate with other children. It is also about developing early communication, literacy and numeracy skills that will prepare young children for key stage 1 of the national curriculum ... All children should be given the opportunity to experience the very best start to their education. We need to ensure that our children enter school having established solid foundations on which they can build. This will help to ensure that they continue to flourish throughout their school years and beyond (DfEE/QCA, 2000: 2).

We have the Foundation stage represented here as doing two jobs – giving children key learning skills and also preparing them for school and the National Curriculum. The unanswered (and probably generally unasked) question is why the key learning skills are not enough on their own (i.e. if they are key learning skills surely they must be sufficient to enable any learner to access any curriculum?).

However, government still works with a narrow model of educational achievement that is essentially a deficit model that expects all children to succeed whilst still using an old-fashioned and, particularly in early years terms, discredited curriculum. Some fundamentally inappropriate and outdated ideas about children's learning remain unchallenged by current political initiatives. Take, for example, the way the Sure Start initiative was announced in

1998. The byline in the *Guardian* was 'Outreach workers to visit newborn as a first step to get them ready for school' (15 July 1998).

It is difficult for governments of any political hue to see early childhood as anything other than preparation for school when one considers the larger agendas with which they are engaged. Moss (1999: 235) sums up the situation rather well:

> . . . early childhood services and young children have become items on the agenda of two major and related [government] projects . . . improving educational standards in school and increasing labour market participation and economic competitiveness. Viewed from the perspective of these imperative projects, young children are understood primarily as dependents of their parents, in need of 'childcare', to enable their parents' employment, and as 'becoming' school children and economically active adults.

Therefore it is easy to see why there may be two competing agendas present in the Foundation Stage guidance document introduced in England in 2000. It requires a significant conceptual shift to begin to see early years as a valid stage in its own right and to understand that if children are to succeed as learners and do well in school the way forward is not to make early years more like school but to ensure that young children have lots of opportunities to form and understand concepts they will need to access school subjects later – in other words, to give them key skills and dispositions towards learning, not to fill them with subject knowledge.

The practitioners and academics on the working group that wrote the guidance had to be assertive about keeping some important elements like play in the forefront rather than the background. Fortunately they were comparatively successful and the guidance is much more popular with early years practitioners than the Desirable Learning Outcomes which preceded it. This is because the principles which inform the document emphasize the importance of knowing about child development and make it less like the National Curriculum. It also brings nursery and reception together as one stage and the National Curriculum now has to wait until Year 1.

As well as the principles there are further sections of guidance entitled 'Putting the principles into practice', 'Meeting the diverse needs of children', 'Children with special educational needs and disabilities, Children with English as an additional language', 'Learning and teaching' and 'Play'. The 'subject' guidance does not appear until page 26 and starts with personal, social and emotional development. Each area of learning is divided into 'early learning goals' to be achieved by the time children finish their reception year and 'stepping stones' colour coded in yellow, blue and green which are stages on the way to the goals. (Interestingly children in Scotland and Northern Ireland do not have to reach goals; they have opportunities to learn in certain areas. Most early years experts would prefer that sort of approach which does not allow one to fail to reach a goal before one is even 5 years old.)

Practitioners can, of course, interpret the guidance in various ways. If one wants to see early years as preparation for school one can focus particularly on core subject areas and pay particular attention to the paragraph on page 27 which refers to making a smooth transition between reception and Year 1 by introducing literacy and numeracy hours by the end of reception. If one wants to focus on the curriculum from the child's point of view then the principles will be more important than a detailed knowledge of every stepping stone, and observation of children's play and responses to structured learning experiences will form the heart of what is seen as important.

Practitioners and academics are increasingly looking to other countries and systems of early years education. Much has been written about the Reggio Emilia approach (Edwards et al., 1993; Abbott and Nutbrown, 2001) and many British educators have either visited Reggio or seen the exhibition which last toured Britain in 2000. The Reggio approach is to follow the child's lead with an emphasis on play, creativity, art and drama. Children in Italy do not start formal schooling until they are 6 years old. Interestingly this approach to education arose from the Italian experience of fascism and a commitment to educate the next generation to think deeply and question those in authority rather than blindly to obey. Educators have also been influenced by the New Zealand national early years curriculum – Te Whariki. This curriculum influenced the group which wrote the English framework for early childhood education entitled *Quality in Diversity in the Early Years* (Early Childhood Education Forum, 1998). It is based on the five foundations of Te Whariki – belonging and connecting, being and becoming, contributing and participating, being active and expressing and thinking, imaging and understanding. Although *Quality in Diversity* was thought too radical to form the basis of the

Foundation Stage guidance (Rodger, 1999: 17), there are echoes of it there. It can also be seen in the four aspects of the new under-threes framework (see above). Wherever they gain their inspiration, good practitioners continue to believe Bruce's (1997) principle that the best way to prepare children for adult life is to give them what they need as children. So how do they do that in the current context?

Good early years practice

Good practice requires good training and this issue is returned to at the end of the chapter when the issues involved in constructing a shared discourse about learning across early years settings are discussed. Good practice is not a universal catch-all concept but what follows is an exploration of the sort of practice that is agreed by the vast majority of early years experts to form the basis of sound life-long learning for all children. It is gathered under five broad headings and really only scratches the surface of many important and linked areas.

Admissions and inclusion

The way in which parents and carers and their children are welcomed to the setting will play a crucial role in how valued they feel and how much they 'belong'. Edgington (1998: 59) points out that, where places are in short supply, staff decisions about which groups of children they prioritize are important. If, for instance, one operates purely on a first come, first serve basis, parents who are unfamiliar with, or unable to cope with, the procedures will be excluded. She goes on (ibid.) to say that 'Offering as far as possible, equal access to nursery education is a start but it is not enough in itself', and discusses the need to examine attitudes and values about equal opportunities. The Children Act 1989, which applies to all settings, lays down the legal duty to take into account children's racial, religious, cultural and linguistic backgrounds. Children's class, gender and the sexual orientation of their parents should also be valued.

Any setting should be welcoming to everyone who uses and visits it. This means ensuring that information about the setting is accessible and also that people see others like themselves represented. It is not inclusive, for instance, to have photos and pictures on the walls, books on the shelves and other resources that only represent typical white middle-class two-parent, two children, non-disabled families. However, the most important factor in valuing children and families is staff attitude. All people, including very young children, know if another person is suspicious, distrustful or uneasy with them.

Of course being welcoming and listening to children, parents and carers may mean that you hear things that are uncomfortable, but it is a first step in moving away from that way of looking at families described by Toynbee earlier in the chapter. It is a long time since Tizard and Hughes (1984) discovered how similar the experiences of working and middle-class children at home with their mothers were and how quickly staff appeared to disempower the working-class children when they went to nursery school and then lowered their expectations of them. Millner (1993) found that by the age of 2 years children notice difference in skin colour and between 3 and 5 years begin to attach values to it.

Early years practitioners have an enormous role to play in countering discrimination and prejudice and in educating not just children but their families as well. For example, calmly explaining to parents why a setting in an almost all-white area is celebrating Divali may answer their questions about the festival itself but also cause them to think about some issues around racism and prejudice. Having the patience to spend five minutes explaining how learning to sign may help, not hinder, both deaf and hearing children's language development and inviting parents to spend some time in the nursery observing signing in action may pay dividends in changing attitudes to disability. These are not earth-shattering actions but they are based on an agreed policy and a sound knowledge of what values translated into action look like.

Intelligence and effective learning

It is through feeling valued that children develop feelings of self-worth and self-esteem. Siraj-Blatchford (1994) and others have shown that lifelong attitudes are set early. Without feelings of high self-worth children may find it difficult to access learning and respond appropriately to challenges. Children who are valued, value others and develop emotional intelligence – the ability to understand oneself, to empathize with others and to understand human relationships and their influence on life. The idea of emotional intelligence has primarily been developed by Goleman (1995), who built on the ideas of Gardner (1983) about multiple intelligences. Handy (1990, quoted in Whitaker, 1993: 35) has developed a list of types of intelligence based on Gardner:

Logical: those who can reason, analyse and memorize.

Spatial: those who can discern patterns in things and create them.

Musical: those who can sing, play or make music of all sorts.

Practical: the person who can pull a carburettor to bits but might never be able to spell a word or explain how they did it.

Physical: the footballers, athletes and dancers among us.

Intra-personal: the sensitive people who see into themselves, the quiet perceptive ones.

Inter-personal: those who make things happen with and through people

As he observes (ibid.): 'It is the tragedy of our schooling that we are led to think that logical intelligence is the only type that matters. Any observation of our friends and colleagues in later life will prove that the other intelligences are at least as important, if not more so.'

Handy argues that we should train ourselves to ask not how intelligent people are but which type of intelligence they have the most of. This would certainly lead to a change in the way we judge children's capabilities. Any early years curriculum should include opportunities to develop all these intelligences. All settings should also involve parents and carers in assessing their children's abilities and interests and in setting targets for their children to achieve which are realistic.

The Effective Early Learning Project (EEL), which is being used across many LEAs (see Pascal and Bertram, 1999), takes some of these ideas about forms of intelligence along with others such of those of Laevers (1994) and Katz (1995) and looks at ways of assessing three other aspects of children's learning alongside academic achievements – dispositions to learn, respect for self and others and well-being. All three of these aspects have been shown to be important in lifelong learning.

Observation and assessment

Whatever form of curriculum planning is used the whole point of it should be to observe, support and extend children's learning (Bruce and Meggitt, 2000). All early years practitioners will have their own theories about how children learn. Crudely, these will probably fall into three broad categories – transmission/behaviourism, laissez-faire and social constructivism. Most practitioners will work with all three models giving more or less emphasis to each depending on context.

The transmission model

The transmission model assumes that the child is an empty vessel and needs to be told what to do all the time. This is closely linked to behaviourism where behaviour is modified by rewarding good behaviour and punishing undesirable behaviour. This model is simple and it is easy to check what has been learnt – for example, you tell the children a story, then you ask some simple questions about it. You praise all the children who are 'sitting nicely' and frown at the ones who are fidgeting – a straightforward application of Skinnnerian ideas about behaviour modification. This approach produces quick results but tends to lead to a lack of open-ended activities and children who only do things if they can get it right. Children are able to make wider connections than we sometimes give them credit for. The following interaction that took place recently between myself and two 4-year-old boys sitting in a coach on the way to the airport illustrates this:

> I was aware that these two boys were not talking about the traffic we could see on the motorway and we were in the middle of a transport topic. So I immediately moved into transmission mode and started asking some questions about what we could see – they answered these in a fairly routine way until Adam suddenly said: 'Elephants are not allowed on the motorway!' This engendered some interest in his friend Cameron who agreed and laughed. I was somewhat nonplussed by this apparently decontextualized statement and, in an effort to elicit more information, suggested that perhaps they would be if they were in a horse box (we had just seen a large one of these). The boys giggled and Adam said patiently – 'No, it would be an elephant box, but they're not allowed anyway.' I then asked Adam how he knew that elephants were not allowed. He replied, to my puzzlement, that he had just seen the sign that said 'Elephants not allowed on the motorway'. I asked him to describe the sign and he was clear that it had an elephant on it, a cross

and writing which said elephants not allowed on the motorway. At this point I was defeated but on the way back I was determined to look out for this mysterious sign. As soon as I saw it I understood. It was a brown tourist attraction sign which had an elephant symbol next to the words 'Twycross Zoo' and underneath crossed swords next to the words 'Bosworth battle site'. Adam had seen the elephant and the cross and, applying the knowledge he had gleaned about road signs during our topic, had assumed the writing said elephants not allowed on the motorway. He may have been wrong about the writing but the incident shows him being able to apply knowledge in a wider context – i.e. being a good learner.

As Bruce (2001: 128) says: 'Learning is only partly about learning *new* things. It is mainly about using what is *already* known, in flexible and imaginative ways.'

The laissez-faire approach

The laissez-faire approach to learning assumes, like the eighteenth-century philosopher, Rousseau, that children are biologically programmed to learn and develop whether adults help them or not. This can be seen in early years settings when children are given resources but the adults do not talk to the children while they are using them and is sometimes linked to the Freudian belief that the unconscious mind influences our behaviour. It can also be seen in Goldschmied's approach to heuristic play (see below). In this approach there will be a lot of observing and support with minimal extension of children's learning.

The social constructivist approach

Most teachers are familiar with the ideas of Piaget, who provided a welcome relief from transmission models when he propounded his ideas that children should be active in their learning. Vygotsky also believed that children constructed their own learning but particularly emphasized the social aspect of that construction. He claimed that interaction with an adult or more competent peer was crucial in children's learning. His ideas have been built on by Bruner, who called the process the adult or more competent peer engaged in with the learner, scaffolding (for a good résumé of these approaches to learning, see Whitebread, 1998). They are known as social constructivist approaches to learning.

All three of these broad approaches can be seen in most settings and will influence the amount of observation, support and extending of learning children get. The social constructivist approach is the most labour intensive for the adult and the most rewarding for the child. The adult must observe what the child can do in order to support or 'scaffold' his or her learning and then come up with ideas for extending it. For example, the practitioner might tell the story of the Bear Hunt, observe children's reactions and ability to join in and then extend the activity into drama, music and sensory experiences (e.g. making caves, feeling the grass, providing small-world scenarios). He or she would use the knowledge gained via observation to encourage different children to extend their learning in different directions.

The way in which adults assess children's learning depends on how much importance they attach to areas of learning outside the subject-based curriculum and how much they are encouraged to use observation and analysis as the basis for showing children's progression and development rather than just ticking boxes as a result of closed questions such as 'what colour is this?' (If it has not been done already, there is a thesis waiting to be written on early years practitioners[1] attachment to knowing one's colours!)

Play and exploration

Much has been written on the importance of children's play for learning and development (Moyles, 1988; 1994; Sayeed and Guerin, 2000; Bruce, 2001; Lindon, 2001). Very young children need time to explore materials. How can one apply paint and glue carefully to make a card for one's mum if one has not had time and opportunity to explore the paintness of paint and the glueness of glue? Good settings allow children time to explore. Holland (1997) recounts her experiences of providing a range of different materials for children to explore with no thought of end-product and no instructions from adults. She has been building on the ideas of Goldschmied and Jackson (1994). Children should be able to play with a range of natural materials as well as commercially produced things. Children can sort shells and pine-cones just as well as plastic cars and get a more enjoyable sensory experience from engaging in the activity.

Children need the opportunity to run, jump and skip, to hide and be found and to find beauty in the outdoors as well as inside

(Bilton, 1998). Through play children make sense of learning. Bruce (1997) developed 12 features of what she calls free-flow play. In her most recent book on play, Bruce (2001: 127) explains how play can help children develop abstract ideas. As they develop a sense of identity and a theory of mind, they begin to talk or sign and the images in their minds become more mobile. This means they can cease to think purely in the here and now and think backwards and forwards. Play also helps children develop empathy and explore emotions. Bruce's advice to practitioners includes the following:

- Enjoy reading or telling stories and poems to children, and singing songs and rhymes with them.
- Make music and dance with children, even if you don't think you can.
- Value the ideas, thoughts and feelings that children have.
- Be relaxed. All this is indirect teaching of the sort that lasts for life.
- Join in, but don't dominate.
- Set up a challenging and exciting environment for play. Visit the park. Play in the garden and create play scenarios indoors too.
- Make dens.
- Develop a workshop area with everything anyone could need for drawing and writing, painting, clay, dough and construction, from found materials and wooden blocks.
- Know when to leave children to develop their own play.

The practitioner who observes play will gain much useful information about the schemas children are using. Piaget used the notion of schema when talking about repeated patterns of behaviour in very young children, and these ideas were further explored by Athey (1990) in relation to 2–5-year-olds and by Nutbrown (1994). Athey (1990: 37) describes schemas as 'patterns of repeatable behaviour into which experiences are assimilated and that are gradually co-ordinated'. Children's first mark-making is for pleasure and often part of a vertical or rotational schema. A vertical schema will be evidenced by lots of straight-line making, jumping up and down, etc., a rotational one by circling, both bodily and in painting and drawing. Being able to draw straight lines and both a circle and a semi-circle are very important for future writing skills. Children gradually then move from mark-making into representation and, eventually, writing.

Language and literacy

'School' literacy seems to turn children off the joy of reading and writing at an early age. As Mills and Mills (1998: 17) claim: '. . . British early years provision rushes children into abstract letters, words and numbers. While elsewhere primacy is given to developing confidence and precision in spoken language, here teaching is dominated by reading, writing and recorded arithmetic.' Early years settings should be giving children lots of opportunities for speaking and listening and developing their own oral responses to events. Anyone who has ever listened to a 3 or 4-year-old conducting a private monologue, perhaps before he or she goes to sleep at night or whilst sitting on the toilet, will know how rich the child's spoken language can be and how much he or she enjoys rehearsing words and phrases and repeating over and over again things heard during the day. The ability to read grows organically and very gradually from oral language and, as Anning and Edwards (1999: 88) say:

> the model of beginning reading that most benefits young children is not the 'disembedded' learning of letter sounds and names and the completion of phonic-based worksheets, but reading within the context of enjoying story and picture books, and delighting in telling and retelling of familiar fairy stories and rhymes. Playing with sounds, rhythms and words whets children's appetite for learning about all aspects of language.

They go on to talk about the ways in which children are exposed to all sort of literacy and literate behaviour in their everyday home lives and how in comparison 'the world of "letteracy" in school must seem rather dull' (ibid.).

In early years settings children should be encouraged to develop confidence in speech and the power to manipulate narrative. As Hendy and Toon (2001: 76) so eloquently put it: 'Drama can be used to speak the silences of stories, or to change the direction of stories, or to create alternative endings.'

Children's representations will gradually become writing through watching adults and older children writing. Their first written letters and words are usually related to themselves – the letters in their own name being the most common. They then have to learn sound/letter correspondence in order for them to be able to write for an audience. Early efforts usually omit vowels and may be in a mixture of upper and lower case (e.g. BtflY, TmS – Butterfly and

Thomas). It is very important for adults to respond positively to these attempts in what is often called 'emergent' writing and not to get hung up on the secretarial aspects of writing but gently to guide children towards the conventions of print. They are growing up in a world in which the uses of literacy mean different things from the one in which readers grew up. As Baker (1999: 132) says, children born during this millennium 'will be the first generation to have been born since the internet and e-mail revolutionized both the provision of information and the way we see the world'. In nurseries and other settings children have access to ICT in many forms, including the Internet, and they are confident users of a mouse, remote control devices, touch screens, etc. Writing with a pen or pencil is just one aspect of communication.

Training

Training is a huge issue in the early years. The level of qualifications in the field vary tremendously and, although the EYDCPs are providing much-needed cheap, accessible training open to all early years workers, there are still issues around first qualification. In my own place of work and many other LEA-funded nurseries and centres all education and childcare workers are required to have at least NVQ 3. However the national standard is 50 per cent of workers trained to NVQ 2. The National Training Organization, which is developing a 'climbing frame' of qualifications, unfortunately does not include teacher training. Teacher training is improving in that there are now more BEd and BA QTS (qualified teacher status) courses offering advanced study of the early years as a specialist subject. Primary postgraduate courses also offer early years as a specialism and recognize the BA Early Childhood Studies as an appropriate degree with which to commence the course. However, we have a long way to go before all training meets the high standards laid out by David (1998: 25).

> Probably the most important implications for training, apart from high levels of knowledge in a range of relevant disciplines, involve the need for early childhood educators to de-centre (to view the world from another's viewpoint); to 'problematize' their favoured theories and to engage in reflexivity (examining how their own thinking, views and actions influence their ecological niche). Thus, training should not be about acquiring facts and knowledge, but about exploring bodies of

knowledge and submitting them to critical analysis in the light of real-life experience. There should be opportunities for experiencing and reflecting on teamwork with other adults, leading to open, depersonalized self-evaluation of strengths and weaknesses. In particular ... there should be discussion of ways in which societies construct different versions of early childhood and the services they deem appropriate as a result.

Conclusion

This chapter has sketched in some of the important issues for children, families and staff involved in the early years of care and education. Some tensions between competing ideas of curriculum and differing concepts of childhood and learning have been discussed. These tensions both inform (and, some would say, deform) everyday practice in care and education. It seems that a major difficulty is a reluctance on the part of adults to rethink their ideas about children and childhood. Clearly this is not a problem confined only to the early years.

Pollard and Filer (1999: 6) talk, in the context of primary education, about this continuing ideological struggle around the conceptualization of children and learning:

> While conservative politicians of both major political parties have asserted the need for more rigorous curriculum specification and *teaching* of 'pupils' (with implicit assumptions of passivity and deficiency), the defensive teaching profession was loath to give up its developmental conceptions of 'children' (with implicit assumptions of innocence and dependency).
>
> In our view, the assumptions of passivity, deficiency and dependency remain significantly embodied in the social representation of 'pupil' within much common sense thinking. Indeed they can be seen as having underpinned the subject-based teacher-dominated emphasis of changes in curriculum and pedagogy of the 1990s. It is assumed, that if standards need to rise, the curriculum must be specified more clearly and pupils should be taught more effectively. There is little talk of trying to engage with pupil imagination or empowering them as learners.

Good early years practitioners need the confidence both to engage with children's imagination and to empower children to think about their own learning. Let's look at Zoe aged 4 years who, although fully engaged in re-enacting the story of the Bear Hunt, stood back momentarily and said to the teacher: 'We're doing a lot of laughing even though its scary'. Zoe is becoming a good learner – she can join in readily with others and test herself with scariness and she can already engage in some meta-analysis, in this instance connected with the comfort and seeming contradiction of laughter. Most importantly she feels able, and is given space, to share her perception with the adult. This seems to me to sum up an important aspect of early years education for both children and adults – the fun of risk-taking and using imagination and the importance of standing back, reflecting on and articulating one's understanding of experience. Whatever ideologies compete for our attention we need to safeguard this creative space or children enter school already uncreative and unexcited by their own power as learners.

Glossary of terms

Childminder Someone who cares for children aged from birth to school age in his or her own home. He or she is usually paid by the children's parents although sometimes social services pay for places for children in need.

Children in need According to the Children Act 1989 definition, these are children whose health or development is likely to be significantly impaired without the provision of services. This definition includes children with special educational needs.

Community nursery A nursery set up by community members, often in areas of high social need and run by a democratic management committee.

Crèche Often attached to a workplace, a crèche is usually staffed by qualified people who offer sessions working parents pay for.

Early excellence centre An early years centre which has been awarded this status on the grounds of the quality of care and education provided and other services to the community.

Early years centre A centre which integrates education and social services provision under one roof and provides a variety of service for families, including nursery education.

EYDCP Early Years Development and Childcare Partnership – these exist in every local authority and are charged with implementing the National Childcare Strategy.

Family centre Usually a social services nursery centre run along similar lines to an early years centre providing care, education and family support.

Family support This can cover a variety of services ranging from supervised contact and parenting assessment programmes (where there is concern for child protection) to adult education classes.

Nursery class A nursery which is attached to a primary school – the first class in the school.

Nursery school A free-standing school with its own headteacher which provides a foundation stage curriculum for children aged 3–5 years. It may also offer other services similar to an early years centre.

Playgroup Most of these are now known as preschools and many belong to the *Pre-school Learning Alliance (PLA)*. They are not-for-profit organizations often run by local parents. They offer morning or afternoon sessions during the week usually for children from 2 years upwards. Some also offer before and after school sessions.

Practitioner A useful catch-all term to include anyone who works with very young children. In practice it may mean nursery nurse, teacher, playgroup leader, childminder, health visitor, social worker, family support worker, etc.

Pre-reception class One of the ways in which schools introduce 4-year-olds to school. Often to be found in schools with no nursery class. Attendance is usually part time.

Private day nursery A nursery run as a private business. Some are part of large chains (e.g. Leapfrog, Jigsaw). They usually open early in the morning and close late in the evening to suit working parents.

Reception class The first class in the primary school. Children start in reception the year they are 5.

Setting Any place where young children and practitioners are to be found.

Small world play Pretend play with miniature people, animals, buildings and places made to scale with the figures.

Student tasks

1 Think about the different settings where you spent time between birth and going to school (do not include your own home but include anywhere else you can remember). Which place(s) can you remember most clearly? Why? Discuss your memories with another person – how do they compare?

2 What effect do you think the fact that the vast majority of early years workers are female and on low pay has on their professional status and on society's attitudes towards childcare and education? Should low-paid and non-graduate workers claim to be professionals?

3 Decide what age you think children should:

- say please and thank you
- know the names of colours
- come out of nappies
- boil a kettle
- use a saw

Compare your answers with other peoples' – what do the results tell you about your own and other's ideas about child development? (*Hint*: There are no right answers and many of the answers given will depend on culture and experience.)

4 Observe a group of children between the ages of 2 and 4 years playing together. What do you notice about their social interaction?

5 What was play like in your childhood? Who were your favourite playmates? Do you find it easy to play now? Would you ever feel embarrassed playing a fantasy game or acting out a story with children? Do adults ever play?

Suggested further reading

Bruce, T. (2001) *Learning through Play: Babies, Toddlers and the Foundation Years*. London: Hodder & Stoughton. A short, accessible text that covers some very important aspects of play from birth onwards, that points readers in other directions, accesses the Foundation Stage guidance and uses photos very well.

Bruce, T. and Meggitt. C. (2000) *Child Care and Education*. London: Hodder & Stoughton. If you only read one book make it this one – it has everything you need. As well as a thorough look at child development it integrates such vital issues as equal opportunities, health and safety, working with parents and carers and SEN.

DfEE/QCA (2000) *Curriculum Guidance for the Foundation Stage*. London: QCA publications. This is a ring binder that all settings with 3–5 year olds are *required* to use. Since August 2002 this guidance is statutory and part of the national curriculum.

Gura, P. (1996) *Resources for Early Learning: Children, Adults and Stuff*. London: Hodder & Stoughton. Ideas for play and about play and what to play with. Lots of interesting case studies.

Millam, R. (1996) *Anti-discriminatory Practice. A Guide for Workers in Childcare and Education*. London: Continuum. A good introduction to the area – includes useful information and tasks on a range of issues.

Murray, L. and Andrews, L. (2000) *The Social Baby*, Richmond: CP Publishing. Using picture sequences from video footage, this fascinating book gives a unique insight into the complex social world of babies. It should make you think about the beginnings of communication and language skills.

Nutbrown, C. (1996) *Respectful Educators, Capable Learners*. London: Paul Chapman Publishing. A thought-provoking text about how children's rights can influence curriculum and attitudes.

Siraj-Blatchford, I. (1994) *The Early Years: Laying the Foundations for Racial Equality*. Stoke-on-Trent: Trentham Books. If you have any doubts about the need for anti-racist education in the early years, read this.

Wolfendale, S. (ed.) (2000) *Special Needs in the Early Years*. London: RoutledgeFalmer. The authors of the various chapters in this book are practitioners and researchers and bring different perspectives to issues of inclusion and integration for a range of children.

Note

1 This chapter focuses on provision in England. Early years education in Scotland, Wales and Northern Ireland, although broadly similar, is different in various important respects.

References

Abbott, L., Ackers, J., Gillen, J. and Moylett, H. (2000) *Shaping the Future: Working with the Under Threes*, (video training and resource package). Manchester: Mancherster Metropolitan University/Open University Press.

Abbott, L. and Moylett, H. (eds) (1997a) *Early Interactions – Responding to Young Children's Needs*. Buckingham: Open University Press.

Abbott, L. and Moylett, H. (eds) (1997b) *Early Interactions – Training and Professional Devlopment*. Buckingham: Open University Press.

Abbott, L. and Nutbrown, C. (eds.) (2001) *Experiencing Reggio Emilia*. Buckingham: Open University Press.

Anning, A. and Edwards, A. (1999) *Promoting Children's Learning from Birth to Five*. Buckingham: Open University Press.

Athey, C. (1990) *Extending Thought in Young Children*. London: Paul Chapman Publishing.

Baker, P. (1999) If this was on the computer we'd hear the lion go roar – ICT in early years education' in L. Abbott and H. Moylett (eds) *Early Education Transformed*. London: Falmer.

Bilton, H. (1998) *Outdoor Play in the Early Years*. London: David Fulton.

Bruce, T. (1997) *Early Childhood Education*. London: Hodder & Stoughton.

Bruce, T. (2001) *Learning through Play: Babies, Toddlers and the Foundation Years*. London: Hodder & Stoughton.

Bruce, T. and Meggitt, C. (2000) *Child Care and Education*, (2nd edn). London: Hodder & Stoughton.

Bruner, J. (1996) *The Culture of Education*. London: Harvard University Press.

David, T. (1998) Changing minds: young children and society. In L. Abbott and G. Pugh (eds) *Training to Work in the Early Years*. Buckingham: Open University Press.

David, T. (1999) Valuing young children. In L. Abbott and H. Moylett (eds) *Early Education Transformed*. London: Falmer Press.

DfEE/QCA (2000) *Curriculum Guidance for the Foundation Stage*. London: QCA.

Donaldson, M. (1981) *Children's Minds*. London: Fontana.

Early Childhood Education Forum (1998) *Quality in Diversity in the Early Years*. London: National Children's Bureau.

Edgington, M. (1998) *The Nursery Teacher in Action*, (2nd edn). London: Paul Chapman Publishing.

Edwards, C., Gandini, L. and Forman, G. (eds) (1993) *The Hundred Languages of Children: The Reggio Emilia Approach to Early Childhood Education*. Norwood, NJ: Ablex.

Gardner, H. (1983) *Frames of Mind: The Theory of Multiple Intelligences*. London: Fontana.

Goldschmied, E. and Jackson, S. (1994) *People under Three*. London: Routledge.

Goleman, D. (1995) *Emotional Intelligence*. London: Bloomsbury.

Gopnik, A., Meltzoff, A. and Kuhl, P. (1999) *How Babies Think*. London: Weidenfeld & Nicolson.

Hendy, L. and Toon, L. (2001) *Supporting Drama and Imaginative Play in the Early Years*. Buckingham: Open University Press.

Holland, R. (1997) Exploratory play. In L. Abbott and H. Moylett (eds) *Early Interactions: responding to children's needs*. Buckingham: Open University Press.

James, A. and Prout, A. (eds) (1997) *Constructing and Deconstructing Childhood: Contemporary Issues in the Sociological Study of Childhood* (2nd edn). London: Falmer Press.

Katz, L. (1995) *Talks with Teachers of Young Children: A Collection*. Norwood, NJ: Ablex.

Kessen, W. (1979) The American child and other cultural inventions', *American Psychologist*, 34(10): 815–20.

Laevers, F. (1994) *The Leuven Involvement Scale for Young Children*, (manual and videotape). *Experiential Education Series* 1. Leuven: Centre for Experiential Education.

Lindon, J. (1999) *Working with young children*. London: Hodder & Stoughton.

Lindon, J (2001) *Understanding Children's Play*. Cheltenham: Nelson Thornes.

Makins, V. (1997) *Not Just a Nursery ... Multi-agency Early Years Centres in Action*. London: National Children's Bureau.

Manning-Morton, J. and Thorpe, M. (2000) *Key Times*. London: Islington Media Services/University of North London

McCalla, D., Grover C. and Penn, H. (2001) *Local Nurseries for Local Communities*. London: National Children's Bureau.

Meggitt, C. and Sunderland, G. (2000) *Child Development: An Illustrated Guide*. Oxford: Heinemann.

Millner, D. (1993) *Children and Race – Ten Years on*. London: Ward Lock.

Mills, C. and Mills, D. (1998) *Britain's Early Years Disaster (Survey of Research Evidence for Channel 4 TV Programme* Too much, Too Soon). London: Channel 4.

Morss, J. (1996) *Growing Critical: Alternatives to Developmental Psychology*. London: Routledge.

Moss, P. (1999) Renewed hopes and lost opportunities: early childhood in the early years of the Labour government. *Cambridge Journal of Education*, 29(2): 229–38.

Moyles, J. (1988) *Just Playing? The Roles and Status of Play in Early Childhood*. Buckingham: Open University Press.

Moyles, J. (ed.) (1994) *The Excellence of Play*. Buckingham: Open University Press.

New Zealand Ministry of Education (1996) *Te Whariki: Early Childhood Curriculum*. Wellington: Learning Media.

Nutbrown, C. (1994) *Threads of Thinking: Young Children Learning and the Role of Early Education*. London: Paul Chapman Publishing.

Pascal, C. and Bertram, T. (1999) Accounting early for lifelong learning. In L. Abbott and H. Moylett (eds) *Early Education Transformed*. London: Falmer.

Pollard, A. and Filer, A. (1999) *The Social World of Pupil Career*, London: Cassell.

Rodger, R. (1999) *Planning an Appropriate Curriculum for the Under Fives*. London: David Fulton.

Sayeed, Z. and Guerin, E. (2000) *Early Years Play*. London: David Fulton.

Siraj-Blatchford, I. (1994) *The Early Years: Laying the Foundations for Racial Equality*. Stoke-on-Trent: Trentham Books.

Sylva, K., Melhuish, E., Siraj-Blatchford, I. and Sammon, P. (1999) *Effective Provision of Pre-school Education (EPPE Study)*. Technical Papers. London: University of London, Institute of Education.

Tizard, A. and Hughes, M. (1984) *Young Children Learning*. London: Fontana.

Trevarthen, C. (1992) An infant's motives for speaking and thinking in the culture. In A.H. Wold (ed.) *The Dialogical Alternative*. Oxford: Oxford University Press.

Vincent, C. and Ball, S.J. (2001) A market in love? Choosing pre-school childcare. *British Educational Research Journal*, 27(5): 633–51.

Whitaker, P. (1993) *Managing Change in Schools*. Buckingham: Open University Press.

Whitebread, D. (1998) *Teaching and Learning in the Early Years*. London: Routledge.

3

Differentiation of Schooling and Pedagogy

Diana Burton

This chapter examines the structural and pedagogical manifestations of differentiation primarily within the UK context. Differentiation developed as a new educational construct in pedagogical terms during the 1990s. However, the division of pupils and students within education systems is as old as the hills and is highly politicized. Discussions about equality of opportunity and comprehensive schooling have been replaced by an agenda which emphasizes 'diversity' and 'choice' within education.

Introduction

It is becoming possible for each child to be educated in a way and at a pace which suits them, recognising that each is different, with different abilities, interests and needs (DfES, 2001: 20).

The pedagogical discourse of the 1990s established 'differentiation' as a seminal term. It became a key focus for school inspection (NFER, 1995) and Ofsted reports made repeated calls for its use as a teaching strategy (Bowen, 1995). Professional development days in schools increasingly focused staff on the use of teaching strategies which supported the differentiated classroom (Weston et al., 1998). A National Foundation for Educational Research (NFER) survey (Weston, 1996) revealed that 60 per cent of secondary school managers considered differentiation important compared with less than

20 per cent in 1992–3. Heads justified the priority status afforded to differentiation in terms of raising attainment. The term differentiation 'is widely understood to be an aspect of a teacher's professional, pedagogical competence, a shorthand for all the methods which teachers try to use within the classroom to enable each pupil to achieve intended learning targets' (Weston, 1996: 2). However, in its broadest sense, differentiation is a construct which describes a whole host of educational phenomena, from the ways in which schooling systems are organized within societies, how learners are divided up for teaching and assessment, the extent to which teachers observe policies of inclusion, right through to the particular teaching and learning strategies a teacher or lecturer employs with individual students. This chapter will examine these various manifestations of differentation; the reader will see that they are inextricably bound up with the socio-political and ideological contexts in which they exist.

Structural approaches to differentiation

Organizing schools by ability

In the 1960s and 1970s the political agenda was dominated by issues of social equality, with the introduction of comprehensive schooling designed to play down the effects of class differences between pupils (Gewirtz et al., 1995; Tubbs, 1996). Intelligence testing in the form of the '11 Plus' had been used to differentiate between pupils for their secondary schooling. On the basis of this norm-referenced test, pupils were sent either to the local secondary modern or grammar school and given a different educational diet accordingly. In secondary modern schools the emphasis was on basic literacy and numeracy and on practical subjects, some even having a vocational focus. Grammar schools tended to replicate the curriculum established within public schools, emphasizing learning for its own sake and thus including such subjects as the classics and Latin. Expectations of pupils on leaving these schools were quite clearly different. A simple distinction would be that from the former were expected to come the unskilled and semi-skilled workforce and, from the latter, those who would proceed into higher education and thence to the professions. Governments of both political persuasions put forward social class arguments for an end to differentiation via selection, with a Labour government finally implementing the change in the mid-1960s by permitting LEAs to reorganize their grammar and secondary modern schools into a single system of comprehensive schools. However, the selection continued within the comprehensives as pupils were often divided into streams based on their mathematics or English achievement. The pupils remained in these streams for all subjects and there was little movement in and out of streams, leading to increasing worries about what Rosenthal and Jacobson (1968) famously described as the 'self-fulfilling prophecy' whereby pupils lived up to the teachers' expectations of the stream and attempted no more.

Selection and division of learners on single ability measures can also lead to inequality of treatment and performance. Darling-Hammond (1994) reported the effects of 'tracking' in the US system whereby instructional programmes based on test scores effectively ration the challenging curricula to a small proportion of pupils. Disproportionate percentages of poor and minority groups (black and Hispanic) are found in the lower tracks. Madeus (1994) has written of the 'grave negative impact' of such 'quantitative reductionism' on minority groups, warning that it undermines pluralistic views of education (p. 86). However, Biemiller (1993) has argued that ignoring the reality of developmental diversity in achievement may amplify the problems which it implies for pupils in classrooms. He called for the grouping of US elementary-grade pupils (aged 5–12 years) to be organized partially on ability lines in order that the less advanced pupils could be given opportunities to master skills. In Britain a research review by Gillborn and Youdell (2000) found that organizational mechanisms, such as setting by ability, tend to produce bottom groups of black and working-class pupils.

There was a period in Britain in the late 1960s and into the 1970s when mixed-ability grouping of pupils, which kept pupils of all abilities together in classrooms, became the favoured organizational strategy within comprehensive schools. However, neither research nor HMI reports could find evidence to support the strategy. HMI findings (DES, 1978) indicated that, in the main, teachers were teaching to the middle via whole-class teaching with the needs of the less and more able pupils being ignored. Both HMI (DES, 1978) and a study by Kerry (1984) found little evidence of task differentiation.

Where attempts had been made to cater for the range of abilities in one class, these had of necessity to be so teacher directed that they limited the extent to which the pupil could be intellectually challenged. Despite some innovative developments by individual teachers (Hart, 1996), there were few systematized approaches either within schools or LEAs to galvanize these strengths and disseminate good practice. Consequently, in the 1980s, mixed-ability teaching declined.

The effect of free market policy on school organization

Although the political agenda of the twentieth-first century differs from that of the 1960s in as much as the class debate has been replaced by one about individual freedom, enterprise and self-fulfilment, the current educational scene, dominated as it has been during the past 15 years by a plethora of legislation, now replicates the selection issues of 30 years ago. Legislation introduced in the Education Reform Act 1988 (ERA), which entitled parents to choose the school their children attend rather than be limited to a catchment area, led to an unofficial decomprehensivization of schooling (Gewirtz et al., 1995) whilst espousing the rhetoric of equal opportunities as its rationale – meeting the needs of all 'according to age, ability and aptitude' (DES, 1989a: 9).

Declared Conservative government policy in the 1980s and 1990s was guided by a belief in the potential of the individual and the need for a free choice in the type of school which would best support this. Meanwhile, the Swann report (DES, 1985a), which looked at equal opportunities issues, explained that differences in learning needs should take account of factors other than simple ability and attainment measures, including interests, work rates and preference for a practical approach. In 1992 the then Prime Minister, John Major, made a speech in which he confirmed 'choice' and 'diversity' as the two key themes of differentiation and the means by which equality of opportunity could be achieved (Hart, 1996: 13). However, popular schools attracted more of the able pupils whose parents could afford to transport them, which in turn brought these schools greater funding and better examination results. Meanwhile the less favoured schools were attended by the local children, for whom parental aspirations and support might be lower, leading to a downward spiral of school achievement and success (see, for example, Ball, 1994). Bridges (1994: 77) explained that the policy encouraged parents to 'secure positional advantage for their children'. Such choices were further complicated by legislation in ERA allowing schools to bid for grant-maintained status (now foundation schools) where they opted out of local government control and were funded directly by central government. Financial incentives given to encourage schools in this direction strengthened the resource base of these schools making them increasingly attractive to parents (Downes, 1994). In tandem with this was the policy of publishing GCSE results in league tables to enable local and national comparisons of school performance. Darling-Hammond (1994) has studied the effects of the trend for using assessment as a lever for school change in the USA, which began earlier than in Britain. She reported (ibid.: 8) 'unhappy results' for teaching and learning generally and for low-scoring pupils in particular:

> Research on these initiatives has found that test-based decision-making has driven instruction towards lower order cognitive skills. This shift has created incentives for pushing low scorers into special education . . . In addition, school incentives tied to test scores have undermined efforts to create and sustain more inclusive and integrated student populations, as schools are punished for accepting and keeping students with special needs and are rewarded for keeping such students out of their programs through selective admissions and transfer policies.

Specialist schools

In 1997 the Conservatives had planned to legislate for some schools to select greater numbers of pupils by ability. The 1997 general election was called, however and, in order to safeguard the less contentious elements of the bill, the selection clauses were removed. Ironically, despite a change of government, the power to select up to 10 per cent of a schools's intake has since been granted by Labour to schools which have won specialist status as a sports, arts, language or technology college. Stark policy differences separate the Labour governments of the 1960s and the early twenty-first century, which reflects both the changed social and political mores of the two eras and the ideological distinctions between them. Thirty-five years ago Labour promoted the establishment of comprehensive schools where pupils of all abilities were taught together. By contrast, the current Labour government is committed to differentiation through the endorsement of faith schools which select pupils on the basis of their faith and the establishment of specialist schools at secondary level, which sport distinctive profiles in terms of their curriculum subject emphases. Schools can bid for specialist status and, if successful, they receive extra funding. Cynical commentators might suggest that schools are really bidding for the funding and that the need to demonstrate specialist status is simply a means to an end. Hattersley (2002) has noted that faith schools are regarded by ambitious parents as superior to secular schools but questions whether respecting cultural difference should mean organizing culturally different schools or welcoming cultural diversity within common schools. Charlot (2002) describes how the push for schools to take into account the cultural specificities of pupils is happening globally. In France there is a demand for a recognition of the regional languages and cultures; in Brazil there is a strong movement for recognition of the African roots of Brazilian culture; in Belgium, Algeria and other African countries, etc., there are similar calls for diversity to be recognized and embraced.

Research by the NFER, which compared examination results of comprehensive, specialist, single-faith and selective (grammar) schools, discovered only minor score advantages for specialist and faith schools over comprehensives (Schagen et al., 2002: 5). However, as Hattersley (2002) has noted:

> the creation of selective schools establishes a hierarchy of esteem in the public mind. Specialist schools are regarded as special. They become parents' first preference. In consequence the notion of good schools and bad schools is established. Once that idea gets into a community's collective unconscious it turns from myth to reality.

As we have seen, this free-choice or free-market approach is precisely what happened when league tables were published in the 1990s. The NFER study also found that able pupils do as well at GCSE level in comprehensive schools as they do in selective schools whilst the middle-ability pupils fared better at Key Stage 3 (age 11–14 years) in selective schools than those in comprehensives (Schagen and Schagen, 2002). In the DfEE's own study, however, which compared the GCSE and GNVQ (General National Vocational Qualification) results of grammar school pupils with those of the top achieving 25 per cent of pupils in comprehensives, the comprehensive school pupils did as well if not better (Jesson, 2001).

This finding has done nothing to diminish the government's commitment to partial selection to specialist schools. In 2002 the then Secretary of State for Education, Estelle Morris, outlined plans for five levels of secondary school. The most successful secondaries, those with the best examination results, will become leaders of educational reform and possibly manage less successful schools. At the next level, there will be advanced specialist schools; below them, specialist schools, then schools working towards specialist status, and finally failing schools where fewer than 20 per cent of pupils gain five A–C grades at GCSE. These proposals are claimed to be more appropriate to the needs of the twenty-first century than the 'one size fits all' comprehensive, some of which Estelle Morris claimed she 'would not touch with a bargepole' during her speech to the Social Market Foundation (Mansell, 2002). It is interesting to consider how the differentiated choice which the government is attempting to provide through specialist schools will find expression in more rural or geographically far-flung communities, many of which only have one secondary school.

In addition to the diversity of provision manifest through different types of schools such as the specialist schools described above, and beacon schools, chosen for their demonstration and dissemination of best practice, the white paper which heralded these developments (DfES, 2001) described a range of ways in which structural diversity was to be pursued. These included the use of different types of adults in classrooms (e.g. classroom assistants and learning mentors), investment in ICT equipment, online curriculum materials 'catering for children of all abilities' (p. 5) and training in its use for teachers, and the facility for the most able pupils to progress at a faster pace. The Centre for Public Policy Research (2002) comments that the white paper also uses diversity in a second way, – i.e. to describe parental preferences and individual talents, assuming that diversity of provision is a means to achieving the latter: 'In eliding the two senses of the term, the document is attempting to contribute to the construction of a new commonsense, one in which selective and differentiated provision is accepted as the most effective means of meeting everyone's needs' (ibid: 18).

Of particular note in the quest for structural change to promote diversity and differentiation is the establishment of the Gifted and

Talented Academy to support the progress of very able pupils (aged 11–16 years) through specially targeted activities. The academy has all the hallmarks of prestige – based in a top-rated university and led by a professor, the very term 'academy' sets it apart from ordinary schooling. In 2002 a hundred pupils were whittled down from 520 applications on the basis of National Curriculum assessment tests, the American College entry test, world-class tests and teacher recommendations to attend a three-week summer school. Over a third of the chosen students were non-white British and over a third were from deprived urban areas. Here we see the coming together of Labour's drive to 'modernize' school approaches with its agenda for social justice. This might be juxtaposed, however, with the government's commitment to the development of world-class tests which have been designed to help universities distinguish between 18-year-olds with straight A grades. There are also plans to develop a distinction or A* grade for A-level (DfES, 2002). In the first round, a third of those taking the world-class tests were from private schools which educate just 7 per cent of the England's pupils (Henry, 2002a).

Thus, although the concept of differentiation by innate ability, tested via the 11-plus, has ostensibly been replaced by differentiation by individual potential, tested via GCSE, GNVQ, A-levels and by national assessment tests, current policy in England is driving schools back to a selective system predicated on measures of single ability. This, despite the growing research evidence which supports a more sophisticated understanding of how people learn using multiple intelligences (Gardner, 1993) and individual learning styles (Riding and Rayner, 1998) – for a full discussion, see Bartlett et al., (2001). In Japan studies have indicated that ability is a much less central concern than effort (Purdie and Hattie, 1996). The western notion of ability is turned on its head; hence 'intelligence is viewed as an expression of achievement; it results from experience and education' (ibid.: 848).

The English National Curriculum and differentiation

In Britain the introduction of the National Curriculum focused the attention of teachers closely on the concept of differentiation. During the 1980s teachers had been striving for a broad and balanced curriculum and for the celebration of the achievements of all pupils through Records of Achievement as opposed to traditional academically focused reports. The DES document *Better Schools* (1985b) reflected this drive in its ideas for raising standards of attainment, asserting breadth, balance, relevance and differentiation as the four key principles which should underpin effective curriculum planning. The introduction of the GCSE in 1986 (first examination 1988), as a means of creating the same examination opportunities for all by replacing GCE O-levels and CSE examinations with a single qualification, was generally applauded by teachers.

It was hoped that the National Curriculum would consolidate these equal opportunities gains through the endorsement of a curriculum which provided the full range of subjects for all pupils (NCC, 1990). Pupils with special educational needs were much hailed as prospective beneficiaries by the architects of the National Curriculum since for the first time they were to be entitled to access to the full curriculum (Stakes and Hornby, 1996). The DES (1989b: para. 4.15) claimed that progression through the attainment targets encouraged differentiation since they allowed 'pupils to make identifiable progress through the levels at their own pace and from their own starting point'. Instead, the reduction of funding for pupils with a statement of special educational need and the publishing of league tables of pupil performance led to a reluctance on the part of school managements to cater for such children. In response the government established a code of practice governing the identification and treatment of pupils with special educational needs (DfE, 1994). One of the fundamental principles underpinning this was that 'the needs of most pupils will be met in the mainstream classroom, alongside their peers' (ibid.: 2).

The extent to which the educational attainment of all children was raised by the National Curriculum was hotly debated in the 1990s since many children with learning difficulties or emotional and behavioural problems 'have been subjected to curricula much of which have been irrelevant to their needs' (Stakes and Hornby, 1996: 215). Subsequent legislation has established the notion of 'individual education programmes' for pupils with special needs which is a highly differentiated approach predicated on individual assessment of particular learning difficulties by expert teachers. The practice of inclusion – teaching pupils in mainstream classes – has been strengthened, with pupils receiving dedicated in-class individualized support from teaching assistants.

Circular 5/89 (DES, 1989a), in its outline of the levels of attainment prescribed in the original National Curriculum, placed great emphasis on continuity and progression of learning. It suggested that, where necessary, pupils might be taught outside the age range so that the work would be commensurate with the level they had reached in a particular attainment target. The reality of this for schools where pupils might be at different levels for different subjects, not to mention different attainment targets within subjects, has meant that the practice of grouping youngsters with different age peers is rare. The effect on a pupil's social and emotional progress is also a deterrent to this approach. Darling-Hammond (1994) reported on American research which found that when students were kept down a grade their scores on both achievement and social-emotional measures were consistently lower than students of equal attainment level who were promoted to the next grade.

Although early guidance on the implementation of the National Curriculum was alert to the need to discuss pedagogy which supports progression in learning, Kerry and Kerry (1997) commented on the paucity of 'official' guidance for teachers on differentiation. This extract from the *Science* document is typical:

> Providing appropriate learning experiences for the full ability range of pupils is a difficult task. It requires careful planning and sensitive teaching by teachers with a broad understanding of science and the ability to match the work to their pupils' capabilities. Activities must challenge all pupils and, at the same time, provide them all with success at some meaningful level. The National Curriculum for science provides scope for challenge within a common framework and the definition of progression within the statements of attainment is a useful device for gauging the scope of work appropriate to different levels of understanding and competence. Some schools may consider organising classes according to ability (NCC, 1989: para. A 7.3).

The guidance goes on to note the problems of low expectations of girls in science, the need to take account of the ethnic and cultural diversity within schools and society and the accessibility of science to learners with difficulties. The general message emerging from the guidance was the need to group pupils by ability in order to facilitate groups with homogeneous ability levels. This approach is known as *setting* – a structural device which separates pupils within subjects based on end-of-year tests and other achievement scores.

Setting by ability

A change of government from Conservative to Labour did not alter
the commitment to setting by ability. In 1997 the DfEE asserted
that, by 2002, setted groups should be the norm at secondary level;
this has been almost entirely met. Again we see that, paradoxically,
it is a Labour government that at the turn of the century supported
the almost exclusive use of setting by ability whilst the Labour government in the late 1960s and 1970s had promoted the adoption of
mixed-ability settings for learning. There are, however, subject differences in the use of setting. Chyriwsky's (1996) research into the
opinions of mathematics teachers in 355 English secondary schools
indicated very clear support (92 per cent) for setting (the separation
of pupils by subject-specific attainment) as a means of responding
to the needs of able pupils. A survey by Ofsted in 1996 indicated
that 94 per cent of schools use setting in the upper secondary years
for mathematics (Boaler, 1997). By contrast, in creative and practical subjects, such as art, PE or music, setting is seldom thought to
be appropriate.

Boaler (1997) has reviewed research into setting, finding that,
whilst there was a small but not statistically significant advantage
for the most able pupils if they were setted, the losses for the less
able when setted were great. Their attainment was significantly
lower than the attainment of the less able who were in mixed-
ability groups. Boaler's own three-year study (1996) compared the
GCSE mathematics results of 310 pupils in two schools, one of which
set the pupils whilst the other taught pupils in mixed-ability groups.
She found that results were significantly better amongst the latter
group even though test results from Year 7 indicated the pupils were
of similar ability. When Boaler asked Year 11 pupils in the setted
school about mathematics lessons the responses revealed a dissatisfaction with the fixed pace of progress. Some pupils, especially girls,
found the pace too fast which occasioned them to become anxious;
more of the boys reported that the pace was too slow. This was the
case across the eight sets which is a striking finding, given that one
would assume a limited range of ability within each set. The pupils
preferred the arrangements lower down the school when they had
been able to work at their own pace in mixed-ability groups because
they gained a better understanding. Many of the pupils who were
negatively affected by setting were the most able. Boaler (ibid.: 585)
concluded that 'a student's success in their set had relatively little to

do with their ability, but a great deal to do with their personal preferences for learning pace and style'.

In primary schools structural changes to the curriculum (i.e. the introduction of the literacy and numeracy hours, which require classes to spend an hour a day on each of mathematics and English), have also spawned the grouping of pupils by ability within classes. MacIntyre and Ireson (2002) investigated whether these groupings had an effect on pupils' self-concepts. They discovered that pupils in higher-ability groups had higher mathematics self-concepts than those in lower-ability groups and that a significant number of pupils were incorrectly grouped according to their mathematical skills. They concluded that within-class grouping can actually inhibit rather than facilitate children's learning. Kutnick et al. (2002) also found problems in within-class groupings across 187 primary classes. Particularly interesting is the finding that for nearly half of the time that the low-ability pupils (mainly boys) had an adult with them it was a classroom assistant or someone other than the teacher. By contrast, when an adult worked with the high-ability groups (mainly girls) there was a much greater likelihood that the adult was a teacher.

Differentiation, curriculum status and assessment

The grouping of pupils via setting and their assessment via national tests and GCSE have, then, become far more differentiated. Teachers can enter pupils for different tiers of the GCSE examination; thus some pupils will be denied the opportunity to attempt the higher-level examination papers. This development is paradoxical when one considers that the whole purpose of the GCSE was to consolidate into a single examining system the previously differentiated examinations of CSE and GCE. GCSE tiering separates chidren and enforces systematic inequalities in curriculum coverage and examination opportunities (Gillborn and Youdell, 2000). Current proposals (DfES, 2002) also include the option for schools to 'capitalize on accelerated learning in Key Stage 3' and allow pupils to take GCSE early on a more general basis than is currently the case.

There has also been a growing differentiation in the status of the English National Curriculum subjects. At primary-school level, statutory changes to the curriculum have inadvertently led to differentiated status for subjects. The core subjects, particularly maths and English and to a lesser extent science, are now over emphasized as a consequence of the National Literacy and Numeracy Strategies which specify two hours daily of prescribed curricula work in mathematics and English. This is at the expense of children working on foundation subjects such as geography, history, art, design technology, music and physical education. Most primaries now spend all morning on these two subjects, 50 per cent of the total school time, leading to a narrowing of the activities for pupils and a far less differentiated curriculum experience. At secondary level the National Curriculum has undergone several amendments such that at Key Stage 4 the only compulsory subjects are now the core subjects, religious education, design technology (DT), information communication technology (ICT), modern foreign languages (MFL), physical education (PE) and citizenship (new from September 2002). There are plans to reform the curriculum further to make MFL and DT an entitlement rather than a compulsory subject and to introduce work-related learning (DfES, 2002).

This degree of flexibility within the curriculum and its assessment inevitably leads to status differentials for subjects, their assessment, their teachers, their esteem amongst pupils, parents and employers. Career opportunities for teachers of the core subjects are likely to be greater than those for teachers of arts or language subjects. Pupils' attitudes towards homework in the core subjects could be more serious than in non-core subjects. Assessment results of compulsory subjects are likely to be esteemed by employers more than those of non-compulsory subjects. Thus a hierarchy of subjects, similar to that in existence at Key Stage 4 before the inception of the National Curriculum, is emerging.

Differentiation and post-compulsory education

At post-compulsory level, Ainley (2002) has described Labour government policy as a divisive strategy since he interprets its consultation proposals (DfES, 2002) as the implicit division of pupils at the age of 14 years into three tiers each following a distinct curriculum route through to the age of 19. Ainley explains that the proposals will lead to the top tier of pupils focusing on an academic diet of traditional A-levels and then proceed to the top research universities funded for this purpose. The second tier will follow a work-based route which will combine work with study through modern apprenticeship schemes and on to two-year foundation degrees. The third non-advanced further education tier who are not expected to go on to higher education (50 per cent of young people) will, in Ainley's (2002: 16) view, 'join those with special needs, refugees, adults on basic skills courses and others on "learningfare" like Welfare to Work where benefits are conditional upon attendance'. This may be an extreme view but Ainley is cynical about the government's insistence that the further education curriculum will be more flexible and responsive to students' needs, suggesting instead that this tertiary tripartism will unofficially differentiate between students on grounds of race, class and gender. In support of his point he cites the fact that most of the older esteemed universities attract the younger, white, middle-class high-achieving students. Proportionately more students from working-class and ethnic minority backgrounds attend the newer, more vocationally orientated universities than attend the old universities.

Gillborn (2001), too, is sceptical about the extent to which student choices at the age of 14 years are real choices because of the pressure which is put on pupils to study for the most 'appropriate' examinations despite any cosmetic changes to their names. Some pupils are thus marked out for high-status academic study and others for lower-status vocational options. He explains that research suggests that there is a greater proportion of black, Bangladeshi and Pakistani pupils in the latter group which limits their post-16 opportunities for advanced study and progression to professional occupations. Thus an apparent attempt by policy-makers to address differential access to further and higher education and to develop parity of esteem between vocational and academic qualifications through structural change may actually run counter to equality of opportunity. Largely this is due to the ideological context in which the free market ideals of Thatcherism have persisted and been extended under New Labour such that money buys access to 'better' education, greater extra-curricular opportunities, state-of-the-art educational equipment and more conducive social interactions which in turn place young people more favourably for top-tier progress.

We see the social justice agenda again at the higher-education level where the government's goal is to widen participation rates in further and higher education to 50 per cent of 18–30-year-olds by

2010. This policy aim is designed to reduce the effect of social and financial differentiation amongst young people. Reaching the low-achieving students, however, proves very difficult despite financial incentives for the students and post-code premiums for colleges and universities. Retention rates amongst these students is poor which may imply that the diet of study or the way in which it is delivered does not suit them. Differentiation of the student experience will be needed if the wider range of student needs and interests is to be catered for. This will require a sea-change in the attitudes and approaches of many lecturers. Engaging in online and distance learning is a highly differentiated way of learning since it it usually individualized. There is now much more emphasis in schools and colleges worldwide on developing the learning technologies and software to support such strategies but there also remains a commitment to group interaction which is so necessary for consolidating and extending learning. This takes us from a discussion of structural or organizational issues to an examination of the pedagogical strategies relevant to differentiated learning and teaching.

Pedagogical approaches to differentiation

Two principles can be identified as underpinning a differentiated approach to learning – first, that pupil performance is a function of contextually dependent sets of skills and aptitudes and not of simple 'ability'; and, secondly, that the focus of the teacher is the learning process not its product. These governing principles are helpful in promoting a shared understanding of the term differentiation which has been fraught with terminological confusion. However, the emergence of a definitive version of the differentiated learning environment runs counter to a commitment to teachers' ownership of pedagogical decisions. An examination of differentiated approaches and their associated pedagogy reveals a rich variety of strategies and approaches each of which can also be critiqued. Whilst there is apparent consensus amongst educators about what differentiation is in principle, practice varies enormously. Differentiation is particular to the teacher, pupils and context in which it exists and, to that extent, might elude generalized definition. A common distinction is differentiation by task or by outcome; both will be considered here. Consideration will also be given to the use of group work because of its fundamental place in the differentiated classroom and to whole-school strategies which signal a commitment to differentiation.

Differentiation by task

This is where the teacher provides tasks of differing complexity relating to the same learning topic (Hart, 1996; Tubbs, 1996). Thus tasks will vary in the media of expression they employ, in the depth of focus and intellectual challenge they provide and in the level of independence they require. Written tasks designed to provide a high level of challenge might include survey design, research reports, novel or extended essay writing. Reading might focus on personally chosen books, quality newspaper cuttings, journal articles or independent research via a library topic loan or the Internet. Pupils might be guided to co-ordinate the principles found in different texts (Freeman, 1996). Oral work at this level would emphasize group discussion, political debate and the use of Open University broadcasts. Opportunities for the higher-order problem-solving and hypothesizing called for by Montgomery (1996) could be created through the design of a mathematical or scientific experiment or model and so on. The emphasis is on long-term goals, intellectual challenge and independent learning. Kerry and Kerry (1997) have discussed the use of cognitively demanding questions and self-marking to this end, pointing out the advantages they have for developing reasoning skills, pupil centredness and freedom of expression. They warned, however, of the potentially divisive nature of these strategies. Teachers also have to remember that pupils need attention and monitoring to move their learning on, however great the challenge of the task. One of the greatest dilemmas in extending and enriching the learning experiences of those pupils who are advancing well is in ensuring that they are not just given more of the same. Freeman (1996: 227) has described enrichment as 'the deliberate rounding-out of the basic curriculum subjects with ideas and knowledge that enable a pupil to be aware of the wider context – not a supplementary diet which depends on whether there is enough money for "extra" material and tuition'. George (1995: 51) too, saw enrichment as a natural part of a skilled teacher's methods which led directly to differentiation as 'a function of the teacher's flexibility, sensitivity to individual needs, a sense of timing, and a mastery of subject area'.

The challenge of meeting the needs of the most able cannot be underestimated. Kerry and Kerry (1997) conducted research into secondary and primary-school teachers' views on the use of differentiated teaching strategies. They reported that teachers found teaching the more able through differentiated work difficult because of the lack of appropriate resources and the time required to prepare them; the tendency of some pupils not to want to be treated differently from their peers; and the demands of catering for a wide range of abilities at once. Similarly, Simpson and Ure (1994) identified three key factors seen by secondary teachers to inhibit the development of differentiation: class size, the range of attainment and lack of time.

The pupils who broadly comply with the rules of the classroom and expectations of the teacher usually comprise the largest group in the class but may be the most easily overlooked. There can be a danger of providing work which is 'busy' yet which encourages little thinking and, in turn, little cognitive development (Adey, 1992). Significantly, even in research projects which seek to explore the range of learner competence in classrooms, these are the pupils who are ignored because of a preoccupation with finding ways of responding to the most and least effective learners rather than with a focus on individual competence. In terms of task differentiation, these pupils may need structured guidance such as prompt sheets to help scaffold their ideas or guide them through software; their reading material may include interest and age-related books, local newspaper cuttings and worksheets of an appropriate reading level (sentence length and complexity, familiarity with vocabulary, etc.). Written tasks might include comprehension exercises, diary construction, short stories/reports and work summaries. Oral work would capitalize on pair and small-group discussion/activities. Problem-solving tasks would move from the concrete to the abstract with examples provided to work from – for example, game design might constitute a task in humanities or database interrogation a focus of science. The emphasis is on monitoring progress to ensure tasks are appropriate – that is, challenging yet achievable. As it is seldom the case that secondary teachers spend long enough with their classes to develop an awareness of each learner's processing style, these generalized strategies can be engineered to employ a range of presentation modes so that there is an increased chance of individuals engaging with the tasks using their predominant processing style.

Where pupils require a much greater level of support and guidance the task will be structured to rely on materials which are simple yet age relevant. The biggest challenge can be in not patronizing pupils whose literacy skills are limited but whose level of 'street wisdom' is as great if not greater than that of their peers. Thus teachers may use youth culture books and magazines alongside worksheets of an appropriate reading level (large type, short sentences, few key ideas, jargon-free terminology). There might also be heavy reliance on audio and video media as a means both of expression and stimulus. Forms of writing could include sentence completion, free writing, subject-specific word games, cloze procedure, list making, word searches and crosswords. Specific literacy and numeracy skills software could be employed as well as subject-specific packages which facilitate progression from simple to more demanding tasks. In oral work a small group might work with the teacher or classroom assistant and an emphasis would be placed on rehearsal, repetition, question/answer and pair discussion. Problem-solving tasks would focus on concept consolidation and graphical representation of new concepts, games playing and scenario completion. The emphasis with pupils requiring more support is on short-term goals, positive reinforcement, repetition and incremental development of understanding.

Differentiation by task requires a great deal of forward planning by teachers and a thorough knowledge of each learner's needs. Whilst commercially produced material can be of some value, case-study research (McGarvey et al., 1996) has shown that teachers still need to devise their own differentiated support materials to meet each pupil's needs. In a study of over 200 primary schools in Northern Ireland, over two thirds of the curriculum support staff visiting the schools reported that teachers were finding it difficult to provide suitable resources for both low and high-attaining pupils. Over 55 per cent also said that there were problems in preparing appropriate core and extension materials for the spread of ability in the middle band. Simpson and Ure (1994) explored the match between pupil competence and tasks provided by a small group of Scottish primary teachers nominated as good differentiators. Results were very similar to the findings of a study in England (Bennett et al., 1984). Both studies revealed that the more able pupils were capable of greater challenge than they were set. This may be because the planning of differentiated schemes of work does not usually start from a knowledge of the assessed competence of particular pupils but from a generalized notion of three levels of ability (Weston, 1996). Withers and Eke (1995) expressed scepticism about the preoccupation with matching the right materials and task to each pupil because of what they perceived to be a concern with outcomes rather than with experience and understanding.

The danger of pupils becoming associated in teachers' minds with a certain task level, leading to the re-emergence of the self-fulfilling prophecy problem, has been identified by Kerry and Kerry (1997). Tubbs (1996) summarized the dilemma with differentiation by task as being the necessity to predict ability in advance in order to match tasks to need. He was uncomfortable about the inevitable separating of pupils one from another and the differences in educational opportunities which this creates. The studies reviewed have indicated, either directly or indirectly, a need for teachers to have a detailed knowledge of each pupil's learning needs. As Weston (1996: 5) feared, however, 'consistently matching work to the capacities of *each pupil in every class*' is an ideal which can be achieved only by 'a few very well-endowed schools'.

Differentiation by outcome

Essentially the teacher provides the same task or stimulus for all pupils, who engage with it at their own pace and using their own interpretation, leading to different learning outcomes. The stimulus might be a radio or TV broadcast, teacher exposition, a reading, a demonstration, a visit or special experience, mixed-ability discussion groups, a class meeting, a picture, photograph or object and so on. Montgomery (1996) has proposed the use of games and simulations for the differentiation of learning outcomes. Across the range of presentation media pupils' responses will vary. For example, a reading about fox-hunting by the teacher in an English lesson might elicit oral responses ranging from a class debate to single-word answers to a series of tape-recorded questions. Within DT the teacher might be looking for the levels of sophistication different pupils apply to the design of a household item, having set the class the same task; the PE teacher, levels of co-ordination within a skills task and so on. Riding and Read (1996), in a study of 12-year-old pupils' preferences for ways of working, found that less able students preferred open-ended tasks that allowed for a wider range of responses and which promoted discussion.

It has been argued by this author (Burton and Anthony, 1997) that the challenge of meeting the intellectual needs of pupils within a mixed-ability class can be met by the use of carefully structured open-ended tasks. Anthony's French class of 25, predominantly Muslim girls, in a 13–18 inner-city comprehensive was set the task of creating a scene in a florist's shop using the transactional language learnt in the unit. A basic set of phrases was provided and pupils were advised that they could work on their own or in groups and could use the teachers as a resource alongside books and displays. The aim was to provide a framework for successful performance amongst pupils of a wide range of ability. The performances were recorded on video tape. Having taught the necessary procedural knowledge to complete the task, it was postulated that the follow-up use of an open-ended task would provide opportunities to extend and communicate meaning beyond the prescribed text.

The findings were convincing: despite some evidence of task resistance due to the novelty of the task specification, all pupils in the class achieved success and were able to alter or add to the given structure of the transactions in some way. The greatest extension of ideas and language occurred amongst the pupils of high ability who went far beyond the basic task, adding meanings taken from their significant personal experiences and previous learning. The open-ended task clearly acted as a catalyst for the meaningful construction and communication of both declarative (knowing that) and procedural (knowing how) knowledge.

Differentiation by outcome is not universally applauded, however. Tubbs (1996: 58) claimed it favours 'an abstract equality' over responding to individual needs. Daw (1995) said teachers take refuge in it, failing to appraise critically their own practice and, like Tubbs, suggested that the tasks or materials were not sufficiently targeted to individual needs. Dickinson and Wright (1993) recognized the notion of differentiation by outcome, avoiding the problems referred to above by concentrating their analysis on how differentiation by resource, by support and by response can lead to different outcomes. Weston's (1996) research revealed that, at secondary level, most pupils were working on the same programme of work, with teachers differentiating by response: 'picking up on answers and comments, observing and assisting individuals and interacting with small groups' (p. 5). Weston (ibid.: 5) explained that the strength of this approach lay in the teacher's capacity 'to adjust constantly to individual pupils' difficulties and insights'. When the activity took a whole-class, teacher-directed approach, such as an interactive talk-based lesson, Weston's lesson observations indicated that the responsive approach was more effective in adjusting to individual differences than when pupils had been given a written task to work on individually. In the latter context, certain pupils repeatedly did not finish the main task; others finished early or adjusted their work pace to fit the time available. The success of the responsive approach 'depended crucially on the teacher's detailed, internalised knowledge of each child's strengths and weaknesses, and on his/her ability to monitor each one's progress as the lesson progressed' (ibid.).

This highlights the centrality of the individuality of pupil learning and teacher response. Given the time to target individuals who are engaged in common tasks, teachers can facilitate greater match between learners' needs and their instruction, which in turn can lead to greater cognitive gains. The individuality of cognitive processing style is more likely to be exposed within this relationship and, with appropriate training, to be responded to by the teacher so that it can be effectively harnessed or mediated by the learner. In addition to differentiation by response emerging, during lesson observation, as the most effective strategy, it was also the strategy most frequently cited in Weston's survey of secondary heads of department in 292 schools. Over half the respondents referred to it as the only strategy used to differentiate. English teachers were found to be more likely than mathematics and science teachers to employ individual target-setting and review as a regular part of their differentiation agenda.

Group work

Organizing learners into small groups within classrooms has been common in primary classes for many years and has also been more widely adopted in secondary classes in recent years. Group work is a strategy which can be used whether teachers are differentiating by task or by outcome. Research using the ideas of psychologists such as Vygotsky (1978) and Bruner (1983) has testified to the learning gains which can be made when talking is facilitated amongst pupils working in pairs and groups (Burton, 2001). Pupils can be mixed by competence at a certain skill, by friendship, by interest, by need and so on; the group membership will depend on the purpose and nature of the lesson. Teachers' views of how to establish groups within classes vary but it is usually recognized that a static group structure may inhibit progress because pupils' roles within their groups can become entrenched. Changing groups around can encourage pupils to adopt different roles – for instance, the pupil who would not ordinarily fall into the group leader role but for whom the teacher considers such an experience would be beneficial. Both the membership and the task of groups need to be carefully thought through beforehand by the teacher if there is to be cognitive gain. Group work is a vehicle through which to encourage and value pupil talk. Dowrick (1996: 16–17) has explained that:

> The standard co-operative learning method has been to employ heterogeneous grouping. The argument in its favour has been that high-ability pupils benefit from mentally organising their thoughts in order to explain them to their less able partners, and from reformulating them to make their explanations clearer when necessary, as well as from initially having studied new material more carefully in order to explain it later. Low-ability pupils are said to learn from their partners' explanations, especially as the explanations are likely to be more accessible than those given by a teacher, and from monitoring their own understanding before asking for help.

A recent study (Black et al., 2002) trained 24 mathematics and science teachers in London to use structured questioning and to encourage all pupils to discuss their understanding of concepts rather than be constrained to find the single correct answer to a teacher's question. At the end of the project pupils of all abilities scored on average half a grade higher in their National Assessment Tests or GCSEs than pupils in ordinary lessons. Group work also facilitates support from the teacher for individuals and inventive group-work activities can help pupils take responsibility for their own work, raise their self-esteem and consolidate and extend their understanding of new material (Le Metais and Jordan, 1996). However, some secondary school teachers are reticent about using group work because they fear a loss of control and direction but their role in monitoring progress, intervening to help scaffold emerging ideas and pointing groups to new information and appropriate sources is essential if learning is to be progressed. Riding and Read (1996) found that most pupils in their study preferred group or pair work to individual tasks but noted that the predominant method used in most secondary schools is the completion of individual tasks.

At primary level, a teacher in McGarvey et al.'s (1996) study of teachers' views on the practicalities of differentiated teaching in over 200 of Northern Ireland's primary schools expressed the view that 'grouping is the closest you'll get to matching tasks to the child' (p. 78). The problems associated with group work, according to McGarvey et al.'s sample, are the differing rates at which pupils work, the heavy organizational demands, difficulties in determining what is 'productive chat' and what contribution individuals are making to a collaborative exercise, and keeping records of individual progress. Le Metais and Jordan (1996) have suggested that many of the problems which teachers experience with group work result because the pupils are not taught how to work co-operatively. When such training is given within the context of the academic subject, it is claimed that pupils' motivation, behaviour and cognitive achievements are enhanced. Gillies and Ashman (1995) argued that their research with 440 Year 6 Australian children in 22 different classes showed that 'children can learn to work very effectively together in the classroom using co-operative learning techniques' and that children can be taught appropriate small-group skills with relative ease (p. 223). In a recent British study of 187 primary classes, Kutnick et al. (2002) found that teachers provided little training for the pupils to develop group-work skills and to practise these in pursuit of learning. They suggested that teachers may not think strategically about the size and composition of groups in relation to the tasks assigned and called for the social pedagogy of pupil grouping to receive attention from educationalists.

Whole-school strategies

The extent to which schools recognize the need for a whole-school approach to differentiation is an important factor in its success. Large class sizes, small teaching spaces, lack of time to prepare and evaluate, shortage of human resources, the pressure of other educational innovations and greater stress on assessing pupils via National Curriculum tests at the end of Key Stages all militate against the maintainance of a fully differentiated approach. A whole-school approach to differentiation through the identification of learning gains, investment of time in organization and planning, motivational strategies for group work and the adoption of new teaching methods is more effective than a piecemeal approach. Long sessions of time, for instance, can facilitate flexibility which is useful for arranging trips or one-off stimuli and the regrouping of pupils according to emerging need (Freeman, 1996). Recent reports suggest that some secondary schools have adopted these longer time sessions by 'introducing two-hour lessons and scrapping homework to do logic and philosophy projects. Timetable overhauls for 11 to 14-year-olds have been implemented by headteachers who argue that the daily grind of unconnected, hour-long subject lessons is not working' (Henry, 2002b: 9).

Small group sizes would clearly also assist any teacher's efforts at differentiation. Jameson et al. (1995) have stressed the need to utilize learning support teaching expertise at the planning stage as well as during the execution of lessons. The development of team teaching and mutual support systems where teachers collaborate on resources, materials and ideas makes for economies of scale as well as for a shared commitment to the school's pedagogical ideals. In-service training, professional development programmes, whole-school language, equal opportunities and assessment policies and well established monitoring and evaluation procedures can all contribute to differentiation of approach.

Summary

An examination of pedagogical strategies for differentiation has revealed the difficulties associated with matching tasks to pupil competence. Even within setted groups there is little evidence that task matching is appropriate for all pupils, although some teachers feel better able to attempt it. It has been suggested that the use of open-ended tasks, combining elements of differentiation by outcome, support, presentation mode, grouping, task and resource, is both more successful and more manageable than task matching, whether pupils are setted by ability or are in mixed groups because they have more opportunity to use their individual processing styles. The call for such an eclectic approach is borne of the fact that no particular method of organizing material or pupils can in itself improve learning. Each learning situation is unique with a host of variables that can be different, from the obvious things like the teacher, pupils, subject matter, environment and motivation levels, to apparently less significant ones such as time of day, absentee pupils, the weather, pupils' previous lesson and so on. However, the one constant factor which can make a significant difference to pupils' learning is, of course, the teacher. A survey of 60 pupils from 15 secondary schools identified the quality of the interaction with the teacher, the explanations the teacher provided and the support and assistance the teacher gave them with their problems as the key factors in enhancing the quality and level of the pupils' learning (Simpson and Ure, 1994).

Conclusion

In spite of its exponents not sharing a common view of what differentiation means, the 1990s vogue for the construct led to a more sophisticated focus on ways of helping individual learners thrive. Thus, teachers learnt about flexible learning, learning styles, the potential of ICT, the need for pupil talk, the importance of group work and so on. It is contended, then, that, in pedagogical terms, differentiated approaches have evolved from concerns about designing teaching as a consequence of the grouping strategy, to the development of a range of strategies which facilitate individual pupil access to the material to be learnt. Creating task variety and intellectual challenge constitutes the goal of teaching in setted classrooms as much as in mixed-ability classrooms. The context is now different because at institutional level teachers are preoccupied with the achievement of targets set for classes, subject departments and year groups as a consequence of data comparison with schools of similar types (see Chapter 6 for more detail). Within this pressurized situation it is to be hoped that individual learning needs are not sacrificed at the altar of teachers' performance score objectives.

In exploring the various manifestations of differentiation, the socio-political determinants of structural forms of differentiation from the 1980s to the present day have been compared with those driving the comprehensive schooling movement of the 1960s and 1970s. Both have claimed equality of opportunity as their rationale although the political mores of each period were quite different. The 1960s was a time of largesse, as a result of economic boom, and a time of social conscience wherein the drive was for equality of treatment in terms of schooling, social opportunity, gender rights and ethnic grouping. The 1980s and early 1990s were again a time of economic progress but this was seen to be driven by personal enterprise, endeavour and resourcefulness and was not the responsibility of the state. Equality of opportunity in education was ostensibly provided by creating the appearance of choice of schools, this choice promoted by an expectation that schools should be more publicly accountable for their 'performance' through comparative league tables of examination results. In fact the choice for pupils of low-income families has been reduced and that of high-income families increased with pupils from the latter group being transported to schools with the best results. We have seen how this 'choice and diversity' agenda has been perpetuated into the new century through government legislation to establish, for example, specialist schools and an academy for gifted and talented pupils and through proposals to diversify the 14–19 curriculum and its assessment. Readers will draw their own conclusions about how far such choice is real and how well such diversity will improve the educational opportunities of all individuals within the UK's very diverse communities of learners. My own view is consistent with that expressed in Linda Croxford's (2002) conclusion to her research article comparing school differences and social segregation in England, Wales and Scotland. She writes (ibid.: 16):

> The research suggests that the more uniform system of comprehensive schooling in Scotland, that was introduced in a whole-hearted manner, has reduced social segregation and led to a high quality of education for the vast majority of pupils. In contrast, the introduction of comprehensive schooling in England was piecemeal and perpetuated a system of differentiated and socially segregated schools. Open enrolment in England has exacerbated school differences. Middle class parents compete to gain access to the most privileged schools. Where there are differences associated with selection, denomination or gender there are differences in social composition and resulting differences in average attainment. This evidence suggests that the proposed expansion of specialist schools in England will lead to greater social segregation and erode still further the comprehensive ideal.

Student task

To what extent are your learning experiences differentiated? Think about:

- tutor's strategies
- assessment opportunities
- differentiation by task, outcome, resource, support
- groupwork
- scaffolding.

This task can be applied to any visits you make to other educational environments, such as nurseries, schools, further education colleges and so on.

Suggested further reading

Bearne, E. (ed.) (1996) *Differentiation and Diversity in the Primary School*. London: Routledge. Published in the 1990s at the height of interest in differentiation as a means of raising educational achievement, this edited collection covers several subject areas and generic themes. Contributors write either about the principles of diversity or the practices of differentiation.

Hart, S. (ed.) (1996) *Differentiation and the Secondary Curriculum: Debates and Dilemmas*. London: Routledge. Another edited collection of the same period, this text examines some of the ideological and pedagogical issues around differentiation. It includes contributions on learning styles and bilingualism as well as on pedagogical strategies in context.

Weston, P., Taylor, M., Lewis, G. and MacDonald, A. (1998) *Learning from Differentiation: a review of practice in primary and secondary schools*. London: NFER. This research review draws on case study and national survey evidence to explore how schools have responded to professional and policy imperatives for differentiated approaches.

References

Adey, P. (1992) The CASE results: implications for science teaching. *International Journal of Science Education*, 14: 137–46.

Ainley, P. (2002) A divisive strategy. *The Times Higher Educational Supplement*, 7 June: 16.

Ball, S.J. (1994) *Education Reform: A critical and post-structural approach*. Milton Keynes: Open University Press.

Bartlett, S., Burton, D. and Peim, N. (2001) *Introduction to Education Studies*. London: Paul Chapman Publishing.

Bennett, N., Desforges, C., Cockburn, A. and Wilkinson, B. (1984) *The Quality of Pupil Learning Experiences*. London: Erlbaum.

Biemiller, A. (1993) Lake Wobegon revisited: on diversity and education. *Educational Researcher*, 22: 7–12.

Black, P., Harrison, C., Lee, C., Marshall, B. and Wiliam, D. (2002) *Working inside the Black Box: Assessment for Learning in the Classroom*. London: King's College, University of London.

Boaler, J. (1996) A case study of setted and mixed ability teaching. Paper presented at the *British Education Research Association Conference*, Lancaster University, September.

Boaler, J. (1997) Setting, social class and survival of the quickest. *British Educational Research Journal*, 23: 575–95.

Bowen, P. (1995) Secondary history teaching and the OFSTED inspections: an analysis and discussion of history comments. *Teaching History*, 80: 9–13.

Bridges, D. (1994) Parents: customers or partners? In D. Bridges and T.H. McLaughlin (eds) *Education and the Market Place*. London: Falmer Press.

Bruner, J. (1983) *Child's Talk: Learning to Use Language*. Oxford: Oxford University Press.

Burton, D. (2001) Ways pupils learn in S. Capel et al. (eds) *Learning to Teach in the Secondary School* (3rd edn). London: Routledge.

Burton, D. and Anthony, S.A. (1997) The differentiation of curriculum and instruction in primary and secondary schools, *Educating Able Children*, Spring: 26–34.

Centre for Public Policy Research (2002) Achieving success? Discursive strategies and policy tensions in New Labour's white paper for schools. *Education and Social Justice* 4(1): 15–25.

Charlot, B. (2002) Education and cultures. *Education and Social Justice*, 4(1): 11–14.

Chyriwsky, M. (1996) Able children: the need for a subject-specific approach. *Flying High*, 3: 32–6.

Croxford, L. (2001) School differences and social segregation: comparison between England, Wales and Scotland. *Educational Review*, 15(1): 68–73.

Darling-Hammond, L. (1994) Performance-based assessment and educational equity. *Harvard Educational Review*, 64: 5–30.

Daw, P. (1995) Differentiation and its meanings. *The English and Media Magazine*. 32: 11–15.

DES (1978) *Mixed Ability Work in Comprehensive Schools: HMI Matters for Discussion* 6. London: HMSO.

DES (1985a) *Education for All (Swann Report)*. London: HMSO.

DES (1985b) *Better Schools*. London: HMSO.

DES (1989a) *The Education Reform Act 1988: The School Curriculum and Assessment*. Circular 5/89. London: HMSO.

DES (1989b) *National Curriculum: From Policy to Practice*. London: HMSO.

DfE (1994) *Code of Practice on the Identification and Assessment of Special Educational Needs*. London: Central Office of Information.

DfES (2001) *Schools Achieving Success*. Nottingham: DfES Publications.

DfES (2002) *14–19: Extending Opportunitites, Raising Standards*. Nottingham: DfES Publications.

Dickinson, C. and Wright, J. (1993) *Differentiation: A Practical Handbook of Classroom Strategies*. Coventry: NCET.

Downes, P. (1994) Managing the market. In D. Bridges and T.H. McLaughlin (eds) *Education and the Market Place*. London: Falmer Press.

Dowrick, N. (1996) 'But many that are first shall be last': attainment differences in young collaborators. *Research in Education*, 55: 16–28.

Freeman, J. (1996) Teaching highly able children. In R. Andrews (ed.) *Interpreting the New National Curriculum*. London: Middlesex University Press.

Gardner, H. (1993) *Multiple Intelligences: The Theory in Practice*. New York: Basic Books.

George, D. (1995) *Gifted Education: Identification and Provision*. London: David Fulton.

Gewirtz, S., Ball, S.J. and Bowe, R. (1995) *Markets, Choice and Equity in Education*. Buckingham: Open University Press.

Gillborn, D. (2001) Race equality and educational policy. *Educational Review*, 15(1): 21–6.

Gillborn, D. and Youdell, D. (2000) *Rationing Education: Policy, Practice, Reform and Equality*. London: Oxford University Press.

Gillies, R.M. and Ashman, A.F. (1995) The effects of gender and ability on students' behaviours and interactions in classroom-based work groups. *Educational Psychology*, 65: 211–25.

Hart, S. (ed.) (1996) *Differentiation and the Secondary Curriculum: Debates and Dilemmas*. London: Routledge.

Hattersley, R. (2002) Education, education, education. *Education and Social Justice*. 4(1): 1–6.

Henry, J. (2002a) Bright test is magnet for private pupils. *The Times Educational Supplement*, 28 June.

Henry, J. (2002b) Longer hours boost learning. *The Times Educational Supplement*, 19 July.

Jameson, G., Maines, B. and Robinson, G. (1995) *Invisible Support: Delivering the Differentiated Curriculum*. Bristol: Lame Duck Publishing.

Jesson, D. (2001) Selective systems of education – blueprint for lower standards? *Educational Review*, 15(1): 8–14.

Kerry, T. (1984) Analysing the cognitive demands made by classroom tasks in mixed ability classes. In: E.C. Wragg (ed.) *Classroom Teaching Skills*. Beckenham: Croom Helm.

Kerry, T. and Kerry, C. (1997) Differentiation: teachers' views of the usefulness of recommended strategies in helping the more able pupils in primary and secondary classrooms. *Educational Studies*, 23: 439–57.

Kutnick, P., Blatchford, P. and Baines, E. (2002) Pupil groupings in primary school classrooms: sites for learning and social pedagogy? *British Educational Research Journal*, 28(2): 187–206.

Le Metais, J. and Jordan, D. (1996) Groups or rows? A co-operative learning perspective. *TOPIC*, 15: 1–6.

MacIntyre, H. and Ireson, J. (2002) Within-class ability grouping: placement of pupils in groups and self-concept. *British Educational Research Journal*, 28(2): 249–63.

Madeus, G.F. (1994) A technological and historical consideration of equity issues associated with proposals to change the nation's testing policy. *Harvard Educational Review*, 64: 76–95.

Mansell, W. (2002) Five steps to create an elite. *The Times Educational Supplement*, 28 June.

McGarvey, B., Morgan, V., Marriott, S. and Abbott, L. (1996) Differentiation and its problems: the views of primary teachers and curriculum support staff in Northern Ireland. *Educational Studies.* 22: 69–82.

Montgomery, D. (1996) Differentiation of the curriculum in primary education. *Flying High*, 3: 14–28.

National Curriculum CounciL (1989) *Science Non–Statutory Guidance.* York: NCC.

National Curriculum Council (1990) *The Whole Curriculum: Curriculum Guidance Three.* York: NCC.

National Foundation for Educational Research (1995) *Differentiated Teaching and Learning in Primary and Secondary Schools (Research Information).* Slough: NFER.

Purdie, N. and Hattie, J. (1996) Cultural differences in the use of strategies for self-regulated learning. *American Educational Research Journal*, 33: 845–71.

Riding, R.J and Rayner, S. (1998) *Learning Styles and Strategies.* London: David Fulton.

Riding, R.J. and Read, G. (1996) Cognitive style and pupil learning preferences. *Educational Psychology*, 16: 81–106.

Rosenthal, R. and Jacobson, L. (1968) *Pygmalion in the Classroom.* New York: Holt, Rinehart & Winston.

Schagen, S., Davies, D., Rudd, P. and Schagen, I. (2002) *The Impact of Specialist and Faith Schools on Performance.* London: NFER.

Schagen, S. and Schagen, I. (2002) *The Impact of Selection on Pupil Performance.* London: NFER.

Simpson, M. and Ure, J. (1994) *Studies of Differentiation Practices in Primary and Secondary Schools. Interchange* 30. Edinburgh: Scottish Office Education Department, Research and Intelligence Unit.

Stakes, R. and Hornby, G. (1996) Special educational needs and the National Curriculum. In R. Andrews (ed.) *Interpreting the New National Curriculum.* London: Middlesex University Press.

Tubbs, N. (1996) *The New Teacher: An Introduction to Teaching in Comprehensive Education.* London: David Fulton.

Vygotsky, L.S. (1978) *Mind in Society: The Development of Higher Psychological Processes.* London: Harvard University Press.

Weston, P. (1996) Learning about differentiation in practice, *TOPIC* 16(4).

Weston, P., Taylor, M., Lewis, G., and MacDonald. A. (1998) *Learning from Differentiation: A Review of Practice in Primary and Secondary Schools.* London: NFER.

Withers, R. and Eke, R. (1995) Reclaiming 'match' from the critics of primary education. *Educational Review*, 47: 59–73.

4

Special Educational Needs and Inclusive Education: Origins and Current Issues

Peter Clough and Philip Garner

This chapter begins with a brief introduction to clarify what is meant by the term 'special educational needs (SEN). We follow this with a discussion of four themes:

1   A historical overview of SEN from the 1950s to the present.
2   The extent to which SEN are created by educational systems.
3   Issues of exclusion.
4   Initiatives to support children with learning difficulties in inclusive educational cultures.

Our aim in this chapter is to draw attention to policy-related experiences in the education of pupils with learning difficulties.

Introduction: what do we mean by SEN?

Special educational needs (SEN) is a familiar term to virtually every-one involved in education. Its importance as a policy issue has been confirmed by the recent initiatives on the part of government to foster an inclusive approach to education. The green paper *Excellence for all children: Meeting Special Educational Needs* (DfEE, 1997) and the subsequent *Programme of Action* (DfEE, 1998) have resulted in an emphasis on the capacity of teachers to accommo-date a far greater range of learners in classrooms. The revised *Code of Practice on the Identification and Assessment of Special Educational Needs* (DfES, 2001a) has confirmed this shift in thinking, and a succession of official publications has ensured that SEN and inclusion will remain at the forefront of the policy agenda for the foreseeable future.

We need to say a brief word about the nature and extent of the phenomenon. According to the code, a child has *special educational needs* if he or she has a *learning difficulty* which calls for *special educational provision* to be made for him or her. Such a learning difficulty may be apparent if a child:

- has a significantly greater difficulty in learning than the majority of children of the same age;
- has a disability which prevents or hinders the child from making use of educational facilities of a kind generally provided for children of the same age in schools within the area of the local education authority; and
- is under 5 years of age and falls within either definition above or would do so if special educational provision was not made for the child.

A child must not be regarded as having a learning difficulty solely because the language medium of communication of the home is different from the language in which he or she will be taught.

The *Code of Practice* op.cit now accepts there are four principal areas of special educational needs relating to:

1 communication and interaction;
2 cognition and learning;
3 behaviour, emotional and social development; and
4 sensory and/or physical impairment.

Estimates vary as to precisely how may children in England and Wales experience these difficulties. Many still uphold the calculation that 'one in five' children are likely to fall into these groupings, an estimate originally made in the Warnock Report of 1978. Of this 20 per cent, about 2 per cent would have a formal 'statement' of entitlement, a term which describes the statutory entitlement of children with SEN to explicit and dedicated resource provision.

Recent statistics regarding 'pupils with statements of SEN' help to show something of the extent of SENs and some indication of current placement policy. Thus:

- Approximately 260,500 pupils had statements of SEN in January 2001.
- The percentage of pupils with statements placed in maintained mainstream schools (nursery, primary and secondary) increased from 57.2 per cent in January 1997 to an estimated 61.4 per cent in January 2001.
- The percentage of pupils with statements placed in maintained special schools or pupil referral units (PRUs) decreased from 37.9 per cent in January 1997 to 34.2 per cent in January 2001.

It is against this contextual background and definition of SEN that we shall now provide a historical overview of SEN, discuss the extent to which SEN are *created* by educational systems, consider issues of exclusion and, finally, look to current initiatives to support inclusive educational cultures.

Historical developments: from SEN to inclusive education

It is worth taking a moment to trace the development of the education of pupils with learning difficulties from provision for SEN to inclusive education. This historical location is important in helping us to understand some of the issues of the present and helps us to see how we have come to use the term 'inclusion'. Here we shall identify some of the roots of present policies which determine the education career of pupils with a variety of curricular, physical, emotional and social needs. The examination of the recent history of SEN-related provision is useful for a variety of reasons, not least in that it enables us to gauge the rapid progress that has been achieved within a relatively short period of time. In particular, it illustrates the crucial shift away from a 'within child' version of provision to one which is emphatically delineated by a 'systems based' approach in which a far greater number of actors and events is implicated.

Inclusive ideology and practice has emerged – in only 50 years – from within a tradition of statutory, categorical exclusion. Special education itself has been transformed from the outside by civilizing forces which have deconstructed and reconstructed its meanings and effects. The move – from segregated special education in special schools, to integration and the development of 'units' within schools, to inclusion of pupils in 'mainstream' settings – has been fuelled by the various ideologies and perspectives which marked their 'moments' in history (Clough, 1998).

At the time of the Education Act 1944 the concept of what is now termed SEN was essentially restricted to those children then described as 'educationally subnormal' or 'physically handicapped'. The Act identified a series of 'categories of handicap', a process which facilitated the easy removal of children into schools or training centres provided for the atypical child. Moreover, in 1994, the permanence of any disabling condition was taken for granted and the acceptance of the concept of intelligence quotient (IQ) as both a valid measure of ability and as an unchanging characteristic justified permanent placements as well as the sharp division of the 11-plus. There were three groups of children who received little or no attention in the Education Act 1944. The severely educationally subnormal (idiots and imbeciles) were outside the educational system altogether, being regarded as 'unsuitable for education in school'. Most were in hospitals for the mentally subnormal and some were in training centres where they were, until 1971, taught and cared for by untrained supervisors. The expectation for these children and young people was that they would live in large hospitals, 'colonies' or asylums and their education consisted of self-help skills and low-level occupational activities. Their parents had even less contact with supervisors than parents of children in mainstream schools had with their children's teachers. Although the general requirement for categorization as 'severely mentally subnormal' was an IQ below 50, some groups (such as those with Downs' syndrome), were identified as 'severely subnormal' purely on the basis of medical diagnosis. In many people's minds, the description 'subnormal' and 'mongol' were synonymous. Even where an IQ score 'justified' it, children with Down's syndrome were excluded from schools for the 'educationally subnormal' (ESN) on principle as the schools tried to preserve their image as educational rather than training establishments.

A second group of children who were recognized but for whom provision was minimal were those identified as 'maladjusted' – a blanket term to describe those children who behaved in ways that schools deemed as inappropriate. The 'category' was notoriously indeterminate and undoubtedly led to misuse, especially given that many of these children were sent to ESN schools (Kysel, 1985).

Thirdly, the 1944 Act recognized that there were children in 'ordinary' or mainstream schools with SEN. It suggested that such children were those whose attainments were 20 per cent or more below the average attainment of children of the same age – measured in terms of IQ. However, within the then tripartite education system established by the 1944 Act, such children were generally accommodated in secondary modern schools and the remedial classes within those schools.

In all these cases educational decisions were made on the basis of intelligence tests, which presented difficulties for those seen as 'maladjusted'. The unidimensional view of educability, with its heavy inference that the difficulty was solely 'within the child', prevented a more productive approach to special education. The report of the Warnock committee (DES, 1978) resulted in the concept of learning difficulty being established. This reorientation was crucial to subsequent developments as it suggested that the child's learning difficulty could be as much interactional and interpersonal as it could be personal. This 'new' way of thinking was to have a significant effect in enhancing opportunities for children with SEN. Moreover, there was an accompanying recognition that IQ was an unreliable predictor of future performance, leading to more flexible, interdisciplinary assessments of children experiencing SEN (Thomas and Loxley, 2001).

The Warnock Report heralded a shift towards 'integration' for many more children who experienced more complex needs. In the period that followed, an increasing number of cases of children with severe learning difficulties (SLD) began to be integrated into mainstream schools (Hegarty, 1987). More recent history would suggest that, although this has been a major successful change, the provision of the so-called Education Reform Act 1988 appeared to have jeopardized the position of some children with SEN. Thus, whilst children with statements who are integrated bring with them substantial resources to their school, the 18 per cent *without* statements were seen by some schools as an expensive nuisance. Moreover, they were viewed as a threat by schools keen to improve their place in the newly established performance league tables. Nowhere was this more apparent than in the case of the child termed as experiencing 'emotional and/or behavioural difficilties' (EBD).

In summary, then, the Warnock Report of 1978 represents the start of SEN in its 'modern' idiom. It introduced the term 'special educational needs', replacing terminology which was both outmoded and pejorative to children with learning difficulties.

Expressions such as 'backward', 'educationally subnormal' and 'maladjusted' were widely used within education prior to the report. Warnock, in contrast, adopted a much more positive approach which was not driven by deficit and determinism. It also signalled the beginning of the more widespread 'integration' of children with SEN into 'mainstream' schools – itself a forerunner of educational inclusion. Furthermore, parents and carers would have a new right to contribute to their child's assessment and the resulting statement of SEN would then be subject to periodic (annual) review – to which parents and carers were entitled to contribute. Interestingly, at the end of 1999, Mary Warnock announced: 'If only we had known then ... The *statement* has been a disastrous mistake.' Reflecting on the effects of the committee's work, Warnock (ibid.) said:

> looking back on the days of the committee, when everyone felt that a new world was opening for disadvantaged children, the most strikingly absurd fact is that the committee was forbidden to count social deprivation as in any way contributing to educational needs ... The very idea of such a separation now seems preposterous.

If Warnock was right in her reassessment of her committees work, the statementing of, and educational provision made for, many thousands of children is called into question.

Throughout the 1980s and 1990s, post-Warnock education provision in England and Wales for children with SEN was continuously affected by major policy changes. Special education occurs within the same policy contexts as all state education and is subject not only to the same structures but also to many of the same impositions, opportunities, dilemmas and conflicts. For all in education, the last 15 years of the twentieth century saw the following trends:

- The increasingly explicit politicization of educational structures and processes.
- Wide and deep-ranging development of legislation which increases the regulation and control of education through central policies.
- The elaboration of systematic inspection processes and criteria.
- The development of certain areas of responsibility (most importantly, funding) to schools.
- The consequent 'marketization' of schooling.

- The complication and, sometimes, conflict of the 'rights' of children, parents and of the consumer generally.
- The increasing separation – both within schools and in the broader institutions which maintain them – of managers from professionals.
- The development of an accountability ethos which effectively promotes instrumentalism within the curriculum (adapted from Clough, 1998).

Thus the twentieth century ended with extensive policy developments and an education culture of constant change. Clough (2000: 8) sketches a rough history of the development of inclusive education, identifying five major perspectives which, though never wholly exclusive of each other, demonstrate historical influences which shape, in part, current views and practices:

1 *The psycho-medical legacy (1950s onwards)*. This is understood as the system of broadly medicalized ideas which essentially saw the *individual* as being somehow 'in deficit' and, in turn, assumed a need for a 'special' education for those individuals.
2 *The sociological response (1960s onwards)*. This broadly represents the critique of the 'psycho-medical legacy', and draws attention to a social *construction* of SEN.
3 *Curricular approaches (1970s onwards)*. This emphasized the role of the *curriculum* in meeting – and, for some writers, effectively *creating* – learning difficulties.
4 *School improvement strategies (1980s onwards)*. This emphasized the importance of systematic organization in pursuit of truly *comprehensive* schooling.
5 *Disability studies critique (1990s onwards)*. This offered perspectives which, often from 'outside' education, elaborated an overtly political response to the exclusionary effects of the psycho-medical model.

This can be represented diagrammatically (Figure 4.1; Clough, 2000) to show the overlap and continuity of various influences 'towards' inclusion. By looking 'back' through the disability studies critique of the 1990s at the influences of the psycho-medical model, the sociological response, curricular approaches and school improvement measures, it is possible to look *forward* to the emergence of a more homogeneous response to inclusive education where individual children's *rights* to inclusive education (as well as *needs for* individually appropriate education) are at centre stage *from the start of their educational career.*

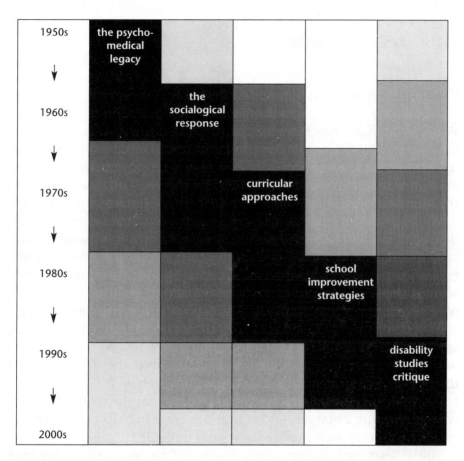

Figure 4.1 *The development of inclusive education*

Looking back we can see how tests, labels and deficits dominated the identification of pupil's learning needs – a legacy from the psycho-medical model dominant in the 1950s and perpetuated by assessment-led curriculum reform of the 1990s. As Sebba and Sachdev (1997) point out, educational 'labels' rather than categorization 'labels' (for example, 'reading difficulties' rather than 'Down's syndrome') lead to more inclusive responses to pupil's learning needs. In the move towards inclusive education, recent developments in England and Wales have hinted at a convergence of thinking about inclusion and about how best this can be achieved. But before we can fully understand the importance of inclusion for *all* pupils, it is important to understand the ways in which SEN are created and how policies and practices *construct* circumstances which lead to exclusion.

Creating needs: constructing difficulty

We suggest that a special educational need is often not a 'given' but can be a 'creation' of educational systems, environments and services. That is to say, it is by virtue of the setting of targets for pupil attainment and levels of pupil achievement and the measures taken to ensure that pupils reach those targets that learning needs are highlighted. Pupils who do not achieve the designated level in, say, literacy or numeracy, may be categorized as having a 'learning difficulty' simply because the standards have been set at a particular level. For example, if it is expected that 80 per cent of 11-year-olds will achieve a certain level in mathematics, it follows that the 20 per cent who are not expected to achieve this fall short of the 'norm' and are somehow inferior in their achievement. Such pupils may well be excluded from mainstream classes as they are placed in segregated settings or units with lessons designed to redress the deficit. Whilst this may be for only part of the school timetable, such separation can create the notion of difference and educational difficulty. In these ways the setting of targets and action designed to help pupils achieve those targets may well *create* educational difficulty.

The assessment-driven curriculum of England and Wales may well be held responsible for the creation of additional concerns about pupil achievement. Children are assessed (often at 4 years old) on entry to the state education system. Though such baseline assessment has been criticized for its distortion of children's capabilities at this age (Nutbrown, 1998), considerable attention has been paid to the use of baseline statistics to measure the 'value-added' by the school, to predict later achievement and to compare school achievement with those of other schools and with previous cohorts of children (see Strand, 1997). Similarly, the Standard Assessment Tasks at 7, 11 and 14 also create non-achievers. There have been many initiatives, as we noted earlier in this chapter, to 'combat' 'underachievement'. Boys' underachievement in English set alarm bells ringing in the later 1990s. Low achievement in literacy inhibits access to the rest of the curriculum and pupils struggling in English are likely to struggle in other aspects of learning at school. In 1997 national strategies were put in place to address issues of underachievement with the publication of a government white paper on education, *Excellence in Schools* (DfEE, 1997b) closely followed by a Green Paper (DfEE, 1997a) which set the tone for consultation on future government policy on SEN. The white paper (DfEE, 1997b: 9) stated: 'Education is the key to creating a society which is dynamic and productive, offering opportunity and fairness to all. It is the Government's top priority. We will work in partnership with all those who share our passion and sense of urgency for higher standards.' Many of the boys who left school in 1997 with no GCSE passes had not achieved what the school wanted for them and, many having experienced occasional exclusions from school, they were likely to experience exclusions from parts of wider society too. Thus, systems and structures can create difficulties which perpetuate through school into adult life.

But it is not the education system and structures alone which create SEN; increasingly, environmental factors affect the health of children and young people. In one broadsheet paper on 10 May 2002, three articles warned of heath risks to young children: danger of skin disease from overuse of chemicals in children's bath gels; poor diet affecting the health and growth of pupils; and closure of public playgrounds for fear that parents might sue local authorities if their children (under the age of 11 years) were injured whilst playing. On the same day, *The Times Educational Supplement* published a special report on autism, alerting (amongst other things) the possible link with the MMR vaccine.

Nutbrown (1998) has argued that early education at its best *is* inclusive education because it is often the experience of those who work within the Foundation stage (QCA, 2000) that many children with learning difficulties and/or disabilities are included *as a first option*. Many such settings would argue that inclusion is as much about *attitudinal* response as it is about *practical* response. It is often the case that systems and structures of institutions construct differences and create difficulties.

Teachers, headteachers, educational psychologists and parents (among others) make decisions about pupils and their difficulties and behind every decision made in response to an instance of educational difficulty there lie traditions of practice that more or less evidently affect outcomes. Those traditions of practice derive from an established (and often unquestioned) belief and a 'diagnosis-remedy' attitude that *construct* difficulty. As Herbert (1998) demonstrates in the case of Steven, 'what's wrong and how can I fix it?' is not the question which needs to be asked; rather, it is a case of 'what are the particular educational needs of each one of my pupils?':

> This was the first time in her short career that Steven's reception class teacher had had a child with a statement of Special Educational Need in her class. She was conscious that by choosing the inclusive option Steven's parents had accepted that he needed to interact with his peer group and not become, once more, dependent upon adults. She was reassured by the head that it was not a scenario of 'success or failure' and was given support to evaluate her own practice in a way which led her to believe that her established skills of providing a well structured and stimulating learning environment for all children were particularly relevant for Steven. She realised that it was her duty to attend not only to what was 'special' about Steven but also to what was 'ordinary' and that there was no mystique to analysing tasks. She was already doing this and making them accessible to all children, including children with learning difficulties (ibid.: p. 103).

The decisions made by parents and teachers in the case discussed above by Herbert pointed to an outcome of inclusive practice. How an individual teacher, a school, a local education authority or service constructs both a problem and its solution is determined by their characteristic habits of interpretation. In the example above, Herbert draws attention to the transferable skills of the teacher to 'analyse skills' and present learning situations to pupils in ways which fit their own individual needs. It goes without saying that other interpretations may well be made, dependent upon experience and upon cultural determinants. In a recent study of four children with learning difficulties, Berry (2001) identified attitudes and curricular responses which contributed, in some cases, to the creation of difficulties for pupils and in other cases to the resolution of difficulties through attention to individual educational need. We could ask, when a child 'succeeds' in one setting and 'fails' in another, what has changed? It is most often the case that it is not the child who is transformed but that the response of the school setting in which he or she is placed is fitting to his or her particular needs. The ethos of the school and classroom, and its constructions and responses to difficulty, can make the crucial difference to achievement and to pupil learning and behaviours which foster inclusion rather than exclusion.

Stories of exclusion: 'Martin', 'Simon' and 'Molly'

Pupils (whatever their age) are often excluded from the mainstream because the educational (and wider social) system is not fit to include them. This can be due to lack of knowledge, lack of will, lack of vision, lack of resources or (even) a lack of morality. For some families, exclusion (from wider society) begins at birth. Perera (2000) describes her experiences as a parent of children with disabilities and discusses the social exclusion which children and their parents can face. Introducing her study of the experiences of five mothers, she writes (ibid.: 91–2):

> I've always believed that parenting is a tough job and an even tougher job is parenting a child with special needs. Until I became a mother in a similar situation I had always thought that having a child with a disability always happened to someone else and possibly could never happen to you. I'd wondered how these families coped with such an unexpected event contrary to all the dreams and expectations of having a healthy child. There were times when I did not understand my mother's friend not wanting to send her daughter to school in the 1960s. The society thought that keeping her at home was the cause of her 'retardation' and spoke critically of the parents. There was another view that the child's 'retardation' was the result of having too much money and too many servants. There were other instances when I'd met doctors who professionally diagnosed the child and dictated terms to these families without empathy. 'Your daughter is brain damaged. There is nothing you can do. Just keep her in a chair and clothe her and feed her as long as she lives' was an instance that haunts me to this day. It was when I found myself to be one of those mothers that I realised the daunting task of bringing up a child with disabilities and the yawning gap between these families experiences and the rest of the world.

Perera continues, in her report, to discuss the diminishing number of invitations to family parties and informal gatherings of mothers and children.

In our discussion of educational exclusion we draw on the experiences of three pupils – Martin, Simon and Molly – who, in their different ways, demonstrate how policy legacies and current policy initiatives are played out in the real lives of pupils in (or on the edge of) the education system.

Nutbrown (1998) gives an account of a nursery teacher who, reluctantly, tried to include a child with autism in her nursery. Things went badly wrong because of endemic difficulties within the setting itself:

> Martin was admitted to a nursery full of children with damage and dislocation in their lives – physical and sexual abuse, overwhelming poverty, disproportionate ill-health, numerous wet beds, and no end of broken hearts.
>
> Martin stayed for two weeks. Each day his teacher talked with his mother. Each day she told her what Martin had enjoyed, and of the struggle he had with his peers in the nursery. There were many troubled children in Martin's company, and though Martin was interested, bright and he was able, the nursery disabled him. In that setting he was not being included in a calm, ordered society. He was not a member of a predictable community, he was appended into a community of children and adults in chaos.
>
> After two weeks Martin left. His teacher hoped he had not been harmed, but she knew the harm it had caused his mother. Martin went to a nursery a few miles away which had a special unit for children with special educational needs and which worked to include children from that unit into mainstream classes once they had become established in the school community (ibid.: 170).

Martin's story is a warning that schools themselves must be fit to include and education professionals equipped with appropriate professional development and management support. Berry's (2001) study of four children demonstrates that inclusion *can* work for some children and not for others and that the factors for success depend upon the children's responses as well as those of educators and parents and on the ability of the adults so involved to listen to the voices of pupils as well as parents and teachers. Berry tells 8-year-old Simon's story of 'exclusion' in a mainstream setting and his move to an inclusive community in a special school. Simon and his mother talk of their experiences:

> *Of his old 'mainstream' school:* I don't like it . . . Well, I liked playing football but the work was too hard. I got into trouble and it made Dad shout and it made Mum cry . . . My sister still goes there and she likes it. It was boring a lot cos I had nothing to do when everyone else was working, but I liked playing with Karen. Karen didn't come all of the time though. She was my friend.
>
> *Simon transferred to a special school of which he said:* It is loads of fun. I play football every week and sometimes I win. Claire lets me play on her

computer too. The work is okay and Maureen or Paula or Jenny help me with my work.

Simon's mother reflected: Simon has been categorised as having Attention Deficit Hyperactivity Disorder (ADHD) but I think it is more than that. There are so many aspects to him and I think he is definitely on the Autistic Spectrum. He needs a school that understands him and works with him, rather than trying to change him. Inclusion can be good and it can be bad. It is a necessary evil probably. It is lovely to keep them protected in a special school. It doesn't do them any good in the long run. They need to be integrated at some point. It is finding the right point. It is definitely finding the right point and doing it for the right reasons. You cannot just plonk them in the catchment area school. They have got to go to the right place for the right reasons, not because it is their time to go, but because they are ready to go – at whatever stage, at whatever point. Mainstream inclusion has got to be good but it has got to be individual and not just across the board. Individual needs need to be looked at (Berry, 2001: x).

So – as Perera, Nutbrown and Berry have demonstrated – difficulty in schooling can begin for many in the early years of life and schooling. The various inequalities which pervade the education system in England and Wales are especially entangled in any discussion of children with difficulties whatever the age of the pupils concerned. Clough (2000) tells the story of Molly, in a comprehensive school and climate of endemic racism bound up with clashes of culture and struggles of the working class and unemployed:

Tim Booth [see below] asked me: *How do you give a voice to people who lack words?*

My problem with Molly is not that he *lacks* words, but rather that they can spill out of him with a wild, fairground pulse; they are sparklers, he waves them splashing around him. And my other problem with Molly's words is that many of them are not very nice; they are squibs that make you jump out of the way. For the moment I think that these are my only problems.

I have been sitting with Molly for some ten minutes and he has explained why the pond at Tenby Dale has been closed for re-stocking. The tale is so parochial, has such artless warmth and polish that I feel that Molly and I are like something out of 'Kes'. I think I am quite skilled at not patronising the Mollies, so I don't entirely aspirate my h's, but I think that Molly will know somehow that I'm alright; or 'o'reet' I would want him to say to his mates; *e's o'reet that researcher bloke – 'im wi t'leather jacket.* But at this, my first meeting with Molly, I am unprepared for the sudden lash that I later come to know him by. So – and God knows where this comes from – I find myself of a moment saying

– *Look here, Molly: you're intelligent, you're bright, you could* . . . and I don't finish my sentence before Molly raps:

– *What an' become a twat like thee? No offence but common sense/self-defence/off-a dat fence what? – what?*

And my audience with Molly is over for today. He is already on his feet and moving *through*, somehow – rather than round – the desks between him and the door. No longer Billy Casper, he is become Anthony Burgess' – Alex? – of Clockwork Orange – *Widdy-widdy-widdy-boom-boom*, and his hands beat a tattoo on the desks as he passes them. *Widdy-widdy-widdy*.

I notice that I am disappointed at being called a 'twat'.

Molly is fifteen years old, nearly sixteen when I meet him. His face bears traces of a prettiness that he will soon properly lose as his complexion yields fully to adolescence; for the moment, though, let him still be pretty, though his voice is at odds: mostly broken (though still sometimes – in excitement, I come to learn – there are light flecks in with the gravel).

His name is Francis Molinari, and there is a number of reasons why I appear to pick him out from John Francis (Tosser), Des Bailey, Tom McPhee (Toffee) and a host of indifferent others. The first of these reasons – when I think about it – has to have something to do with Molly's brightness. You can see this in his face, but not in *this* sort of brow, *that* sort of nose; or a sparkling eye, or any such. Unless it closes down – and just occasionally it does – this face is simply open with mirth. At nine he would have looked mischievous; at fifteen he is not yet watchful – though this will surely come later, after careful and before baleful; these things, too, are written in his face – no, he is not yet watchful so much as alert to possibility.

As the story unfolds, Molly's difficulties are compounded by his confrontations with staff, his eventual exclusion and his own brightness. (A footnote to the story informs readers that Molly died joy-riding a few years later.)

We can see, in the stories of Martin, Simon and Molly, first, how history has influenced the development of practice towards inclusion and, secondly how policy impacts on present experience. So what can we learn from the stories of Martin, Simon and Molly? These stories confirm for us that educational difficulty is complex and responses to those difficulties must be individual, but they also suggest that the *culture* of a school can make a difference to the ability of that school to cater for individual needs and difficulties.

In our final section we want briefly to discuss recent initiatives to support the growth and development of inclusive educational cultures.

Initiatives to support children with learning difficulties in inclusive educational cultures

As we said earlier, the SEN *Code of Practice* (DfES, 2001a) took effect from January 2002. This provides advice to LEAs, maintained schools, early education settings and others in carrying out their statutory duties to 'identify, assess and make provision for children's special educational needs'. Numerous updates and guidance have since been issued in order to support schools in the development of practices to realize this new policy development. We do not intend in this chapter to discuss the detail of those developments for they unfold with the flow of government, and readers can update themselves on such policy shifts through various DfES documents and its official website.

Nevertheless, it is worthwhile to map the range of initiatives which the green paper entitled *Excellence for All Children. Special Educational Needs* (DfEE, 1997a) heralded and which were operationalized by the subsequent *Programme of Action* (DfEE, 1998). Not only do its component activities illustrate the complexity of the territory we have surveyed in this chapter but the *Programme of Action* also offers an opportunity to reflect on the rate of change that has taken place within SEN in England. In considering these points, readers may wish to consider whether the *actions* in the 'programme' are necessarily concomitant with a shift in the way in which disability and educational difference is now conceptualized.

The *Programme of Action* both reported on the progress being made and the future planning in each of five key areas of SEN activity, and we now briefly highlight some of these. Unsurprisingly it placed great importance on a greater involvement of parents in the processes of identification and assessment. This collaboration was to be formalized locally in a series of 'parent partnerships'. Moreover, and given the frequently adversarial nature of some SEN issues, plans were implemented to establish conciliation arrangements for disputes. Perversely, this heading in the programme sought 'more involvement of children in the process', implying that children remained the almost Victorian chattels of their parents or carers.

Major changes were to be advanced in the way in which SEN was organized. We have already mentioned the *Code of Practice* (DfES, 2001a) which updated – with a supposed 'simplified' approach – the initial version. Greater LEA accountability was to be forthcoming – and this in spite of the draconian reduction in powers and financial capabilities of LEAs subsequent to the Education Act 1988, notably the introduction of local financial management of schools.

There was to be greater emphasis on developing knowledge and skills within the field of SEN. Central to this were plans to place greater emphasis on SEN in teacher training – an approach which appeared not to recognize that the Warnock Report (DES, 1978) had long since identified this as a key 'change issue' in SEN and which had, over the years, been met with a studied indifference by central government (Garner, 2001). Attention was due to be directed towards the continuing professional development of teachers, another area of indeterminate effectiveness in the post-Warnock period (Davies and Garner, 1997).

The position of so-called learning support assistants (LSAs) or teaching assistants (TAs) was to be enhanced. Hitherto these had been poorly paid 'dogs-bodies' possessing little status and no career structure (O'Brien and Garner, 2001). Noticeably in ongoing discussions about LSA/TA roles in the classroom there has been a sharp indifference to the need to involve the child or young person in how they should be deployed. 'Working in partnership' represented a further broad theme within the *Programme of Action*. It was planned to extend the regional co-ordination of SEN provision in a series of 'Regional Partnerships', whose role was to promote inter-LEA and inter-agency collaboration – for example, with health trusts and voluntary agencies.

But there is one initiative within the *Programme of Action* which is deserving of more detailed and explicit attention. The New Labour administration in England used the programme to signal its policy and practice intentions in respect of developing a more inclusive education system. LEAs were required to publish their intentions in respect of inclusion and there was to be a review of the statutory arrangements promoting inclusive practice. The latter was realized in the adventurously entitled circular, *Inclusive Schooling* (DfES, 2001b). Schools would be required to demonstrate fair and equitable treatment of SEN children in the admissions process – a move which appears to be inhibited by the continued preoccupation with 'league tables' based (primarily) on academic performance in a limited range of school subjects. The paradox, it seems, escapes the notice of most politicians and parents alike, whose perversely merito-cratic view of the educational process seems rooted in a pre-1944 mind-set.

But if we accept that the creation of inclusive cultures is a key factor in a positive response to learning difficulty, whatever its cause, schools need support in examining their ethos and institu-tional culture in order to address the areas of potential difficulty. The *Index for Inclusion* (CSIE, 2002) is one such tool, designed to help schools understand what they *mean* by inclusion as well as to identify their inclusive practices and blocks to those practices.

Booth et al.'s (2000: 64) position is that inclusive education is about education for all members of the community – all minority and oppressed groups:

> Some continue to want to make inclusion primarily about 'special needs education' or the inclusion in education of children and young people with impairments but that position seems absurd ... If inclusion is about the development of comprehensive community education and about pri-oritising community over individualism beyond education, then the history of inclusion is the history of these struggles for an education system which serves the interests of communities and which does not exclude anyone within those communities.

The *Index for Inclusion* is a tool for school development. It is sum-marized as follows:

> The *Index* is a set of materials to guide schools through a process of inclu-sive school development. It is about building supportive communities which foster high achievement for all students. The process of using the *Index* is itself designed to contribute to the inclusive development of schools. It encourages staff to share and build on existing knowledge and assists them in a detailed examination of the possibilities for increasing learning and participation for all their students.
>
> The *Index* involves a process of school self-review on three dimen-sions concerned with inclusive school cultures, policies and practices. The process entails progression through a series of school development phases. These start with the establishing of a co-ordinating group. This group works with staff, governors, students and parents/carers to exam-ine all aspects of the school, identifying barriers to learning and sustaining and reviewing progress. The investigation is supported by a detailed set of indicators and questions which require schools to engage in a deep, and challenging exploration of their present position and the possibilities for moving towards greater inclusion (Booth et al., 2000: 2).

Clough and Nutbrown (2002) reviewed the experience of education professionals who used the Index and found it to be a positive tool for staff teams in reviewing their environments and practices to assess their ability to include all involved in the life of their school. So, the index is intended to enable schools to 'sample' their cultures, policies and practices to see how they measure up to the view of inclusion articulated above by Tony Booth and colleagues – a view which embraces inclusion of *all* and addresses aspects of gender, class, race, religion, sexuality and social class as much as learning difficulty or disability.

Conclusions

In this chapter we have attempted to draw from the archive of SEN as well as to delineate its contemporary features. It is, necessarily, an incomplete and simplified working of an aspect of education which is at the forefront of the social and political agenda, whether institutionally, locally or at a national level. At various points throughout our account we have highlighted sharp differences between practice and experience and the overarching ideologies, belief systems and interests which impact upon them.

Nowhere is this more apparent than in the tension between individuality and standardization, between local actions and centralized control. Examples of these abound in SEN and inclusion: the National Curriculum has access for all as its defining motif, yet progress of children (and schools) is measured in 'league tables – the epitome of a competition in which there will be losers as well as winners. The *Code of Practice* (DfES, 2001a), whilst it allows for local interpretation, nevertheless compels schools to adopt particular approaches to provision by its positioning as 'statutory guidance'. And the ongoing school inspection regime, with its capacity to 'name and shame' supposedly 'failing schools', seems oblivious to the fact that many such schools cater for an above-average number of 'at-risk' children. Noteworthy illustrations of all these can be drawn from the voices of those with lead roles in this perpetual drama – the young people and the adults who work alongside them in schools. Whilst there is little doubt that the 'inclusive vision' for those experiencing SEN will remain a feature of our education system for some time, it is the *nature* of that vision which is contentious. In a word, have we become providers of a more socially acceptable – indeed, politically correct – version of an unreconstructed, pre-Warnock service? The discourse, we argue, needs to shift more honestly to an empowerment model, based on individual needs and expectations.

Student tasks

1 Study Figure 4.1 on page 84 where Clough (2000) sketches five 'eras' or routes towards inclusion. Where does your own experience as a learner fit into this 'map'? How have these phases of development affected your own education, and how you currently view inclusive education?
2 Increasing emphasis is placed on the involvement of parents of children with learning difficulties in the decision-making about their children's education. List the strategies in current policy on SEN which allow for parental participation.
3 Take a look at a copy of the *Index for Inclusion* (Booth et al., 2000). Try using one of the questionnaires in an institution you know – which may well be your own school or college. To what extent is your institution an inclusive one?

Suggested further reading

Blamires, M. (1999) Universal design for learning: re-establishing differentiation as part of the inclusion agenda? *Support for Learning* 14(4): 158–63.
Dyson, A. (1997) Social and educational disadvantage: reconnecting special needs education. *British Journal of Special Education*, 24(4): 152–7.
Farrell, P. (2001) Special education in the last twenty years: have things really got better? *British Journal of Special Education* 28(1): 3–9.

References

Berry, T. (2001) Does inclusion work? A case study of four children. Unpublished MA, University of Sheffield.
Booth, T. (2000) Reflection. In P. Clough and J. Corbett (eds). *Theories of Inclusive Education: A Students' Guide*. London: Paul Chapman Publishing.
Booth, T., Ainscow, M., Black-Hawkins, K., Vaughan, M. and Shaw, L. (2000) *Index for Inclusion: Developing Learning and Participation in Schools*. Bristol:

Centre for Studies in Inclusive Education (the *Index* is available from CSIE, 1 Redland Close, Elm Lane, Redland, Bristol BS6 6UE).

Centre for Studies in Inclusive Education (2002) *Index for Inclusion* (2nd edition). Bristol: CSIE.

Clough, P (ed.) (1998) *Managing Inclusive Education: From Policy and Practice.* London: Paul Chapman Publishing.

Clough, P. (2000) Routes to inclusion. In P. Clough and J. Corbett (eds) *Theories of Inclusive Education.* London: Paul Chapman Publishing.

Clough, P. and Nutbrown, C. (2002) *The Index for Inclusion: personal perspectives from early years educators.* Early Education, Spring, 2002.

Davies, J. and Garner, P. (eds) (1997a) *At the Crossroads: Teacher Education and Special Needs.* London: David Fulton.

DES (1978) *The Warnock Report.* London: HMSO.

DfEE (1997a) *Excellence for All Children: Meeting Special Educational Needs.* London: HMSO.

DfEE (1997b) *Excellence in Schools.* London: HMSO.

DfEE (1998) *Meeting Special Educational Needs. A Programme of Action.* London: HMSO.

DfES (2001a) *Code of Practice on the Identification and Assessment of Children with Special Educational Needs.* London: HMSO.

DfES (2001b) *Inclusive Schooling.* London: DfES.

Garner, P. (2001) Goodbye Mr Chips: special needs, inclusive education and the deceit of initial teacher training. In T. O'Brien and M. Blamires (eds) *Enabling Inclusion: Blue Skies . . . Dark Clouds.* London: HMSO.

Hegarty, S. (1987) *Meeting Special Educational Needs in Ordinary Schools.* London: Cassell.

Herbert, E. (1998) Included from the start? Managing Early Years Settings for all in P. Clough (ed.) *Managing Inclusive Education: from policy to experience.* London: Paul Chapman Publishing.

Kysel, F. (1985) Characteristics of pupils in special schools and units. In F. Kysel (ed.) *Educational Opportunities for All? Research Studies for the Fish Report. Volume 2.* London: ILEA.

Nutbrown, C. (ed.) (1996) *Respectful Educators: Capable Learners – Children's Rights and Early Education.* London: Paul Chapman Publishing.

Nutbrown, C. (1998) Managing to include? Rights, responsibilities and respect. In P. Clough (ed.) *Managing Inclusive Education: From Policy and Practice.* London: Paul Chapman Publishing.

O'Brien, T. and Garner, P. (2001) *Untold Stories. Learning Support Assistants and their Work.* Stoke-on-Trent: Trentham Books.

Perera, S. (2000) Living with Special Educational Needs – A Mother's Perspective, in P. Clough and C. Nutbrown (eds) *Voices of Arabia.* Sheffield: University of Sheffield.

Roffey, S. (2001) *Special Needs in the Early Years: Collaboration, Communication and Coordination* (2nd edn). London: David Fulton.

Sebba, J. and Sachdev, D. (1997) *What Works in Inclusive Education?* Ilford: Barnardo's.

Strand, S. (1997) *Pupil progress during Key Stage 1: a value added analysis of school effects.* British Educational Research Journal. 23, (4), 471–87.

Thomas, G. and Loxley, A. (2001) *Deconstructing Special Education and Constructing Inclusion*. Buckingham: Open University Press.

Warnock, M. (1999) *If only we had known then*. Times Educational Supplement, 31 December, 1999.

Wolfendale, S. (ed.) (2000) *Special Needs in the Early Years: Snapshots of Practice*. London: RoutledgeFalmer.

5

Education for Citizenship

Dean Garratt

This chapter seeks to explore the nature of education for citizenship. It begins by outlining a framework of the traditions that have influenced the development of modern citizenship before drawing upon a range of theoretical models to present an analysis of recent educational policy in Britain. The analysis is contextualized alongside the Convention on the Rights of the Child, which raises critical issues regarding the suitability of different models relating to children's rights to particular freedoms. The chapter closes with discussion of how these rights are to be found in relation to contemporary models of citizenship, and suggests how they might best be recognized so as to empower rather than constrain young people.

Introduction

What is the nature of education for citizenship? The question posed is deliberative since it brings together two concepts – education and citizenship that are both prized and promiscuous. They are prized because each has the ability to 'lead out' something valuable and worth while, for children, adults and society as a whole. Yet they are also promiscuous since both are difficult to pin down, bringing an ineradicable vagueness and ambiguity to the question of what precisely each is supposed to mean. Answers are far from straightforward, for education and citizenship have in common the ability to seek legitimation from positions that draw upon a variety of different perspectives, none of which are hermetically sealed but are

often overlapping and sometimes conflictual. That competing positions share different values gives rise to internal tensions
concerning how education and citizenship are properly understood. Increasingly this situation is one in which scholars are
encumbered to explore their purpose and meaning, seeking out the
core principles, key features and basic assumptions that contrasting
perspectives tacitly presuppose. Education and citizenship are
essentially practical concepts yet, tantalizingly, both are susceptible
to the vagaries of political whim or intellectual obfuscation, neither
of which, pragmatically speaking, has helped provide clarity on the
growing body of divergent views. Just as many have questioned the
purpose of education in the broadest and most general terms (see,
for example, Peters, 1966; 1973; White, 1982; 1990; Laura and
Cotton, 1999), increasingly teachers, politicians, social scientists
and students of education alike are questioning the nature and purpose of citizenship (see, for example, Crick, 2000; Miller, 2000;
Osler, 2000). What does it mean? How is it to be defined? For
whom is it intended? Which model(s) of practice are appropriate or
desirable? In the end, answers to such questions can find no philosophical resolution. As Crick (2000: 3) reminds us: '[Important] social
and moral concepts always get defined in different ways by different
groups for different purposes. They are what a philosopher has called
"essentially contested concepts" . . . and definitions, whether by individual thinkers or by committees, do not settle arguments.
"Citizenship" can carry significantly different meanings.' Yet surely
it is incumbent upon scholars of education to attempt to understand the meanings and purposes that are implicit in a range of
recognized models. If so, such an understanding may require the
opening up of debate between competing positions that, in their
different ways, seek to define the meaning of citizenship. In turn
this entails the recognition that different models confer a heritage
of different social, cultural and political values and beliefs, and that
these form the constituents of the philosophical traditions of
which they are part. Such traditions or 'worldviews' create the
foundation for the concept of citizenship, which has led, in various
guises, to its construction and explication within different educational contexts.

   It is with these issues in mind that this chapter will attempt to
outline a framework of the traditions that have influenced the
development of modern citizenship. The analysis locates itself within

the context of recent educational policy in Britain and the Convention on the Rights of the Child, and examines this relationship at a time of renaissance for citizenship – both internationally and in Britain under New Labour.

Internationally, the last 15 years have brought into focus the issue of what it means to be a citizen, both from a civil rights perspective in terms of nationality and legal status and from a cultural point of view, where issues of belonging and identity have attracted considerable attention (Isin and Wood, 1999). The fall of the Berlin Wall and liberation of East Germany, the dissolution of the old Soviet Union and fragmentation of the Balkans, formerly recognized as Yugoslavia, to mention a few examples, in many ways characterize what has been referred to as the 'postmodern condition' (Lyotard, 1984) – a condition in which fragmentation and pluralization abound, not only in European states but across many nations globally. At the same time, overlapping this condition, the 'riddle' of modern life introduces a subtle interconnectedness and globalization between nation-states. In Europe this has gathered momentum through the affirmation of the European Union and European Parliament, creating greater interdependence between political and economic factors as well as closer social ties. These developments are set against a backdrop of people's growing awareness of human rights and their wider recognition of the difference between partial and full membership of nation-states. Countries like Norway, for example, have been quicker to respond to the consequences of the ratification of the Convention on the Rights of the Child by holding a 'children's hearing' in Bergen in 1990. This hearing and other later ones challenge traditional notions of children as 'becomings', perceiving them instead as 'beings' in their own right – i.e. citizens with a voice that should be listened to (John, 1996). Others, including Britain, have been slower to acknowledge the rights of both children and adults and many would claim that being conceived as a subject creates a situation in which individuals are deliberately disenfranchised and/or perpetually subjugated by the state. Somewhat paradoxically, these factors have conspired to create social conditions in which struggles for independence and self-governance are situated with calls for increased political and social cohesion, creating tensions between positions of individual autonomy and established forms of collective authority. Movements, debates, struggles and in some cases even wars concerning the future of modern societies have precipitated the timely rebirth of citizenship, reviving notions of rights and corresponding responsibilities within frameworks of equality, liberty and community.

Seizing this opportunity, in Britain New Labour have made no secret of their desire to embrace the concept of citizenship and have sought to articulate its potential contribution towards social and curriculum ends. Following the white paper, *Excellence in Schools* (DfEE, 1997), these ambitions found expression in the government's commissioning of several working parties, one of which was intended to provide 'advice on effective education for citizenship in schools – to include the nature and practices of participation in democracy; the duties, responsibilities and rights of individuals as citizens; and the value to individuals and society of community activity' (QCA, 1998: 4). The findings and deliberations of the Advisory Group on Citizenship were subsequently published as the report, *Education for Citizenship and the Teaching of Democracy in Schools* (QCA, 1998), and provided a foundation for the development of a statutory order for *Citizenship* (QCA, 1999). Together, these documents represent the most recent, and perhaps first serious, attempt at generating a framework of possibilities for the future of education for citizenship in Britain. The following analysis, therefore, will be presented through an examination of the ideological perspectives that are reflected in this current thinking. Throughout this analysis critical issues are raised concerning the intentions of different approaches as they connect with other putative models, and to the Convention on the Rights of the Child. In raising issues that have important bearing on the recognition of these rights, the chapter closes with a discussion of how they are positioned in relation to models that dominate contemporary thinking. The chapter begins, however, with the first of two parts of a historical overview. For heuristic and pedagogical reasons, it presents a simple dichotomy of the philosophical traditions that have influenced the way in which education for citizenship has evolved.

Background

Historical context: part 1

Questions of meaning, intention and action are bound together with ideas of purpose and delivery. Their philosophical roots lie

within the traditions of different political and educational ideologies, many of which are interwoven and can often be seen as
overlapping. Indeed, it is through the interlacing of the social and
cultural with the political and economic that education for citizenship acquires its reason for being. As far back as Plato's *Republic*, for
example, the social and political were combined in producing a
curriculum plan that would prepare children for the responsibilities
of adult citizenship. An important feature of this early model is that
it derived its intellectual energy from the ideology of classical
humanism, where notions of elitism and claims to social power conspired to produce the central tenets of a hierarchical and socially
ordered theory. As Skilbeck (1976: 15–16) asserts: '[Invariably], in
classical humanist doctrine, the potential leaders are given a different and separate education from that of the masses . . . [it] has
drawn significant distinctions between the classes who are to be
educated . . . [relating] to either intellectual potential or social class
or both.' Commensurate with the philosophy of Plato, then, only a
tiny elite was granted the privilege of an authentic education in
which the spirit of critical inquiry and intellectual freedom was pas-
sionately endorsed. In contrast, the masses were bequeathed a
cultural heritage that would prepare them, in less noble ways, for
the responsibilities of becoming law-abiding citizens in a well
ordered society.

This perspective has strong resonance with the history and evolution of the concept of education for citizenship in Britain. At the
end of the nineteenth century, for example, it is argued that whilst
state-supported schools were predictably reliable in their purpose of
teaching civics, public schools (now private schools) were much
more focused on fostering education for leadership. This first wave
of citizenship that led up to the beginning of the First World War
had its intellectual roots in the movement of idealism, which was
prevalent in Britain at the time (Rees, 1996) and which had borrowed its ideas from the earlier philosophy of Plato. It generated a
vision of citizenship in which young people were intended to
become 'upright and useful members of the community in which
they [lived], and worthy sons and daughters of the country to
which they [belonged]' (Heater, 1990: 85). Underpinning this was
the conservative idea that the purpose of education for citizenship
was to nurture loyalty and obligation to the nation-state, deference
towards the social and political elite and a strong sense of pride in

the Empire (Oliver and Heater, 1994). As these basic, but vigorously implemented, ideas gradually evolved they brought with them a more direct and systematic training in the duties of citizenship for young people (Batho, 1990). The use of the term 'training' here is entirely deliberate, for the inculcation (or indoctrination) of citizenship was intended principally for ordinary young citizens, where teachers conveyed 'simple virtues of humility, service, restraint and respect for personality' (Ministry of Education, 1949: 41) upon their pupils.

In these terms education for citizenship is afforded only a narrow definition. It is seen as largely functional, with emphasis devoted exclusively towards the rote learning of civics. Among other things, this might involve the study of how to become a law-abiding citizen, of legal rights and responsibilities, of government and the salient features of the British Constitution, and of the necessity to obey established social norms. In more open and critical ways, however, this raises a question about whether the aim of nurturing respect for the law and deference towards the social and political elite actually constitutes 'good citizenship'. From a different standpoint this may easily be construed as a deliberate and systematic attempt to engineer passive citizenship; of grooming young people for their role as passive subjects[1] in a society perceived as stable and typified by consensus. This issue will be revisited later, but for now it serves as a powerful reminder of the possible tension developing between citizenship as a legal status, in which a contractual agreement of political and economic ends is followed, and the purpose of achieving genuine personal and social development, serving to empower the individual. Are 'good citizens' those who merely understand and obey or those who are encouraged to question and challenge?

The rights of the child

The question posed has more than mere rhetorical force. For, expressed another way, it presents the issue of whether 'good citizens' are to be socially engineered or actively empowered. Purposely indoctrinated or critically emancipated? Prospective answers to these questions raise serious issues concerning the developmental outcomes of citizenship in young people and, further, have implications for the type of educational experience they might enjoy. This point is not insignificant since, as Verhellen

(2000: 33) suggests, children have historically been seen as 'not yets .
. . not yet knowing, not yet competent, and not yet being'. In contrast, a more critical perspective of citizenship might suggest that
children are moral agents from the moment they are sentient and,
in any case, certainly from the time they begin attending school. To
this end, Article 28 of the Convention on the Rights of the Child
(CRC) is unequivocal in stating that all children have the right and
free access to education. In addition, Article 29 provides a perspective on the translation of this entitlement in practice. As Verhellen
(2000: 39) considers:

> Article 29 contains detailed provisions concerning the aims and values
> involved: the development of the child's personality to its fullest poten-
> tial; the preparation of the child for a responsible role in society; the
> development of respect for nature; mutual understanding and friendship
> among all peoples; and especially the development of respect for human
> rights and fundamental freedoms.

These rights are crucial to the development of citizenship in young
people. In particular, the aim of preparing the child for a responsible role in society has been incorporated within the order for
Citizenship, where it is stated that schools should enable pupils to
'develop a critical appreciation of issues of right and wrong, justice,
fairness, rights and obligations in society' (QCA, 1999: 7). This suggests that beyond the child's legal right *to* education are further
rights *in* education, which embrace important political and social
dimensions that encourage the development of critically informed
views. These aspirations are consonant with the canons of Articles
12–16 of the CRC which, in reflecting the ideas of a western, liberal
democracy, articulate important fundamental freedoms to which
children are legally entitled. Some examples include the freedom to
express opinions, freedom of thought, freedom of conscience and
religion and freedom of association (Verhellen, 2000). Such freedoms are empowering for they create opportunities for the young
to question, challenge and raise issues around important social and
political themes. They generate an educational context in which
the desire to know, explore and understand is positively promoted.
More than fostering notions of obedience and conformity, they
present opportunities to pursue critical and socially enlightened
perspectives of citizenship. But what would such a model look like?
And what sorts of values would inform its philosophy?

Historical context: part 2

One model that has attempted to influence a critical disposition towards the development of citizenship, in ways that are essentially self-willed and uncoerced, is featured in the ideology of progressivism. This philosophy has its educational roots in the work of the eighteenth-century social philosopher, Jean-Jacques Rousseau. In Rousseau's *Emile* there is an elaborate account of the various ways in which the casual transmission of cultural heritage is made subservient to the developing impulses of the inquisitive child (Skilbeck, 1976). Within the context of education for citizenship, this could mean that whereas more traditional models might, for example, present the requirement to obey the law without question (in tandem with the notion of the 'passive subject'), more progressive models might allow for the questioning and modification of unjust laws, or perhaps seek to promote the democratization of voluntary bodies (Crick, 2000). In these terms, progressivism, a movement that found clear expression in the Plowden Report (DES, 1967) and pedagogy of child centred education during the 1960s and 1970s, presents a striking antithesis to more traditional ideologies which the concept of citizenship has historically embraced. In turn education for citizenship becomes something in which individuals are not merely equipped with a knowledge and understanding of all that is necessary to function competently in modern society, but are also empowered to partake in the active process of political democracy; a process that may lead, in various ways, to their becoming able and effective members of a community. This is a central feature of modern, progressive citizenship in which there is an active relationship between the developing child and the school and wider community to which he or she belongs. This modern notion, notably absent from the early philosophy of Rousseau where individual and tutor formed an intimate and separate relationship from the rest of society, invokes a union that extends beyond any simple model of integration. Rather, it attends to the idea, *vis-à-vis* CRC, that children may be courted in a critical and creative role in which they are enabled reflexively to question fundamental values and beliefs that shape public life.

Historically, this open and participatory perspective was embodied in the work of the Politics Association during the 1960s (Heater, 1969), whose concerns surrounding the participation of young people in debates of social significance led to intense calls for increased political education. Interestingly, it is now endorsed in citizenship's latest reincarnation, where the perceived benefits are identified accordingly:

for pupils   – an entitlement in schools that will empower them to participate in society effectively as active, informed and critical and responsible citizens . . .

for society   – an active and politically literate citizenry convinced that they can influence government and community affairs at all levels (QCA, 1998: 9)

This perspective subsequently found expression in the 'light touch' statutory order for *Citizenship*, where it was reinforced, if not as boldly as before, that pupils should be taught about: 'the importance of playing an active part in democratic and electoral processes . . . [and] the opportunities for individual and voluntary groups to bring about social change locally, nationally, in Europe and internationally' (QCA, 1999: 15). What is manifestly lacking from these latter statements, however, is a clear expression of their meaning, for the embedding of the term 'active' in the rhetoric of the order may not be as complete as it seems. It is necessary, therefore, that such statements are interpreted alongside the Advisory Group's Report and, moreover, the broader ideological context in which they were seen to emerge. Yet before proceeding further an important caveat must be issued.

Since it is rarely true that contrasting models of citizenship exist in forms that are exclusively one thing or entirely another – classical humanist or progressive – a more detailed examination of the relationship between citizenship and ideology is required. Whereas earlier, for heuristic reasons, a simple dichotomy of ideal types or historical caricatures was used to elucidate the juxtaposition of two opposing theoretical stances, in practice models of citizenship are seldom polarized between active and passive camps. Rather, they run along a continuum, marking out territory in which different settlements display, with differing degrees of emphasis, tendencies towards active or passive status. In recognizing this complexity, a new framework is required that is capable of illuminating the dominant conceptions of modern citizenship as they relate to the rights of the child. These are liberal, libertarian, republican and communitarian and will be set against the documents *Education for Citizenship and the Teaching of Democracy in Schools* (QCA, 1998) and

Citizenship (QCA, 1999), as well as the wider political context in which their ideas were deliberately constructed.

A framework for modern citizenship

The liberal conception

The embodiment of the liberal view is contained within T.H. Marshall's (1950) seminal text, *Citizenship and Social Class*, in which three strands of citizenship – the civil, the political and the social – are identified. These are played out through a reciprocal relationship of rights and corresponding obligations that are enjoyed by every citizen as a legal entitlement. This status may confer, for example, the rights to freedom of speech and to vote, as well as rights for the protection of the sanctity of contracts and for ensuring personal welfare and security. Yet it may also enjoin citizens to honour obligations like upholding the law and refraining from interfering with the rights of other citizens. This fundamental equality of rights and duties carries with it a potentially redistributive function (Hindess, 1993), for it creates a model of social justice that is intended to counteract the negative consequences of a market economy driven by considerations of efficiency (Miller, 2000). On this view, social, class and economic inequalities are capable of being redressed through the recognition of social rights and basic entitlement to economic welfare (Mann, 1996). In this way the conditions are created in which every citizen may enjoy a common social heritage and the minimum standards of living that prevail within society, including, for example, minimum levels of education, income and housing. In complying with the spirit of CRC, these ideas have recently acquired new life within the Advisory Group's final report, where Marshall's work was adopted as the foundation for developing citizenship and its associated themes: 'social and moral responsibility, community involvement and political literacy' (QCA, 1998: 11). In the following section this relationship is examined through the identification of similarities and differences that are shared between the liberal view and citizenship's latest reincarnation.

The view that Marshall's theory is all but a blueprint for the liberal conception of citizenship is perhaps beyond dispute (see Miller,

2000). However, the link between citizenship's present status and the liberal model is less certain. A point at which common ground is shared is in the emphasis that the Advisory Group places upon the importance of rights and responsibilities, which are subsequently agreed in the statutory order for *citizenship* (QCA, 1999). For example, in the section outlining knowledge and understanding about becoming informed citizens it is suggested that pupils should be taught about: 'the legal and human rights and responsibilities underpinning society and how they relate to citizens, including the role and operation of the criminal and civil justice systems' (ibid.: 15).

However, perhaps more than Marshall, the present view displays a firmer commitment towards the promulgation of responsibilities rather than rights. This is affirmed in the belief that children might be enabled to develop 'socially and morally responsible behaviour both in and beyond the classroom, both *towards those in authority* and towards each other' (QCA, 1998: 12, emphasis added).

The emphasis on demonstrating responsibility to authority, in the view above, is not insignificant. Its juxtaposition with notions of developing active citizenship generates considerable tension, creating conditions that resemble more a contractual relationship between the state (government) and the individual than any pretension towards active citizenship. From the perspective of the child, however, it displays ignorance of the rights and freedoms to which they are entitled. It enforces a view that power and authority should properly reside in the hands of controlling institutions, and that freedoms should rightly be conferred at their bequest. At best this perspective is likely to promote dispositions that engender respect, responsibility and obedience. At worst, it may preclude the development of social rights that are the essential preconditions of political democracy. Returning to Marshall and the liberal view, however, the establishment of social rights is something to be determined by common agreement rather than through any deliberate imposition. Quite how this might be determined in a pluralist society is a matter for some considerable debate and will be revisited later on. For now, it will suffice to say that from the liberal perspective, the privileging of responsibilities over rights is curious for at least two reasons.

First, as foreshadowed, it seems odd that when rights and responsibilities are said within the advisory report to form part of a reciprocal relationship, social rights, in contrast with responsibilities, are not explicitly defined. Of course, while the document *Education for Citizenship and the Teaching of Democracy in Schools* claims to work within Marshall's framework it does not vow to do so slavishly. Nor, for that matter, despite its allusions to democracy, does the Advisory Group's report pledge allegiance to a liberal view, and therefore whilst there may be some overlap with the liberal position there is also some considerable degree of slippage. Secondly, the omission of any discussion of social rights within the Advisory Group's report shares a certain political character with an earlier curriculum document, in which its predecessor – *Curriculum Guidance 8: Education for Citizenship* (NCC, 1990a) – was seen to contain a similar inherent bias. In this document a framework was produced where social rights were virtually ignored and in which the welfare state was completely disregarded (Carr, 1991). At this earlier moment such bias was heavily criticized by the political Left for its excessive emphasis on civic duties (or responsibilities) and what was then seen as non-political voluntary work (Oliver and Heater, 1994). Of course, this interpretation emerged within a particular ideological context, where *Education for Citizenship* was one of five cross-curricular themes, forming part of the whole curriculum (NCC, 1990b), which was itself part of a broader set of educational reforms driven by the philosophy of a market democracy (Carr, 1991).

On the point of failing to acknowledge and make explicit any basis for the elaboration of social rights there is, without question, a strong degree of overlap between the 'old' and the 'new'; and between *Curriculum Guidance 8: Education for Citizenship* (NCC, 1990a) and *Education for Citizenship and the Teaching of Democracy in Schools* (QCA, 1998), later becoming *Citizenship* (QCA, 1999). Indeed, it is in this crucial respect that both depart from the liberal view. However, while the point of departure is undeniably the same, the axes on which they are relocated are clearly substantively different. A clue to this repositioning, for the new model of citizenship, can be found in the following extract from the Advisory Group's Report, in which it is stated that 'We firmly believe that volunteering and community involvement are necessary conditions of civil society and democracy' (QCA, 1998: 10).

The stress on community involvement and voluntarism within the 'new model' suggests a movement away from the liberal view towards one that is affiliated with communitarian thinking. This perspective is presented later on. However, in the case of the 'old' model of citizenship, the departure from the liberal view leads more decisively towards a libertarian ideology and so it is the core principles, key features and basic assumptions of this perspective that will now be considered.

The libertarian conception

In contrast with the liberal view, the libertarian conception of citizenship can be seen to have emanated from the politics of the New Right in which the relationship between the individual and state are conceived in terms that are explicitly contractual (Miller, 2000). A version of this perspective was prominent during the 1980s, in which consumer sovereignty and the pursuit of rational self-interest formed the backdrop to an enterprise culture inspired by an individualist and utilitarian political and moral philosophy. The libertarian position has been summarized in the following way:

> People seek to satisfy their preferences and values through private activity, market exchange and voluntary association with like-minded individuals . . . Citizenship is not valued for its own sake; we are citizens only because we demand goods that require public provision. The citizen, to put it briefly, is a rational consumer of public goods. As far as possible his activities as a citizen should be modeled on his behavior in the economic market, taken to be a paradigm of rationality. In its most extreme version, this means that the state itself should be regarded as a giant enterprise and the citizens as its (voluntary) customers (ibid.: 50).

The preconditions for this model, however, are virtually impossible to achieve in practice. This is because they presuppose the possibility of 'authentic markets' (Tooley, 1997) that are free from interference by the government and in which individuals are disposed with economic resources that enable them to participate effectively in a free market economy. Notwithstanding the fact that these conditions may be inappropriate as the basis for democratic citizenship, since it has been argued elsewhere that they reinforce class, ethnic, and gender inequalities (see, for example, Edwards and Whitty, 1992; Ball, 1993; Gewirtz et al., 1995; Arnot, 1997; Osler, 1997; Sewell, 1997), they also create a context in which the requirement for citizenship may be superfluous. On this view, the libertarian model displays some serious educational inadequacies for it fails to acknowledge, in tandem with the market, children's rights to the freedoms of personality, thought and expression (Verhellen, 2000).

In less extreme forms, however, modes of libertarianism can and have existed. During the Conservative government in the1980s, for example, a less classical version of libertarianism was seen to co-exist happily alongside a socially conservative model of citizenship. Within this model, the basic preconditions of a libertarian perspec-tive – market forces, enterprise and utilitarian philosophy – were conjoined with the social conditions – minimal state intervention, a politically passive citizenry, strong active political leadership cir-cumscribed by the rule of law – necessary to facilitate its functioning. While some of these features can be found within the curriculum document *Education for Citizenship* (NCC, 1990a), and its accompanying rhetoric (see Robinson and Garratt, 1994), they are perhaps best captured in the views of the then Prime Minister Margaret Thatcher. During her famous speech on 'Christianity and wealth', delivered to the leaders of the Church of Scotland, she argued that:

> [Any] set of social and economic arrangements which is not founded on the acceptance of individual responsibility will do nothing but harm. We are all responsible for our own actions. We cannot blame society if we disobey law. We simply cannot delegate the exercise of mercy and gen-erosity to others (Thatcher, 1988: 2).

These views were supported by the affirmation of a traditional moral-ity in which citizens were expected to demonstrate respect for authority, to exhibit social responsibility and self-discipline, and to display a degree of social conformity towards the active political elite.

From an educational perspective that holds aspirations of nurtur-ing active rather than passive citizenship, of developing the qualities that are associated with 'good citizens' as opposed to 'docile subjects', the libertarian model may prove woefully inade-quate. Its problems revolve around assumptions concerning the exercise of civil liberties. Like the liberal view before, this particular brand of libertarianism, embracing simultaneously aspects of social conservatism and elitism, reinforces the notion that civil liberties are a framework of law protecting individuals from, or sanctioning their submission towards, the state. On this view civil liberties are little more than a legal status, devoid of political content and social character. Yet as Marshall (1997) reminds us, from a liberal perspective, such omissions deprive citizenship of its life-blood, denying individuals any positive means of influencing contemporary social affairs through the exercise of rights to which they are entitled. Moreover, even though the education of children may have a positive and direct bearing on the development of citizenship, without the ability to exercise rights citizenship may become a sterile and empty concept. As Marshall (ibid.: 299) elaborates:

> [The] right to education is a genuine social right of citizenship, because the aim of education during childhood is to shape the future adult. Fundamentally it should be regarded, not as the right of the child to go to school, but as the right of the adult citizen to have been educated . . . Education is a necessary prerequisite to civil freedom.

While Marshall is correct in his assumption that education is a genuine social right of citizenship and, by extension, the genuine social right of all children, his assertion that its motivation should be more properly associated with the rights of adult citizens is, for obvious reasons, controversial. More than this, however, it is inimical to the philosophy of the CRC.

Against the libertarian view, then, it is the development of social rights that provides the means by which citizens are able to diminish their status as commodities (Twine, 1994), and hence participate in the active role of democracy. This critique of the libertarian perspective and its underlying philosophy requires, by necessity, a deliberate shift towards a republican conception of citizenship.

The republican conception

In contrast with the libertarian position, but in harmony with the liberal view, the republican model (or civic republicanism as it is sometimes recognized) shares a mutual faith in the fundamental equality of rights and duties. More than this, however, it has been argued that it provides the underlying rationale of the order for *Citizenship* (Crick, 2000) where, in transcending the limitations of the liberal tradition, an appeal is made for greater political participation. Part of this spirit entails willingness on the part of each person to protect the rights of other citizens and to promote, in more general ways, a community's common interests (Miller, 2000). This requirement is implicit in the Advisory Group's Report, where responsibility is construed as an 'essential political as well as moral virtue, for it implies (a) care for others; (b) premeditation and calculation about what effects actions are likely to have on others; and (c) understanding and care for the consequences' (QCA, 1998: 13.) In recognizing this requirement it can be imagined that, in situations where the rights of other citizens are in need of protection, an individual will be motivated to act in his or her defence. This point is perhaps best illustrated in the case of the late Philip Lawrence, the headteacher who, in sensing the threat of danger to pupils in his care, moved outside his school in a brave effort to prevent violence. By acting in this way he did more than he was legally or morally obliged to do and yet with admirable courage displayed what many would regard as good citizenship (Miller, 2000).

A further dimension of the republican model is contained in the idea that citizens are enjoined to an active role, in which they are encouraged to participate in the political spirit of public life. Presumably this was implied when the Advisory Group argued that 'citizenship education is education for citizenship, *behaving and acting as a citizen* . . . it is not just knowledge of citizenship and civic society' (QCA, 1998: 13, emphasis added). Positive participation, therefore, reaches beyond the requirement of the citizen, for example, to check the excesses of government – in, say, preventing the violation of civil liberties. More importantly, it directs the citizen towards the active process of political democracy, in which group and sectional interests, as well as those of the community, are effectively prompted. This feeling is captured in the following statements:

> [Civic] spirit, citizen's charters and voluntary activity in the community are of crucial importance, but individuals must be helped and prepared to shape the terms of such engagements by political understanding and action (QCA, 1998: 10).

> [We] firmly believe that volunteering and community involvement are necessary conditions of civil society and democracy. Preparation for these, at the very least should be an explicit part of education (ibid.).

In presenting a view that embraces the requirement for rights and responsibilities (if appropriated somewhat unequally) on the one hand, and the promotion of community involvement, voluntarism and the common good on the other, the Advisory Group has sketched a framework for citizenship in which liberal and republican positions can be seen to overlap. Yet perhaps more significantly it is the invocation of 'community', in the statements above that is potentially most revealing. For it signals the emergence of a new framework that, in blurring the distinction between liberal and republican models, provides a partial view of citizenship in its present communitarian guise.

The communitarian conception

In the last 20 years or so, the concept of communitarianism has proliferated the globe (Etzioni, 1995; 1997; Putnam, 2000). Its appearance within UK politics, however, has occurred only more recently. Following the 1997 general election, New Labour emerged with its own brand of political ideas, establishing a social agenda that made a firm commitment to issues of citizenship, social welfare and public order. These social issues generated a requirement for collective citizenship that subsequently found expression in the language of community, shared values and civic identity. That citizens cannot be understood apart from the environment into which they are socially embedded is a belief that is fundamentally at the heart of communitarian thinking. It provides the social cement that binds citizens together and forms the basis upon which communal values are established. Yet whilst the central premise of communitarianism has never been in doubt, the means by which consensus is achieved is a moot point. This is because the concept of communitarian thinking is not a unitary school of thought. It is a broad church that encompasses a variety of different positions, many of which share common ground with divergent political views. However, to simplify matters and for the sake of brevity, three relatively crude conceptions will be presented. These have been borrowed and adapted from the work of Miller (2000) and serve to illustrate the left, right and centre positions within communitarian politics.

To the centre right, communitarian thinking can be seen as reinforcing the canons of unity and authority where, in ideal terms, a national community will create the social conditions in which language, history and culture are universally shared. This position has a natural empathy with traditional views that are inclined towards social conservatism and elitism. Communitarians to the left display characteristics consonant with key features of the republican

position, in which the principles of equality and freedom are positively reinforced. Free of the shackles of tradition, communitarians
on the left believe that community is not preordained but, rather,
open to revision. It is to be made as opposed to inherited. In this
crucial respect, centre-left communitarians believe in the evolution
of community in ways that are essentially self-determining and
uncoerced, and in which all members are treated equally regardless
of social standing. The central position in communitarian politics
shares a strong affinity with the liberal perspective outlined earlier,
where the ideas of cultural pluralism and individual autonomy are
pre-eminent. On this view, notions of community are a matter of
perspective according to the various individual values and preferences that inform its construction. This does not deny the fact that
citizens are often born into one or more communities (i.e. family,
religious or ethnic) but that through their own judgement and free
will may enter or leave as they wish. At the heart of this perspective
is the idea of authentic voluntary consent.

The latter has a semblance of meaning alongside the remarks of
Home Secretary, David Blunkett, where, in reflecting upon society,
he argued that:

> [Individual] freedom, the protection of liberty and respect for difference
> have not been accompanied by a strong, shared understanding of the
> civic realm. This has to change. It is vital that we develop a stronger
> understanding of what our collective citizenship means, and how we can
> build that shared commitment into our social and political institutions.
> These shared values cannot be imposed or community cohesion built in
> Whitehall. Local people need to take the lead on local problems because
> no one else has a greater stake in solving them (Blunkett, 2001a: 2).

The line here between voluntary assent to the concept of community and coercive submission through the apparatus of the state is,
indeed, a fine one. For Blunkett's message contains language that
may be interpreted in ways that can be seen to empower or constrain. On the one hand, its vision is empowering since it displays a
commitment to individual freedom, the protection of liberty and
active participation. Yet on the other it is constraining, for appeals
to collective citizenship, shared values and community cohesion
impose a notion of 'social uniformity' to which citizens may not
autonomously subscribe. That this may be the case can be illustrated in calls, by the Prime Minister, Tony Blair, for an 'explosion
of voluntary activity' underpinned by cash incentives to managers

in industry (Blair, 2000: 1). This type of coercion (or persuasion) is oppositional to the idea of developing citizens that are essentially self-determining and autonomous. On this view, the remarks of Blunkett and Blair may together be interpreted with the centre-right perspective of communitarianism, in which unity and authority are seen to gain assent. If this is the case, there may be considerable tension between the expressed view for active citizenship within the Advisory Group's Report and the wider political framework in which that discourse is located.

Either way, in key speeches, New Labour have regularly invoked notions of community:

> If we succeed in making a more active community, I'm convinced that there will also be other benefits – less anti-social behaviour, less crime, less of the corrosion of values that worries so may people (Blair, 2000).

> Today's reports show that too many of our towns and cities lack any sense of civic identity or shared values. Young people, in particular, are alienated and disengaged from much of the society around them, including the leadership of their communities. These are not issues for government alone. They demand a wide public debate on what citizenship and community belonging should mean in this country (Blunkett, 2001b).

These remarks can be read as implying that in some way 'more community' may provide the solution to the myriad social problems, including crime, homelessness, drug abuse, moral relativism and so forth. This is particularly true in relation to the belief that its reification is capable of stemming a 'corrosion of values', and that the recovery of community is a matter for society writ large, and not merely an issue for government alone. Once again, there are two contrasting interpretations. One view is that invocations of community possess a certain intrinsic quality, in which communitarian citizenship may reflect the values of either centre-left or liberal perspectives. On this assumption, individuals can be enabled to make informed, critical choices in the process of becoming active citizens within the communities to which they belong. Yet this raises a thorny issue: how feasible is it within a pluralist society, containing different cultural, ethnic and religious groups, that citizens may, of their own free will, subscribe to the moral ideal of collective citizenship? This issue is further sensitized by the influence of prior political and economic forces that have penetrated the communities in which people live. For ten years, during the 1980s, the hegemony of neo-liberal economic policy and libertarian political ideology systematically reinforced the virtues of individualism, rational self-interest and the creation of wealth (Menter and Whitty, 1989; Quicke, 1992). That communities of citizens may no longer feel able to identify with ideas of collective citizenship, shared values and the moral ideal of community (see Putnam, 2000) can be interpreted as a representation of the legacy of 'Thatcherism'.

This perspective leads towards the second view, which is that notions of community may have instrumental value in providing solutions to society's various social problems. On this more cynical note, community is a convenient rhetorical and social device to allow responsibility to be shifted away from the realm of government and placed at the hands of the individual (Piper and Piper, 2000). Conceived in this way groups of individuals, forming respective communities, are enjoined to deal with the social problems that government itself was democratically elected to address. This point can be further illustrated in relation to the Advisory Group's Report, where it is argued that community: 'is especially important at a time when government is attempting a *shift of emphasis* between, on the one hand, *state welfare provision and responsibility* and, on the other, *community and individual responsibility*' (QCA, 1998: 10, emphasis added).

The politics of communitarianism, and its relationship with education for citizenship, runs into further difficulties when the concepts of pluralism and community are brought into view. Their appearance invokes conditions in which diversity and unity, often seen as diametrically opposed, struggle to find a basis for compromise. This tension is recognized within the Advisory Group's Report where, in response to pressing concerns regarding society's changing social composition, the corrosion of values and proliferation of cultural beliefs, it is argued that

> a main aim for the whole community should be to find or restore a common sense of citizenship, including national identity that is secure enough to find a place for the plurality of nations, cultures, ethnic identities and religions long found in the United Kingdom. Citizenship education creates common ground between different ethnic and religious identities (ibid.: 17).

More recently, this view has found support in the comments of Home Secretary, David Blunkett (2001a: 2): '[There] is no contradiction between retaining a distinct cultural identity and identifying with Britain . . . Citizenship means finding a common place for diverse cultures and beliefs, consistent with the core values we uphold.'

At issue here is the tension between various sectional interests, minority groups and divergent communities on the one hand and the aspiration of collective citizenship, common values and shared national identity on the other. The argument that is sometimes assembled by centre-left communitarians against the liberal position is that if cultural pluralism is allowed to develop unabated, without at the same time attending to the requirement of common social interests, there is a distinct possibility that different communities will become increasingly alienated from, and hostile towards, one another (Miller, 2000). This view gathered political momentum when in response to outbreaks of inner-city violence during the summer of 2001, David Blunkett insisted upon the renewal of a shared civic identity. On this perspective, however, education for citizenship can become a repressive, rather than progressive, social factor, as the status of cultural minorities is defined solely in terms of their membership to the nation-state. This view is in concert with current moves to impose citizenship classes for new immigrants entering into the UK (Blunkett, 2001b). Such cultural imperialism, of course, sanctioned by the authority of the state does little in the way of recognizing that different forms of citizenship have evolved within different social and historical contexts. As Heater (1990: 131) reflects: 'the idea of nationalism and the nation-state have not transferred with any comfort to Asian and African continents. The ethnic and cultural homogeneity which the term "nation" denotes barely exists . . . nationhood has been rejected by minorities with their own powerful sense of community.' As the state presently attempts a more directive approach to education, part of whose function is to convey the established identity and culture of the nation-state, it engenders a sense of belonging that becomes inevitably muted for many ethnic groups (ibid.). Moreover, in moving closer to the centre right of communitarian politics this perspective shifts further away from the idea of active citizenship and turns towards a model that is inherently more passive.

Conclusion

As the beginning of the introduction started with a question, the start of the conclusion begins with several more. Which branch of communitarian politics does education for citizenship assume? What conception of citizenship is dominant in current thinking? And what implications does this have for the development of the rights of the child? The obvious answer to the first two questions is that parts of the current perspective can be interpreted so as to support aspects of a number of different putative models. To complicate matters further, interpretations of citizenship must take place within a political context that alone is capable of generating a collection of different readings around issues of social and educational significance. This has been demonstrated in the preceding analysis, which revealed that the nature and purpose of citizenship could be interpreted so as to suggest links with both centre-right and centre-left positions of communitarian thinking, thereby indicating that such affinities are partly determined by the adopted angle of vision. Since curriculum documents do not interpret themselves, parts of the rhetoric of citizenship can be seen as entertaining either active or passive dimensions, according to particular conceptual frameworks that are used to inform such judgements.

This does not, however, imply that anything goes. For some models of citizenship are clearly more morally and educationally reputable than others from the standpoint of a child's educational entitlement. According to the various articles that comprise the Convention on the Rights of the Child, children have the right to specific freedoms that presuppose the opportunity of a rich and diverse education. Part of this aim requires that children become empowered to make critically informed decisions concerning social and political choices around which their lives are seen to revolve. But what does this mean? And what might it involve?

For philosophers like Wringe (1992), positive freedoms in a democratic and free society amount to more than a mere statement or enactment of one's rights. They require, in concert with the liberal tradition and framework of the CRC, an understanding of freedoms from want, fear, insecurity and constraint. These presume the possibility of enabling the young to understand broad sets of issues concerning, say, the plight of the underprivileged, the development of a healthy scepticism (yet not undue protest) towards the rule of law and the promotion of an ability to respond appropriately to the misfortunes of others. Active citizenship, then, is not a mechanism through which rights are to be defended, for they are, by definition, things to which individuals are already entitled. Rather, they are the means by which young people may be enabled to develop attitudes that lead to purposeful actions in response to concern for fellow citizens.

Following a recent study (Davies and Evans, 2002), it has been suggested that in the light of uncertainty regarding current practice, such freedoms and actions could be operationalized by focusing on content that is relevant and 'real'. This would presume a participative process that is inclusive and which would ensure that outcomes are valued by a wide range of people through activities that are primarily locally based. Others, in contrast, have suggested using global contexts as a means of emboldening young people's understandings of citizenship. Hicks (2001), for example, has argued for the presentation of four separate dimensions of citizenship: personal, social, spatial and temporal. On this model, the spatial dimension is seen to embrace both local and global understandings of contemporary issues, whilst simultaneously drawing upon the requirement of a temporal dimension. The latter assumes that human existence is impossible in the absence of preconditions that reflect upon past, present and future modes of temporality. Opportunities for contemplation for young people of what is possible, probable (i.e. likely to happen) and preferable create the conditions for critical activity that is necessary to the preservation or reconstruction of future lifestyles (ibid.). In this way more active models of citizenship may be preferred to those that are inherently passive, since they engage the young in critical processes that underpin what it means to be active in a political democracy. The real difficulties in meeting this challenge, then, lie not in the perceived dominance of one particular model over another (classical humanism over progressivism, libertarianism over republicanism or centre-right communitarianism over centre-left communitarianism), but rather in the extent to which young people are encouraged to wrestle with the tensions that characterize citizenship's contested terrain. Only when these conditions are satisfied might it be possible for the young to exercise their rights, to engage in the freedom of open and critical debate, and to live their lives in ways that allow them to develop their personalities to the full.

Student task

Given that citizenship can mean different things to different people at different times:

1 Design your own model of a citizenship curriculum. What sort of ideological influences would inform its construction?
2 To what extent does the present national curriculum framework for citizenship support or detract from your conception?

Suggested further reading

Crick, B. (2000) *Essays on Citizenship*. London and New York: Continuum. This book is thought provoking, argumentative and polemical. In eloquent fashion it presents an overview of Crick's thinking on politics, political philosophy and citizenship over the last 30 years, seeking to combine older writing (layered with commentary) with more recent essays. It serves as a useful device for repositioning his early work within the context of the present curriculum and for asking questions regarding the aims and purpose of citizenship today.

Isin, E.F. and Wood, P.K. (1999) *Citizenship and Identity*, London: Sage. This edited collection of essays provides an in-depth account of a range of issues around the associated themes of citizenship and identity. While this book introduces a more abstract perspective of citizenship (away from the curriculum), the depth and clarity with which issues of gender, sexuality and culture impacting on the construction of identities are presented provides an important overview on contemporary issues of citizenship.

Osler, A. (2000) *Citizenship and Democracy in Schools: Diversity, Identity and Equality*. Stoke-on-Trent: Trentham Books. In this edited collection of essays issues of citizenship, race, identity and human rights, and practising democracy are raised. The section on human rights is particularly meaningful and illuminative within the context of citizenship's recent rebirth. It raises important questions concerning the rights to which children are entitled and considers the implications of these for the development of social justice.

Note

1 The use of the term 'passive subjects' invokes a series of tensions associated with common understandings of republicanism (in which people are typically conceived as active citizens) on the one hand and the monarchy (in which members of the state are typically conceived as obedient subjects) on the other. It is not the purpose of this chapter to engage in a full-blown analysis of these tensions, which have been debated elsewhere (see, for example, Wilson, 1989; Donnellan, 1998; Freedland, 1998). Suffice it to say that 'passive subjects' may not be fully able to share in the privileges of citizenship but may none the less be obligated to perform certain civic responsibilities at the request of the state headed by the monarch. There may be certain contradictions, therefore, between the rhetoric of active

citizenship and the practice of living within a monarchy, such as that of the UK, where members of the state may be presumed submissive.

References

Arnot, M. (1997) 'Gendered citizenry': new feminist perspectives on education and citizenship. *British Educational Research Journal* 23(3): 275–95.

Ball, S.J. (1993) Education, markets, choice and social class: the market as a class strategy in the UK and the USA. *British Journal of Sociology of Education*, 14(1): 3–19.

Batho, G. (1990) The history of the teaching of civics and citizenship in English schools. *Curriculum Journal* 1(1): 91–100.

Blair, T. (2000) Blair backs volunteer call with cash (http://news.bbc.co.uk/hi/english/uk_politics/newsid_663000/663918.stm).

Blunkett, D. (2001a) Its not about cricket tests (http:www.guardian.co.uk/Archive/Article/0,4273,4319914,00.html).

Blunkett, D. (2001b) The full text of David Blunkett's speech, made in the West Midlands to highlight the publication of reports into inner-city violence this summer (http://www.guardian.co.uk/Archive/Article/0,4273,4317784,00.html).

Carr, W. (1991) Education for citizenship. *British Journal of Educational Studies*, 39(3): 373–85.

Crick, B. (2000) *Essays on Citizenship*. London: Continuum.

Davies, I. and Evans, M. (2002) Encouraging active citizenship. *Educational Review*, 54(1): 69–78.

DfEE (1997) *Excellence in Schools*. London: DfEE.

DES (1967) *The Plowden Report*, London: HMSO.

Donnellan, C. (ed.) (1998) *Monarchy or Republic*? Cambridge: Independence Educational Publishers.

Edwards, A. and Whitty, G. (1992) Parental choice and educational reform in Britain and the United States. *British Journal of Educational Studies* 40(2): 101–17.

Etzioni, A. (1995) *The Spirit of Community*. London: Fontana.

Etzioni, A. (1997) *The New Golden Rule: Community and Morality in a Democratic Society*. New York: HarperCollins.

Freedland, J. (1998) *Bring Home the Revolution: The Case for a British Republic*. London: Fourth Estate.

Gewirtz, S., Ball, S.J. and Bowe, R. (1995) *Markets, Choice and Equity in Education*. Buckingham: Open University Press.

Heater, D. (1969) *The Teaching of Politics*. London: Politics Association.

Heater, D. (1990) *The Civic Ideal in World History, Politics and Education*, London: Longman.

Hicks, D. (2001) Re-examining the future: the challenge for citizenship education. *Educational Review* 53(3): 229–40.

Hindess, B. (1993) Citizenship in the modern west. In B.S. Turner (ed.) *Citizenship and Social Theory*. London: Sage.

Isin, E.F. and Wood, P.K. (1999) *Citizenship and Identity*. London: Sage.

John, M. (ed.) (1996) *Children in Charge: One Child's Right to a Fair Hearing*. London and Bristol, PA: Jessica Kingsley.

Laura, R.S. and Cotton, M.C. (1999) *Empathetic Education: An Ecological Perspective on Educational Knowledge*. London: Falmer.

Lyotard, J.-F. (1984) *The Postmodern Condition: A Report on Knowledge*. Manchester: Manchester University Press.

Mann, M. (1996) Ruling class strategies and citizenship. In M. Bulmer and A.M. Rees (eds) *Citizenship Today – the Contemporary Relevance of T.H. Marshall*. London: UCL Press.

Marshall, T.H. (1950) *Citizenship and Social Class and Other Essays*. Cambridge: Cambridge University Press.

Marshall, T.H. (1997) Citizenship and social class. In R.E. Goodin and P. Pettit (eds) *Contemporary Political Philosophy*. Oxford: Blackwell.

Menter, I. and Whitty, G. (1989) Lessons of Thatcherism: education policy in England and Wales, 1979–1988. *Journal of Law and Society* 16(89): 42–64.

Miller, D. (2000) *Citizenship and National Identity*. Cambridge: Polity Press.

Ministry of Education (1949) *Citizens Growing up*. London: HMSO.

National Curriculum Council (1990a) *Curriculum Guidance 8: Education for Citizenship*. York: NCC.

National Curriculum Council (1990b) *Curriculum Guidance 3: The Whole Curriculum*. York: NCC.

Oliver, D. and Heater, D. (1994) *The Foundation of Citizenship*. Hemel Hempstead: Harvester Wheatsheaf.

Osler, A. (1997) Black teachers and citizenship: researching differing identities. *Teachers and Teaching: Theory and Practice* 3(1): 47–60.

Osler, A. (ed.) (2000) *Citizenship and Democracy in Schools: Diversity, Identity, Equality*. Stoke-on-Trent: Trentham Books.

Peters, R.S. (1966) *Ethics and Education*. London: Allen & Unwin.

Peters, R.S. (1973) Aims of education – a conceptual enquiry. In R.S. Peters (ed.) *The Philosophy of Education*. London: Oxford University Press.

Piper, H. and Piper, J. (2000) Volunteering and citizenship in communitarian education policy: philosophers' stone and fools' gold. *Education and Social Justice*, 3(1): 48–55.

Putnam, R.D. (2000) *Bowling Alone*. London: Touchstone.

Qualification and Curriculum Authority (1998) *Education for Citizenship and the Teaching of Democracy in Schools*. London: QCA.

Qualification and Curriculum Authority (1999) *Citizenship*. London: QCA.

Quicke, J. (1992) Individualism and citizenship: some problems and possibilities. *International Studies in Sociology of Education*, 2(2): 147–63.

Rees, A.M. (1996) T.H. Marshall and the progress of citizenship. In M. Bulmer and A.M. Rees (eds) *Citizenship Today – the Contemporary Relevance of T.H. Marshall*. London: UCL Press.

Robinson, J. and Garratt, D. (1994) Interdependence and controversial issues: environmental education and economic and industrial understanding as cross-curricular themes. *International Journal of Environmental Affairs and Information*, 13(4): 415–28.

Sewell, T. (1997) *Black Masculinities and Schooling: How Black Boys Survive Modern Schooling*. Stoke-on-Trent: Trentham Books.

Skilbeck, M. (1976) Three educational ideologies. In *E203 Curriculum Design and Development. Unit 3: Ideologies and Values*. Milton Keynes: Open University Press.

Thatcher, M. (1988) Margaret Thatcher speech (http://forerunner.com/forerunner/X0145_Margaret_Thatcher_Sp.html).

Tooley, J. (1997) Saving education from the 'lurching steam roller': the democratic virtue of markets in education. In D. Bridges (ed.) *Education, Autonomy and Democratic Citizenship – Philosophy in a Changing World*. London: Routledge.

Twine, F. (1994) *Citizenship and Social Rights – the Interdependence of Self and Society*. London: Sage.

Verhellen, E. (2000) Children's rights and education. In A. Osler, (ed.) *Citizenship and Democracy in Schools: Diversity, Identity, Equality*. Stoke-on-Trent: Trentham Books.

White, J. (1982) *The Aims of Education Restated*. London: Routledge and Kegan Paul.

White, J. (1990) *Education and the Good Life: Beyond the National Curriculum*. London: Institute of Education, University of London.

Wilson, E. (1989) *The Myth of British Monarchy*. London: Journeyman.

Wringe, C. (1992) The ambiguities of education for active citizenship, *Journal of Philosophy of Education* 26(1): 29–38.

6

The Management of Teachers as Professionals

Steve Bartlett and Diana Burton

Teachers play a central part in 'New' Labour's strategy of raising standards in education as part of the creation of a prosperous and inclusive society. This chapter begins by considering the work of teachers and noting that, far from being a homogeneous group, they vary greatly in terms of what their daily work entails and how they respond to it. This leads us to a consideration of the complexity of teacher professionalism. A history of recent changes in teaching then charts the increasing centralization of the curriculum, the development of markets in education and the corresponding development of managerial forms of control. We conclude by looking at the model of the modernized professional currently being promoted by the government.

Introduction: the work of teachers

Teaching is a varied occupation. For instance, a teacher working with a nursery class will have a very different working day from that of a history teacher in a secondary school. The challenges facing the teacher of very young children differ enormously from those of a secondary 'subject specialist'. Even teachers teaching the same age group of pupils and subject face very different experiences depending upon the type, size and geographical location of the school and the abilities, attributes and motivation of individuals within that particular group. It is no accident that some areas of the country, such as the inner cities, have great difficulty in recruiting teachers whereas in other, more rural and affluent, areas there is no such problem. Thus when considering national developments in teaching and the curriculum and when talking of teachers as a general category of employees, we need to be aware of these great variations in the labour process.

Apart from teachers there are many other adults also employed in schools who are part of the broad education process. School secretaries, caretakers and cleaners all play an important part in the daily life of any school. There are others such as classroom assistants and nursery nurses who have an increasingly important role in the education of children as teachers are encouraged to 'concentrate' upon their task of teaching. Some of these groups are increasingly seen as para-professionals supporting the work of classroom teachers. The growing use of classroom assistants may actually serve to increase the status of the professional classroom teacher. Alternatively, these assistants may be seen as a cheaper alternative to trained teachers and a way of solving the problem of teacher shortages. Teachers must also liaise with other professionals working with young people, such as social workers, probation officers, youth workers, the police and educational psychologists.

The role of the teacher is thus complex and worthy of detailed analysis (Squires, 1999; Newton, 2000; Sugrue and Day, 2002). There is a multitude of skills involved in the daily work of a classroom teacher, and what constitutes 'good' teaching is very much open to debate, the answer depending upon the views of the people responding and where they see the emphasis of a teacher's work lying (see Bartlett et al., 2001, for a discussion of this).

In commonsense terms teaching involves a transfer of knowledge to the pupils. This can be carried out in a variety of ways depending upon the type of knowledge and the reasons for acquiring it. For instance, we may learn some facts rote fashion when they are needed primarily for recall purposes, we may learn by experimenting, we may learn by practising our existing skills. Thus 'lessons' can take many forms depending mainly upon the judgements of the teacher (see Kyriacou, 1998; Petty, 1998; Hayes, 2000, for practical accounts of classroom teaching skills and organization). However, education involves much more than a transfer of knowledge in the subject sense. Many would view education as having a very important moral and social dimension. It involves caring for the pupils in terms of their welfare and also fostering values of mutual respect and tolerance required in a democratic society. A teacher's work may involve them emphasizing particular aspects of this broad role depending upon their subject and pastoral responsibilities.

Teaching style is an important issue in the debate about what makes a good teacher. Some teachers prefer a more informal and relaxed teaching style whereas others feel that learning takes place more effectively in a formal atmosphere. This leads to a considera- tion of discipline in the classroom. Teachers can be criticized for being overly strict and pupils may complain that they feel too fright- ened to learn. However, the lack of discipline in the classroom and its effect upon learning is a more publicized complaint in the media. A certain level of control over the class does need to be exercised by the teacher, but if discipline is too strict it can become oppressive, whereas softness by a teacher may be portrayed as a weakness to be exploited. This discussion reminds us that what can be included as the characteristics of a good teacher or teaching rests heavily upon our ideological beliefs of the nature and purposes of education. Thus there will never be total agreement about 'good' teaching whilst there are ideological differences. Perhaps we should consider the work of teachers as education professionals in more detail.

The professional nature of teaching

The term 'profession' is frequently applied to the work of teachers. It is now worth considering to what extent teachers may be regarded as professionals. Becker (1962) saw professionalism as merely a symbol for an ideology used to justify actions and behav- iours. He noted that many occupations trying to become professions used the symbol in an attempt to increase their auton- omy and raise their prestige. They would try to take on as many parts of the symbol as possible. Becker may well have considered teaching to be such an occupation.

There have been many attempts to identify the features of a profes- sion. Bottery (1996) suggested that at least 17 different criteria have been claimed at one time or another to describe professional behav- iour. Salient characteristics included subscription to a specialized body of knowledge exclusive to the occupation which required learn- ing in higher education. There was a code of professional conduct and ethics with a strong emphasis on service. There was a high degree of self-regulation by the professional body itself over entry, qualifications, training and members' conduct. It is perhaps appropriate to consider how teachers have, or have not, matched up to these professional criteria.

In 1957, Tropp felt that teachers had, since the Second World War, and through steady development, reached the status of 'true' professionals. Teaching was seen as a worthwhile occupation. There were teaching associations whose aim was to raise professional standards. Teachers had fought for educational progress and been engaged in continuous research and evaluation. He felt that at work teachers had gained almost complete independence. They had earned their licensed autonomy and the school's inspectorate (HMI) were regarded as helpful senior colleagues. Tropp (ibid.) saw this professional development and independence within education as a safeguard to democracy and protection against the growth of dictatorship. This position prevailed in the 1960s and into the 1970s but was to alter radically through the 1980s and 1990s.

A number of occupations have developed higher levels of training and standards of practice to enhance their claims to professional status. However, Wilensky (1964) said that many of these groups rested on a knowledge base which was either too general and vague or too narrow. They lacked autonomy and were supervised by those without professional status themselves. Etzioni (1969) preferred to classify these occupations as 'semi-professionals'. These workers, in his view, were characterized as working in bureaucratic organizations, a large number of them were likely to be female, training was usually less than five years and the knowledge base was weak and not directly used by the worker. Significantly, they had restricted autonomy because they were controlled by those in higher ranks. Their working day was tightly regulated and they were subject to checks in areas where their work was least visible. Teachers can be viewed as prime examples of semi-professionals. Such things as the need by teachers to report to parents on their child's progress, school inspections and the publishing of pupil performance in league tables help to regulate the autonomy of teachers.

Perhaps in realization of the fact that teachers did not really match the model of the established or more traditional professions, there have been attempts to redefine the term 'professional' or to present different kinds of professionalism. Much of this discussion has focused on the actual practice of teaching. The modern professional, according to Schön (1983), constantly questioned and reflected upon practice. This involved the professional regarding his or her work from the point of view of the client or as an outsider. The purpose of this was to understand all aspects of the process resulting in greater professional insight. This whole procedure (involving evaluation, criticism and ultimately self-development), required openness and trust between those involved. Schön saw these reflective practitioners, with their critical and innovative approaches, as being important ingredients in modern organizations. However the need for such professionals to operate within environments allowing high levels of autonomy and their tendency to treat clients as individual cases created tensions with managements that saw uniformity and predictability as a key to ensuring quality control in volume production. Hoyle (1980) differentiated between two sorts of teachers. Restricted professionals are conscientious practitioners but are limited in outlook. Extended professionals seek to improve their practice by learning from other teachers and professional development activities. They are keen to be involved in practitioner research and to link theory to practice.

The political context of teacher professionalism

The changing position of teachers in England is worthy of discussion at this point. Post-1944 is often seen as the 'golden age' of teaching (see Lawton, 1989) in terms of the autonomy granted to teachers in all aspects of their work. However in the 1970s misgivings began to arise concerning the curriculum and educational standards. These fears were publicly expressed by the then Prime Minister, James Callaghan, in his Ruskin speech of 1976 which instigated 'The Great Debate' on standards of learning and teaching. Conservative opposition also voiced concern at the state of education, placing the blame at the teachers' door (see Cox and Dyson, 1969a; 1969b).

On gaining power in 1979 the Conservative government radically changed the nature of education over a 20-year period. The policy of the New Right comprised an apparently contradictory mix of increasing central control and the development of market forces in education. In the compulsory sector this policy was manifested through certain significant reforms. The introduction of a National Curriculum increased central control of the curriculum. Greater parental choice was brought about by the introduction of open enrolment, the creation of city technology colleges, grant-maintained status and, later, specialist secondary schools. Schools were allowed to be more adaptable to market demands by gaining control of their own budgets (LMS). Schools, and also teachers, were to be made more accountable for their actions with the introduction of comparative league tables of performance and a rigorous inspection regime under the Office for Standards in Education (Ofsted). By the end of this period teachers had lost their control of the curriculum. Content and assessment were now determined by national bodies, the National Curriculum Council and the Schools Examination and Assessment Council (later combined to form the Qualifications and Curriculum Authority).

Throughout the Conservative administrations of the 1980s and 1990s many changes have been noted in the work process of teachers (see Ozga and Lawn, 1988). Their ability to control pace, content, volume and assessment of work declined. Routine administrative tasks grew in number. Schools' managements became more supervisory and concerned with performance levels, in keeping with their industrial counterparts. Teaching posts became less secure with redundancy, redeployment and retraining issues attacking the professional identity of teachers.

It has been argued (see Ball, 1994) that policies of presenting education as a commodity in the marketplace have steadily transformed the nature of schools as organizations and workplaces. Forms of industrial management came to be seen as appropriate for schools. So we have the development of management cultures emphasizing cost effectiveness, efficiency and competition, as opposed to professional cultures, which prioritize the development of the individual pupil, social relationships and collegiality. Grace (1995) found that as managerialism became more salient there arose a conception of 'senior management' who were distinguished from 'middle management'. Thus teachers within a school became differentiated into a clearer hierarchy as there emerged a line management model of the organization. Reay (1996) saw the development of management discourses in education, such as human resource management and total quality management, which involved a shared set of managerially sanctioned values such as quality, service and innovation, as the beginning of a shift away from professional towards corporate identities amongst teachers. The increasing workload, progressive loss of control over their work, and greater accountability to managerial forms of control led to the analysis of the work process of teachers as undergoing various changes such as intensification (Hargreaves, 1994) and proletarianization (Apple, 1988; 1996).

Within education Hoyle (1995) saw the meaning and use of the term 'professionalism' as having altered. The focus was now in, and not beyond, the classroom. It had come to mean a form of management-assured quality delivery. Teachers had now, in Dale's (1989) terms, moved from licensed autonomy, trusted by the state and allowed relative independence, to a more regulated autonomy, subject to greater external monitoring. Ozga (1995a; 2000) characterized teachers as bureaucratized, state professionals. It was the relationship with the state that she saw as most significant. The state had effectively retained strategic control of teaching, the curriculum and assessment whilst using school heads to develop the market strategy. This process involved the co-option of management and the growth of managerialism. As market success required smooth production and the eradication of problems, Ozga (1995b) suggested that deviations from policy were less likely to be tolerated. Thus under the guise of empowerment and collegiality, teachers were subject to increasing monitoring and surveillance. She suggested that the growth of management teams and supervisory functions may have 'extended' the professionalism of some but deskilled others. Bottery (1996) explained that these changes involved retrenchment due to reduced budgets, increased scrutiny in terms of costs and efficiency, changes in contract which redefined power relationships in favour of management and greater content control over work.

Conservative policy did have its critics. Central controls were seen, by many, as too rigid. The policy of market forces was criticized as being unfair to certain groups and individuals in society. Due to the excess of demand for education over the quality of supply, the market still appeared to be dominated by producers. Labour came to power in 1997 with modernizing education as a central plank of their political agenda. They talked of a partnership between all those concerned in the raising of standards in education. Labour has increased funding for education and created a strategy for professional development of teachers whilst expecting in return flexibility and co-operation from the teaching force in the introduction and development of new initiatives designed to modernize the profession and improve schools (see DfEE, 1997; 1998; DfES, 2001). Whilst the rhetoric has changed from conflict to partnership under Labour, apart from different spending priorities much of the Conservative reforms have been left in place (Docking, 2000).

It could be argued that the Labour government has reduced the emphasis on the market but continued to develop control from the centre (Avis, 1999). Fergusson (2000) suggests that the social and economic policy of the New Right was to 'marketize', giving precedence to economic success and individual enterprise whilst the social consequences were of secondary concern. In contrast, New Labour's modernization agenda can be interpreted as seeking complementarity between its economic and social priorities. Interestingly, Fergusson sees New Labour's mission to modernize as facing comparable problems to those of the New Right when they attempted to marketize the state welfare systems. The difficulty is in changing the culture of state-run enterprises: 'The common strand is the need to drive new objectives down through the institutions' (ibid.: 2000, p. 207). Thus Labour uses the same managerial forms of administration as the previous Conservative government. New Labour's so-called 'Third Way' presents a combination of the ideologies of neo-liberalism and state socialism or alternatively a pragmatic response to the need to please a middle-class electorate whilst operating under the fiscal constraints of the treasury (Phillips, 2001).

Teaching is a key occupation as education plays a crucial part in Labour's endeavour to make the British labour force competitive in the new global economy, whilst at the same time, creating a more socially democratic and inclusive society (there is here a link to government policies in the areas of lifelong learning which are discussed in Chapter 9). The challenge they face is in reconciling the objectives of competitiveness and social justice (Jones, 1996; Phillips, 2001). For Ozga (2000), Labour policy places a heavy emphasis on the economic functions of education, and the modernization of education aims 'to create an enterprising culture of the system, the institution and the self. It privileges waged work as the passport to inclusion, as well as the passport to wealth' (p. 222).

Thus making pupils employable is considered a major strategy in combating social exclusion.

However, given the shortage of teachers and the importance of the teaching force in delivering the reforms required, Labour has recognized the need to improve the public image and the status of these 'new professionals' through, for example, such initiatives as the establishment of the General Teaching Council (GTC), the creation of a National College for School Leadership and the awarding of knighthoods for chosen headteachers (McCulloch, 2001). The GTC is the new professional body for teachers and started work in September 2000. A majority of the council's 64 members are teachers, most of them elected. It is an independent body funded by teachers' registration fees. Teachers in maintained schools are required to register with the GTC. The GTC advises the government on professional development, induction, career progression and performance management in the drive to raise standards of achievement. It has powers to remove teachers from the register for serious misconduct or incompetence. There is still debate about how independent of government control the GTC actually is and how its functions relate to those of the Department for Education and Skills (DfES) and the Teacher Training Agency (TTA).

Current policies of professional development: a managerial approach?

The plans for modernizing the teaching profession announced in the green paper, *Teachers: Meeting the Challenge of Change* (DfEE, 1998), are seen by Ozga (2000) as just a further development in a recent history that involves the redesign of teaching through changing the training, development and career structure of teachers. She suggests that this is a policy design that promotes adherence to the technical/managerial approach that sees just one model of successful teaching and successful school leadership. This increasing standardization of practice is at the expense of innovation and creativity. Furlong (2001) suggests that, in order to reform education, there was a need to change the culture within schools through the structure and content of initial teacher training and continuing professional development (CPD). This was in effect a struggle for the minds of teachers through a managerial approach that emphasizes the technical aspects of teaching and managing rather than the philosophical questions of purpose. The training of senior and middle managers for schools through bespoke pro- grammes is well funded by the government and is threatening to replace the traditional Masters degree qualification that aspiring school leaders formerly undertook. Thus training and teacher devel- opment now takes place increasingly within a tightly managed school environment rather than as part of higher education. The professional development of serving teachers has become far more practical and focused and there is less opportunity for teachers to extend their broader thinking as educationalists. The current emphasis for teacher development is on training as opposed to edu- cation, and inspections of the quality of this training scrutinize closely its impact on pupil progress.

The Labour government launched a major review of professional development in February 2000 that sought to 'transform educa- tional standards and raise achievement in every school' (DfEE, 2000a: 3). It was predicated on ten principles. These include a need for teachers to take ownership of their development, to 'learn on the job' from expert practitioners, to harness the potential of ICT and to plan and evaluate their development programmes. The gov- ernment pledged a commitment to fund and support teachers' professional development through a culture of entitlement. Fundamentally, the goal is to raise standards of pupil achievement. The parameters for this are the individual teacher's needs and aspi- rations, the needs and priorities of individual schools and national strategic priorities.

The government has as its frame of reference for this professional development the sets of national standards it has laid down for teacher competence at various stages of their career. Teacher educa- tion is increasingly conceptualized within an extended framework from initial training, through induction to the newly qualified teacher (NQT) year and beyond into qualified teacher status (Heaney, 2001). The emphasis is on individual teachers charting their way through the stages and phases of this framework of stan- dards whilst their progress is governed by the management of teacher performance. Thus there are standards for subject leaders, for special education needs co-ordinators (SENCOs) and for advanced skills teachers (ASTs) who will be paid at a higher rate to develop and promulgate expert classroom practice. Standards for headship, together with an accredited qualification, are now well established and there are plans to make the qualification a compulsory requirement for all heads. The effect of these plans has been to create a plethora of routes to promotion and a diversification of remuneration for teachers. It is interesting to note the areas that have been determined by the government to be worthy of standards to govern practice. Pastoral care posts in secondary schools, which place teachers in very demanding, key roles, have thus far not been deemed to need standards; similarly, neither have year co-ordinator roles in primary schools.

The changes also include a 'fast track' through the profession to early subject leadership, senior management roles and on to headship (DfEE, 1999). Top-quality graduates and 'the most talented serving teachers' will be selected for their commitment to teaching, excellent subject knowledge and their talent to communicate, inspire and lead. Fast-track teachers will move through a number of designated challenging teaching posts to gain a range of varied experience. They will undertake extra CPD activities out of school hours and during school holidays, such as short work placements outside teaching, and will study for additional higher-level qualifications and courses offered by the National College for School Leadership. In return they will move more quickly through the pay scales and take up senior leadership roles within a few years of joining the teaching profession.

The creation of AST and fast-track posts is controversial as the availability of a few highly paid posts militates against a collegial approach to school improvement. A situation in which a few high-fliers are dubbed experts may lead to the disillusionment of many committed but less ambitious teachers who may leave the development work to those who are better paid. Once again a government is talking of the teacher as a professional. However this may be seen as a restricted view of professional activity (Bottery and Wright, 1999; Burton and Bartlett, 2002). Emphasis is on the classroom and the techniques of teaching.

Evidence-based practice

The government is encouraging teachers to put greater emphasis on 'evidence-based practice' which, at its simplest, means analysing what they are doing with pupils to ensure that there are good reasons for a particular approach or task. This can also be interpreted as 'doing what has been shown to work' rather than being tied to a particular ideological approach to teaching. Each school now receives from Ofsted a PANDA Report (Performance AND Assessment) which shows the school's performance data in comparison with national averages and with schools in similar contexts. Heads are expected to use the data as a management tool in the cycle of evaluation and improvement. Consideration is given to the 'value added' to each individual pupil or group of pupils. 'Performance indicators' are identified for teachers to focus on with the subsequent year's classes in order to make year-on-year comparisons. Data from the school's PANDA are expected to help teachers measure the effectiveness of a department or year group. Whilst such data may be of some use, many would argue that as they are divorced from the particularity of the pupils involved they have limited value. The situated nature of learning in particular contexts with particular pupils is, for many educationalists, a richer focus for research and improvement than a focus on disembedded, generalized performance data.

The DfES is currently making funds available to teachers to conduct small-scale research into good practice in their classrooms through the Best Practice Research Scholarship scheme. These may help teachers focus on the particularity of their learning situations. There is some scepticism within established research communities, however, about whether the methodologies and theoretical frames of reference for such investigations are appropriate. Bottery and Wright (1999) note that the drive to transform teaching into a research and evidence-based profession, whilst being desirable in aiming to improve the craft of teaching, remains narrowly focused. There is little scope for reflection beyond the classroom and for wider pedagogical debate. This remains a 'technical-rational' approach to teaching (see Bartlett, 2002). A tendency is also emerging for headteachers to sponsor teachers' scholarships where they can be clearly linked to issues arising out of the school's PANDA Report. This can detract from the teacher's intended focus and inappropriately privilege quantitative data where qualitative data may elicit richer understandings about the learning situation.

Teacher appraisal and performance management

In 1991 staff appraisal was made compulsory under a teacher's contract of employment. Teacher appraisal, as it was first introduced, suffered from conflicting perceptions of purpose, being seen by some as a means of control over teachers and by others as a tool for professional development (Bartlett, 2000). Its introduction, which came after a prolonged industrial dispute between teachers and the government over pay and conditions, was compromised. Teachers had to take part in appraisal and were required to set personal targets as a result of the process. However, the process was not related to pay and the appraisal statements were to be confidential. Thus what could have become either a system for increasing the accountability of teachers or a means of enhancing their wider professional development was from the start ineffective. Staff appraisal, being costly in terms of time for both management and teachers, was quickly abandoned in school as ineffective.

Labour has now taken appraisal and reintroduced it in the form of performance management. This is part of a strategy designed to improve the performance of schools in terms of identified indicators. Schools have had to devise and implement a performance management system since September 2000. This involves the drawing up of a school development plan that sets clear targets within a realistic time frame. Thus targets are also set for subject departments and for each individual teacher in relation to this whole-school plan. All teachers are now subject to annual performance review. Performance management is seen as an ongoing cycle involving planning, monitoring and review (DfEE, 2000b).

School heads and senior teachers will be expected to set objectives for individual teachers relating to various year groups and subject areas. For example, a teacher might be set the objective of developing a different approach to a teaching topic. Alternatively a small group of pupils not meeting expectations might be targeted for extra attention or a specific classroom management technique. Assessment and benchmarking data derived from Ofsted inspections, Standard Attainment Tests scores and GCSE results will be used to set targets in the school's development plan, and objectives for individual teachers will fit with these overarching goals. The scope of objectives will relate to a teacher's responsibilities, so headteachers will have objectives for pupil progress at school level whilst heads of subject may look at progress by year group and teachers within departments focus on work with cohorts, groups or individuals (DfEE, 1999). Objectives are expected to cover pupil progress and teachers' professional development. The latter might involve observing other teachers' good practice or signing up for some particular training: 'Performance management works best when it is an integral part of a school's culture; is seen to be fair and open; understood by everyone and based on shared commitment to supporting continuous improvement and recognizing success' (DfEE, 2000b: 2).

This model of professional development is controversial because it assumes a simplistic causal relationship between teacher input and pupil attainment. In Hoyle's (1995) terms it encourages restricted rather than extended professionalism. We know that there is a host of factors influencing pupils' performance that are beyond the control of the teacher, from the amount of television they watch to their attendance pattern and the extent of the support they receive from parents. We also know that teachers contribute more to a pupil's development than that which can be measured through examinations. Teachers have a concern for the whole person that includes his or her self-esteem, physical and emotional well-being, and cultural and spiritual development.

Thus performance management, like appraisal, has the rhetoric of professional development. Unlike in appraisal the targets set and their annual evaluation are not confidential. Thus it is now possible to link performance to pay. Teachers can now apply to pass through a 'threshold' of performance once they have reached a certain point on the professional pay scale. They must compile a portfolio of evidence to support their claim that they are functioning at a level deserving of threshold performance. The extra remuneration for reaching this level is £2,000. At least 95 per cent of the teachers who went through this process in 2000–1 successfully achieved threshold status. In the following year, however, the government only granted sufficient funding for 80 per cent of applicants to progress to the next rung of the ladder and to receive a further £1,000 salary increase. This has inevitably raised the question of whether performance is really being assessed against agreed criteria as evidenced in the portfolio. It is clear that success will be circumscribed by the amount of money available. Reconciling the rhetoric of performance management with the realities of funding limits brings into sharp focus the conflicts inherent in the government's model of teacher professionalism. There is here a managerialist assumption that monetary incentives are the prime motivator of employees and that linking targets to financial rewards will lead to more industrious and effective workers. Once again there is a potential conflict of purpose between a process designed to monitor performance for accountability and to promote openness for professional development.

The performance management model also promotes a focus on the individual teacher as opposed to the subject or year team, yet we know that much of the creative pedagogic and curriculum development work emanates from a team approach. This focus on individual development and management by objectives contrasts with a 'total quality management' model of development which emphasizes collaboration and teamwork (Deming, 1986; Scholtes, 1998). They suggest that emphasizing such targets concentrates attention on what is measurable rather than what is important and encourages workers to put their own interests ahead of what may be best for all. Ultimately the more an individual is judged in terms of targets which are often beyond his or her total control, the more threatened and isolated he or she will feel. The linking of individual performance to pay may, rather than increasing the motivation of teachers, have the opposite effect, as suggested by the results of a Mori poll conducted after the first round of applications by teachers to cross the performance threshold (Mansell, 2001). Thompson (2000) suggests that teachers are not enthusiastic about individual pay initiatives and that there needs instead to be consideration of what does motivate teachers, which she cites as a sense of engagement with the school, students and teaching itself. More sophisticated ways of assessing the contribution of a single teacher to a pupil's learning will need to be found if the profession is not to be fractured by what could become a very divisive methodology.

The ideology of performance management sits well within a technical-rational approach and the desire to itemize discrete teaching skills and teacher behaviours through, for example, QTS (qualified teacher status) and NQT standards. It has evolved from a managerialist view which equates standardization with quality assurance. Many have argued that this atomization of teaching provides an impoverished and partial model of the teacher and that the whole is greater than the sum of the parts (Burton and Bartlett, 2002).

This dominant ideology has spawned a report commissioned by the DfEE to determine what makes an effective teacher. It has recently reported findings that come as no surprise to many serving teachers. The government used these early findings to set the standards for the new performance threshold and to inform its performance management appraisal system. HayMcBer conducted detailed interviews with 172 teachers and observed around 120 of them. Five thousand questionnaires, completed by teachers, pupils and others, were also analysed (a summary of the report can be found at www.dfee.gov.uk/teachingreforms/mcber). The findings are grouped into three factors that affect pupil progress: a teacher's 'professional characteristics', 'teaching skills' and 'classroom climate'. The teaching skills thought to be particularly significant amongst effective teachers at both primary and secondary levels are high expectations and effective use of homework. Additionally at primary, strong time and resource management and good pupil assessment were most important whilst good planning was cited at secondary as being a key teaching component (Barnard, 2000). The HayMcBer Report cost a great deal of money yet served only to identify what the teaching profession itself could have told the government. Thus we see a 'legitimation' of teachers' work through a government-controlled management consultancy approach. This resonates well with Hoyle's (1995) analysis that policies which might be seen by some as 'deprofessionalization' could be regarded by the policy-makers as making those occupations more professional in relation to the needs of their clients – i.e. a process of reprofessionalization.

Conclusions

There have been differing views presented as to the nature of teacher professionalism. Whitty (1999: 2) suggests that it is best to see these alternative models existing as competing versions of teacher professionalism rather than 'seeing any one as fitting an essentialist definition . . . and others as detracting from it'. He suggests that the version different individuals support will be influenced by their political beliefs, values and position in relation to government reforms. Similarly, Stronach et al. (2002), whilst criticizing the reductive typologies and characterizations of professionalism, argue for a 'more nuanced account of professional identities, stressing the local, situated and indeterminable nature of professional practice, and the inescapable dimensions of trust, diversity and creativity' (p. 119). Helsby (1996) states that local contexts, and in particular departmental cultures, are influential in shaping teachers' sense of professionalism. She contends that mutual support is important because it engenders self-confidence.

Operating as groups or individuals within schools, teachers are affected by and react to wider issues. However, they are not totally determined by them. They form judgements, take decisions and act according to their own circumstances and perceptions. Many suggest that it is too simplistic to talk of a clear split between managers and teachers in educational organizations and that in fact the picture is far more complex. It has also been pointed out (Grace, 1995) that senior management teams in schools have risen from the ranks of the classroom teacher and hold a great allegiance to those they continue to view as fellow professionals. Undoubtedly the work of teachers became far more regulated during the Conservative administrations. Under Labour the talk is again of teacher professionalism though it would appear to be of a restricted and regulated form. This restricted professionalism may remain a straitjacket or may develop into a more licensed position that existed previously.

McCulloch (2001) notes how the constantly changing relationship between teachers and the state is central in the shaping of ideas about teacher professionalism. The years following Callaghan's Ruskin speech have seen vigorous debate over the issue. Callaghan had stressed the need for increasing accountability of teachers for standards in education. McCulloch (ibid.: 115) suggests that this reorientation proved decisive in the demolition of the ideal of teacher professionalism that had held sway over teachers of that time:

> Meanwhile, into the gap left by the progressive decline of this older professionalism there poured new ideas and precepts, often incoherent and inconsistent, some reformist and pragmatic, others more radical in nature, which jostled with each other and against older ideals in the process of reinventing teacher professionalism.

The last 25 years have thus seen many changes in the nature of teacher professionalism. It can be argued that teachers are no longer encouraged to take a wider perspective and years of criticism have encouraged a culture of the restricted professional. However, although during recent decades teachers have had more controls imposed upon them centrally, the act of teaching itself is still a largely autonomous activity in which the teacher is the final arbiter of his or her teaching and class management approach and through which teachers are able to make a significant long-term impact on the knowledge and skills of other individuals. Notwithstanding the managerial model of professional development which prevails currently, adopting the view that teaching is itself a learning act is more likely to foster lifelong learning amongst pupils and to encourage teachers to take ownership of their own professional development. Ultimately all teachers carry their own philosophy about their work, schools and the education system in general.

Student tasks

1 In small groups, compile in order of priority a list of ten characteristics that make a 'good' teacher. Each group should present their list giving reasons for their choice. Is it possible to identify different ideological approaches to education in these lists?

2 Read *Teachers: Meeting the Challenge of Change* (DfEE, 1998). In groups, discuss the following questions:

- What can you identify as the responsibilities of the 'new professional'?
- How will teachers be rewarded for the efforts required in reform?
- Is the model of professional presented in this document restricted or extended (in Hoyle's terms)?

Suggested further reading

Clarke, J. Gewirtz, S. and McLaughlin, E. (eds) (2000) *New Managerialism, New Welfare?* London: Open University in association with Sage. For the more advanced student, this collection provides a critical reflection of Labour's agenda for the modernization of public services. As such it gives the student an overview of how developments in the education sector are paralleled in other related areas of public administration, such as health and social services.

Philips, R. and Furlong, J. (eds) (2001) *Education, Reform and the State. Twenty-Five Years of Politics, Policy and Practice*. London: RoutledgeFalmer. This is an excellent edited volume that examines significant changes in education that have occurred since the Callaghan speech of 1976. While covering a wide range of policy developments, contributors consider the different sectors of education, professionalism and also issues of equality in particular.

Sugrue, C. and Day, C. (eds) (2002) *Developing Teachers and Teaching Practice. International Research Perspectives*. London: RoutledgeFalmer. This is a very interesting edited collection that considers the nature of teaching and learning in schools and also how teachers learn. Taking a global perspective, it goes on to consider the impact of major policy initiatives on the work of teachers internationally. Each chapter is very much research based and as such will prove valuable to students of education.

References

Apple, M. (1988) Work class and teaching, in J. Ozga (ed.) *Schoolwork: Approaches to the Labour Process of Teaching*. Milton Keynes: Open University Press.

Apple, M. (1996) *Cultural Politics and Education*. Buckingham. Open University Press.

Avis, J. (1999) Shifting identity: new conditions and the transformation of practice – teaching within post-compulsory education. *Journal of Vocational Education and Training*. 51(2): 245–64.

Ball, S. (1994) *Education Reform. A Critical and Post-Structural Approach*. Buckingham: Open University Press.

Barnard, N. (2000) Blueprint for the perfect teacher. *The Times Educational Supplement* 23 June: 22.

Bartlett, S. (2000) The development of teacher appraisal: a recent history. *British Journal of Educational Studies* 48(1): 24–37.

Bartlett, S. (2002) An evaluation of the work of a group of best practice teacher researchers. *Journal of In-Service Education*, Vol 28(3): 529–42.

Bartlett, S., Burton, D. and Peim, N. (2001) *Introduction to Education Studies*. London: Paul Chapman Publishing.

Becker, H. (1962) The nature of a profession. *Yearbook – National Society for the Study of Education*, 61(part 2): 27–46.

Bottery, M. (1996) The challenge to professionals from the new public management: implications for the teaching profession. *Oxford Review of Education*, 22(2): 179–97.

Bottery, M. and Wright, N. (1999) The directed profession: teachers and the state in the third millennium. Paper presented at the annual SCETT conference, Dunchurch, November.

Burton, D. and Bartlett, S. (2002) Professional issues in design technology. In B. Barnes et al. (eds). *Issues in Design Technology*. London: Routledge.

Cox, C.B. and Dyson, A.E. (eds) (1969a) *Fight for Education: A Black Paper*. Manchester: Critical Quarterly Society.

Cox, C.B. and Dyson, A.E. (eds) (1969b) *Black Paper Two: The Crisis in Education*. Manchester: Critical Quarterly Society.

Dale, R. (1989) *The State and Education Policy*. Milton Keynes: Open University Press.

Deming, W. (1986) *Out of the Crisis: Quality, Productivity and Competitive Position*. Cambridge: Cambridge University Press.

DfEE (1997) *Excellence in Schools*. London: HMSO.

DfEE (1998) *Teachers: Meeting the Challenge of Change*. London: HMSO.

DfEE (1999) *A Fast Track for Teachers*. London: DfEE Publications Centre.

DfEE (2000a) *Professional Development: Support for Teaching and Learning*. London: DfEE Publications Centre.

DfEE (2000b) *Performance Management in Schools. Performance Management Framework*. London: DfEE Publications Centre.

DfES (2001) *Schools Achieving Success*. London: DfES Publications Centre.

Docking. J. (ed.) (2000) *New Labour's Policies for Schools. Raising the Standard*. London: David Fulton.

Etzioni, A. (1969) *Readings on Modern Organizations*. Englewood Cliffs, NJ: Prentice-Hall.

Fergusson, R. (2000) Modernizing Managerialism in Education, in Clark, J. (eds) *New Managerialism, New Welfare?* London: Sage.

Furlong, J. (2001) Reforming teacher education, re-forming teachers: accountability, professionalism and competence. In J. Furlong and R. Phillips (eds) *Education, Reform and the State. Twenty-five Years of Politics, Policy and Practice*. London: RoutledgeFalmer.

Grace, G. (1995) *School Leadership: Beyond Educational Management*. London: Falmer Press.

Hargreaves, A. (1994) *Changing Teachers, Changing Times*. London: Cassell.

Hayes, D. (2000) *The Handbook for Newly Qualified Teachers*. London: David Fulton.

Heaney, S. (2001) Experience of induction in one local education authority. *Mentoring and Tutoring*, 9(3): 241–54.

Helsby, G. (1996) Defining and developing professionalism in English secondary schools. *Journal of Education for Teaching*. 22(2): 135–48.

Hoyle, E. (1980) Professionalisation and deprofessionalisation in education. In E. Hoyle and J. Megarry (eds) *World Yearbook of Education 1980. Professional Development of Teachers*. London: Kogan Page.

Hoyle, E. (1995) Changing conceptions of a profession. In H. Busher and R. Saran (eds) *Managing Teachers as Professionals in Schools*. London: Kogan Page.

Jones, K. (1996) Cultural politics and education in the 1990s. In R. Hatcher and K. Jones (eds) *Education after the Conservatives: The Response to the New Agenda of Reform*. Stoke-on-Trent: Trentham Books.

Kyriacou, C. (1998) *Essential Teaching Skills*. Cheltenham: Stanley Thornes.

Lawton, D. (1989) *Education, Culture and the National Curriculum*. London: Hodder & Stoughton.

Mansell, W. (2001) Performance pay saps teacher morale. *The Times Educational Supplement* 21 September: 1.

McCulloch, G. (2001) The Reinvention of Teacher Professionalism, in R. Phillips, and J. Furlong (eds) *Education, Reform and the State. Twenty-five Years of Politics, Policy and Practice*. London: RoutledgeFalmer.

Newton, D. (2000) *Teaching for Understanding. What it is and How to Do it*. London: RoutledgeFalmer.

Ozga, J. (1995a) New age traveller. *Curriculum Studies* 3(1): 190–5.

Ozga, J. (1995b) Deskilling a profession. In H. Busher and R. Saran (eds) *Managing Teachers as Professionals in Schools*. London: Kogan Page.

Ozga, J. (2000) Education: New Labour, new teachers, in J. Clark et al. (eds) *New Managerialism, New Welfare?* London: Sage.

Ozga, J. and Lawn, M. (1988) Schoolwork: interpreting the labour process of teaching. *British Journal of Sociology of Education* 9(3): 323–36.

Petty, G. (1998) *Teaching Today. A Practical Guide*. Cheltenham: Stanley Thornes.

Phillips, R. (2001) Education, the state and the politics of reform: the historical context, 1976–2001. In Phillips, R. and J. Furlong (eds) *Education, Reform and the State. Twenty-five years of politics, policy and practice*. London: RoutledgeFalmer.

Reay, D. (1996) Micro-politics in the 1990s: staff relationships in secondary schooling. Paper presented at the British Education Research conference. Lancaster.

Scholtes, P. (1998) *The Leaders' Handbook: Making Things Happen, Getting Things Done*. New York: McGraw-Hill.

Schön, D. (1983) *The Reflective Practitioner*. New York: Basic Books.

Squires, G. (1999) *Teaching as a Professional Discipline*. London: Falmer.

Stronach, I. Corbin, B. McNamara, O. Stark, S. and Warne, T. (2002) Towards an uncertain politics of professionalism: teacher and nurse identities in flux. *Journal of Education Policy*, 17(1): 109–38.

Sugrue, C. and Day, C. (Eds) (2002) *Developing Teachers and Teaching Practice*. London: RoutledgeFalmer.

Thompson, M. (2000) Performance management: new wine in old bottles. *Professional Development Today*, 3(3): 9–19.

Tropp, A. (1957) *The School Teachers: The Growth of the Teaching Profession in England and Wales*. London: Heinemann.

Whitty, G. (1999) Teacher professionalism in new times. Paper presented to the annual SCETT conference, Dunchurch, November.

Wilensky, H. (1964) The professionalization of everyone. *American Journal of Sociology*, LXX(2): 137–58.

7

Post-compulsory Education: Issues for 16–18-Year-Olds

James Avis

*This chapter explores a number of issues surrounding post-compulsory educa-
tion and training and, to contextualize the discussion, the competitiveness
settlement is explored. The argument that education should play a significant role in developing the skills and knowledge required by the economy is
critically examined. This sits alongside a discussion of the way in which
the economy is currently conceived, as well an exploration of New Labour's
interest in modernizing the economy, and developing a society characterized
by social inclusion, cohesion and justice. This analysis leads to a discussion
of the 16–19 curriculum in relation to the vocational/academic divide,
Key Skills and progressive curricular forms. The chapter concludes with an
analysis of the limits and possibilities for radical practice that reside within
the sector.*

Introduction

Schools of the vocational type, i.e. those designed to satisfy immediate
practical interests, are beginning to predominate over the formative
school, which is not immediately 'interested'. The most paradoxical
aspect of it all is that this new type of school appears and is advocated as
being democratic, while in fact it is destined not merely to perpetuate
social differences but to crystallise them in Chinese complexities
(Gramsci, 1971: 40).

This chapter explores a number of issues surrounding post-compulsory
education and training, in particular, and education in general.

To begin I discuss the competitiveness settlement – that is to say, what role education should play within society. There is a real attempt to universalize these arguments so that they form part of a common sense shared across classes and by leading political parties. This discussion is followed by an examination of the economic relations that are thought either to be developing or are understood as characteristic of leading-edge companies. These latter relations are thought to be ripe for generalization throughout the social formation or society. It may seem strange to start a discussion of post-compulsory education by focusing on economic issues, but these are pivotal to current understandings of education and carry with them particular constructions of the learner, the economy and, indeed, society itself. This discussion raises questions concerning the 'economizing' of education whereby it is seen as servicing the economy. The role of education in this case is to produce forms of labour required by the economic system. But how do notions of social justice fit in with these arguments? One suggestion is that an effective economy provides opportunities for all members of society and that economic success is a precondition for societal well-being. The penultimate section of this chapter examines the 16–19 curriculum in relation to the vocational/academic divide, the notion of Key Skills and, finally, progressive curricular forms are explored. The chapter concludes by examining the limits and possibilities for radical practice that reside within the sector.

However, before addressing the above themes it is necessary to say something about post-compulsory education and training in England. This refers to education and training that is provided at the end of compulsory schooling and is at a level below that normally associated with higher education. It therefore encompass post-16 provision within colleges of further education and adult and community education as well as training provided by private training agencies. Since April 2001, government funding for post-16 education has been distributed by the Learning and Skills Council through its regional offices. This has led the post-16 sector to be redefined as the learning and skills sector. Within the Learning and Skills Council and its local offices 'employers will form the largest single group and will directly influence a far wider range of post-16 provision than they do now, covering academic as well as vocational education' (DfEE, 1999: 24). There are two points that need to be made about the learning and skill sector or post-compulsory education and training. First, there is a degree of slippage in the way in which the terms are understood, with a blurring of boundaries arising across educational sectors. For example, many of the new universities have much in common with further education colleges and in some cases will offer not dissimilar provision. Foundation degrees are a case in point. These are to be vocationally based, are to be at a lower level than ordinary degrees but are to address employer requirements. The second point to be made is that not only is there a blurring between higher and further education but also between secondary education and the learning and skills sector. This has arisen as a consequence of the revival of an interest in 14–19 vocational education with the disapplication of the National Curriculum for those who wish to pursue this particular pathway (see Hodgson and Spours, 1999; DfES, 2001b, and for a historical example, Gleeson, 1988; Dale, et al., 1990).

The competitiveness settlement

It is has almost become a cliché to talk of a settlement or a new consensus formed around post-compulsory education. By settlement I have in mind a generally agreed framework or set of assumptions surrounding the nature of and development of post-compulsory education and training, as well as, crucially, its relation to the economic system (see Avis et al., 1996; Avis, 1993; 1996; 2002). Educational settlements seek to 'organize' a range of constituents from educationalists through to industrialists as well as attempting to take on board the interests of ordinary people in their own economic well-being and that of their children. In the case of post-compulsory education elements of the current settlement have been present for some time and have centred upon a shared analysis of the failings of the English economy and its education system. For a number of years the English economy has been castigated for its short termism and lack of investment in training and education (Hutton, 1995; 1997), whilst the education system has been criticized for its élitism and failure to encourage mass participation in post-compulsory education and training.

What is useful about the notion of settlement, coming as it does out of Gramscian Marxism, is its ability to take on board contradiction/tension/negotiation as well as a recognition of its fragility (see Education Group II, 1991). The notion of settlement embodies a recognition of attempts to create a social bloc or alliance around post-compulsory education whereby the interests of capital are secured. The idea of hegemony sits alongside that of settlement and refers to the organization of consent whereby members of society recognize that there is no alternative but to accept the current economic arrangements. This ensures that the ability of capital to secure its interests is sustained. The notion of settlement refers to similar processes taking place in relation to education:

> Hegemony involves securing both the conditions for future capitalist production and the consent of the subordinated population to the social and cultural implications of 'progress'. It is exercised not only through law and coercion, but also through 'educative' processes in a larger sense, including schooling, the media and centrally political parties. It necessitates the building of new alliances that may be active in promoting new solutions. Hegemony is not uniquely a product of 'the state' but involves the institutions of 'civil society' too.
>
> If hegemony refers to the overall relations of force in a society, we wish to use the term educational settlement to refer to the balance of forces in and over schooling. Settlements entail at this 'regional level' rather than 'global level' some more or less enduring set of solutions to capital's educational needs, the putting together of a dominant alliance of forces, and a more widespread recruitment of popular support or inducement of popular indifference (Education Group, 1979: 32).

It is important to recognize the vulnerability of hegemonic arrangements to challenge as well to be aware that not all members of society will necessarily accept these arrangements as just or valid. However the point is that, whilst we may challenge and contest these ideas, they secure their power through the production of a common sense that claims there is no alternative. The Blairite interpretation of globalization would be a case in point. Here it is claimed we have no choice but to accept the reality of global economic competition and adjust our economic and education systems, as well as our individual orientation to paid labour, in line with that reality (see Chapters 9 and 11). Richard Johnson (1998: 90, emphasis added) captures these ideas well when he writes: 'The hegemonic is not necessarily what everyone *practices*, nor what everyone *believes in*. Hegemony is *not* dominant ideology saturating the whole formation; winning consent is not necessarily agreement. Rather the hegemonic is that for which *"there is no alternative"*.'

We are all very familiar with the orthodox critique of education and the English economic system. At the risk of some repetition it is worth noting the following points drawn from widely held critiques of education which claim the English system is marked by:

- low participation rates in post-compulsory education;
- low standards of education in relation to international competitors;
- an elitist system – characterized on the one hand by excellence and on the other by mass exclusion and low participation rates;
- failure to develop a broadly based education that is inclusive and encourages high participation rates; and
- failure to prepare young people for work and therefore to meet the needs of employers.

In relation to the economic system, Hutton's (1995; 1997) critique has become influential and suggests that the economy has been undermined by the dominance of the City and finance capital. The consequence is that manufacturing has become characterized by low levels of investment in capital equipment, with firms pursuing short-term profit maximization at the expense of long-term investment in either education or training of its workforce. Indeed for much of English industry, training has historically been viewed as an expense rather than an investment in future profitability. For Hutton these features of the English economy derive from the dominance of the City upon the banking system which is characterized by short-term loans that seek to maximize immediate returns on investment rather than an interest in the long-term profitability of a particular company. This is also a characteristic of the stock market and of shareholder capitalism that seeks to maximize investment returns in the shortest possible time.

The previous critiques criss-cross constituents, with some being contested, and it is also the case that their significance changes over time. The point is that settlements are not given but have to be won and continually resecured. The collapse of Thatcherism is salutary in this connection. However, what is important is the way in which these critiques constitute a common sense surrounding the nature of the economy and education resulting in the construction of a framework that we can all 'buy' into – a set of ideas that are taken for granted unproblematically.

The current education settlement accepts globalized economic relations and construes the pursuit of competitiveness as being the route to societal and economic well-being. Within this framework education is to develop the skills and capacities of people so that they can contribute to the success of the economy. What is notable in this case is the way in which education is to service the needs of the economy rather than, as was in the case with the social democratic settlement, when the economy was to provide for the 'good' of wider society (Du Gay, 2000). Within the current settlement, education has been set within an economic logic as can be seen in the emphasis placed on competitiveness.

However, what New Labour has done is to accent the connection between economic success and social well-being. This is set against the Conservative market model which was seen to exacerbate inequality, and it is notable that during the Thatcher years the distribution of income and wealth became increasingly polarized. For New Labour the pursuit of economic competitiveness is seen to offer not only economic but also social benefit. Here lies a resonance with social democracy in which there was also an apparent coincidence between the educational development of individuals and the economy. However what is specific to New Labour is a concern with social inclusion and cohesion as well as an interest in doing something about those who experience social exclusion (see Kennedy, 1997; DfEE, 1998, 1999). These ideas are couched in the language of fairness rather than class antagonism, and the aim is not so much to create an alternative society but to manage the existing society more equitably. New Labour suggests that a competitive economy is capable of delivering a fair, socially just and inclusive society. However, this rests alongside a recognition of the inevitability of capitalist relations – what we used to call the new realism. The capitalist economic system and its relation to globalization are accepted as inevitable and to which there is no viable alternative.

The current Labour project draws together elements of social democracy and Thatcherism. Drawn from Thatcherism is an acceptance of the efficacy of the market and the necessity to engage in competitive practices to win global markets. This rests with an acceptance of and a recognition of the inevitability of capitalist relations as well as the allied concern with the need to sustain the economic viability and vitality of the economy. Similarly there is an acceptance of the break down of the division between the public and private sector in the provision of welfare services. 'Old' Labour had been committed to public sector provision of welfare services, whereas in the current period the party is more interested in 'what works' rather than whether provision is public or private. Thus within post-compulsory education and training there is a plethora of private training providers existing alongside the public-sector, as well as public–private partnerships.

The Labour project can be understood as an attempt to modernize English capitalism as well as to remoralize its population to accept the inevitability of capitalist relations. The remoralization of the population is encapsulated in the emphasis placed upon 'rights and responsibilities' as well as the stress upon 'something for something'. These ideas focus on the individual and his or her responsibilities and seek to undermine dependency culture as well as resistance to waged employment. As Rose (1999: 486) notes: 'Those who refuse to become responsible to govern themselves ethically, have also refused the offer to become members of our moral community. Hence for them harsh measures are entirely appropriate.' For New Labour the emphasis upon rights and responsibilities is part of its strategy to render the social formation economically competitive. Here we encounter the idea of the social investment state – a state which encourages the population to avail itself of the opportunities provided by education and ongoing skill development. In this way members of society, by taking on the responsibility endlessly to reinvent themselves in whatever form the labour market requires, will avoid poverty and escape from dependency on the state. Giddens (1998: 100–101) writes: '. . . redistribution must not disappear from the agenda of social democracy. But recent discussion has . . . shifted the emphasis towards the "redistribution of possibilities". The cultivation of human potential should as far as possible replace after the event "redistribution".' These ideas are also linked to New Labour's concern to develop a form of capitalism capable of encouraging social inclusion and cohesion – a socially responsible capitalism. However for critics, many of New Labour's interventions have a resonance with Thatcherism: both seek to discipline the population into accepting capitalist relations and the individual necessity to seek waged employment.

Fordism, post-Fordism, neo-Fordism and the knowledge economy

David Blunkett, the then Secretary of State for Education, wrote in the Foreword to *The Learning Age: A Renaissance for a New Britain* (DfEE, 1998: 7): 'Learning is the key to prosperity – for each of us as individuals, as well as for the nation as a whole. Investment in human capital will be the foundation of success in the knowledge-based global economy of the twenty first century.' And in *Learning to Succeed: A New Framework for Post-16 Learning* we read:

> The Challenge we face to equip individuals, employers and the country to meet the demands of the 21st century is immense and immediate. In the information and knowledge based economy, investment in human capital – in the intellect and creativity of people – is replacing past patterns of investment in plant, machinery and physical labour. To continue to compete, we must equip ourselves for this new world with new and better skills. We must improve levels of knowledge and understanding and develop the adaptability to respond to change (DfEE, 1999: 12).

Underpinning the competitiveness settlement is a particular understanding of the route to a successful economy and the direction of economic change. The two preceding quotations indicate the stress that has been placed on the development of human capital as well as the allied notion that it is through the skills of the workforce that a vibrant and successful economy can be developed. Human capital refers to the skills and qualification that learners develop through educational encounters and it is for this reason that education and the concern with widening participation play such a key part in the labour project and the competitiveness settlement. The argument suggests that there has been an epochal shift in the route to competitiveness, in part generated by the development of computer-based technologies and other technological developments, which have particularly impacted upon 'advanced' capitalist societies. These changes have, according to pundits, called for the development of industrial and economic systems built around post-Fordist relations. This is set against earlier productive systems that were based on Fordist relations of production.

Fordism characterized manufacturing relations in much of the postwar period (1945 onwards) and can be readily associated with mass and assembly-line production, the prime example being the motor industry. Fordism sat well alongside the social democratic settlement which was characterized by Keynesian economic management – a commitment to full employment and the welfare state. Fordism provided an economic system that was characterized by a demand for semi- and unskilled labour which was partly provided by an education system based upon mass failure. Only a minority of pupils obtained qualifications that enabled progression to higher education. There was an affinity between these educational processes and the labour market. Fordism was characterized by protected national markets, mass production of standardized products and employment relations that were hierarchical and bureaucratic. Workers were involved in fragmented and standardized work tasks and were placed in employment relations in which there was little scope for autonomy or initiative. Employment for the most part was based on low-trust relations where there was little need for any formal training in the majority of jobs. The oil crisis of 1973 and subsequent economic downturn marked the collapse of the social democratic settlement as well as indicating the limitations of Fordism as a route to profitability. The move towards globalized economic relations meant that protective national markets gave way to unregulated market competition. Economic crisis, technological advances, market deregulation and the development of a global economy presaged the collapse of social democracy and the 'apparent' decline of Fordism.

The early analyses of Fordism and post-Fordism struck a particularly optimistic tone: a tone which is reflected within the competitiveness settlement and its relation to the celebration of the knowledge economy and its empowering possibilities (see Table 7.1). These ideas have been rehearsed ad nauseam within the policy rhetoric of the state (see, for example, DfEE, 1998; 1999; DfES, 2001, a, b). They have also been taken up in some of the writing that has addressed the social and economic changes that confront western societies. For writers such as Finegold and Soskice (1988), the British and, in particular, the English economy is marked by a low skills equilibrium whereby a nexus of factors contributes towards its continuation, with employers, young people and the economic system as a whole gaining clear advantages from this pattern of relations.

Table 7.1 *Characteristics of Fordism and post-Fordism*

Fordism	Post-Fordism
Economy competition and production process	
Protected national markets	Global competition
Mass production of standardized products	Flexible production systems/ small batch/niche markets
Bureaucratic hierarchical organizations	Flatter and flexible organizational structures
Compete by full-capacity utilization and cost cutting	Compete by innovation diversification, subcontracting
Labour	
Fragmented and standardized work tasks	Flexible specialization/multi-skilled workers
Low-trust/low-discretion majority employed in manufacturing sector/blue-collar jobs	High-trust/high-discretion majority employed in service sector/white-collar jobs
Little on-the-job training, little formal training required for most jobs	Regular on-the-job training, greater demand for knowledgeable workers
Small managerial and professional elite	Growing managerial and professional service/class
Fairly predictable labour-market histories	Unpredictable labour-market histories due to technological change and increased economic uncertainty

Source: Brown and Lauder (1992: Table 1.1, p. 4)

One need only recall the arguments of Hutton (1995: 1997) in which he bemoans the failings of shareholder capitalism for its short termism. The arguments of Finegold and Soskice (which have been adopted by many others), were that the low skills equilibrium was no longer an adequate route to competitiveness. The deregulation of the world economy meant that low-waged workers could be found elsewhere and that therefore the only sustainable route to competitiveness was through the development of the skills of the population. There was therefore a need to move towards a high skills equilibrium and, indeed, the British economy had no real choice in the matter for, to do otherwise, would lead to secular decline – a decline that would not only render the economy less successful but would be one that undercut the social aspirations of the state.

A not dissimilar argument was forwarded by Brown and Lauder (1992) who, in this case, celebrated the shift towards post-Fordism for its empowering possibilities and the promise of the transformation of work relations. Fordism, through its detailed division of labour, led to alienated work relations which stifled the creativity of workers. In contrast, post-Fordist work relations sought to utilize the skills and creativity of the workforce and, by so doing, value-added waged labour could generate profitability. In this way these new work relations could contribute to national competitiveness, with education and lifelong learning being seen as crucial to these processes.

Post-Fordism required a flexible and adaptable labour force capable of acquiring and developing new skills as and when required. It also necessitated the worker being able to contribute creatively towards production and in this way would aid continuous improvement. Post-Fordism was characterized by high-trust relations with the worker being able to exercise autonomy and creativity at work. For those writers who celebrated the empowering possibilities of these new relations, post-Fordism held the promise of empowered and satisfied workers. Arguments such as these led to the claim that earlier forms of oppression and exploitation at the site of waged labour had been transcended. The false promise of a community of interests between workers and capital in earlier Fordist epochs was now realizable. For within post-Fordist work relations, high skill and high wages went together, as did the exercise of creativity and autonomy. Those employers who offered their workers sufficient space to exercise skill would reap the benefits.

However, this overly optimistic picture carried with it a number of serious flaws. Capitalist economies are characterized by uneven development and, whilst the skill requirements in one sector are increasing, in others deskilling and proletarianization may be taking place. Although post-Fordist relations may characterize some segments of the economy, for example in high-tech industries, this will not be characteristic of all. We need only think of McDonald's and other fast-food outlets as well as much service sector employment as examples. In addition, the high-skills, high-trust route towards competitiveness is not the only way in which firms can generate profitability. Indeed, for much of the postwar period the state has encouraged inward investment to secure increased rates of employment. Often such employment has been relatively low-skilled assembly work. The point is that there is no overwhelming evidence that:

> 'the rules of international competition have undergone a paradigm shift, and that knowledge and skills now represent the sole sustainable source of competitive advantage' (Keep, 1997: 460).

Thus for Keep the competitveness strategy adopted by a particular firm will be based on the way in which a number of factors are made sense of by the individual company. These may include the availability of labour, its skill profile, and the nature of the wider economy in which the firm is located, as well as the characteristics of the particular market for which the product is being produced. For example, markets in which competition is based upon price lend themselves to production strategies that seek to reduce costs, including that of labour, whereas markets in which competition is based upon the quality of goods will tend to adopt production strategies that seek to enhance the value-added aspects of the labour process. Arguments such as these suggest that the model of the economy that underpins the competitiveness settlement is deeply flawed. In addition, overly optimistic post-Fordist arguments underplay the forms of antagonism and exploitation that surround waged labour in capitalist societies. Instead, a model of a consensual society is proposed in which all members share a common interest in economic success. There is a resonance here with the Blairite notion of rights and responsibilities in that we have a duty to contribute to national well-being through the exercise of our labour power. Another difficulty surrounding those arguments that call for the increased flexibility and adaptability of the workforce is that these can easily slip into highly exploitative economic relations which merely serve the interests of capital at the expense of wider social interests. Sometimes neo-Fordist work relations were misrepresented as post-Fordist. Brown and Lauder (1996: 5) usefully draw out the distinction between neo- and post-Fordism: 'Neo-Fordism can be characterized in terms of creating greater market flexibility through a reduction in social overheads and the power of trade unions, the privatisation of public utilities and the welfare state, as well as a celebration of competitive individualism.' And Beck (1999: 12) valuably points to the way in which flexibility is a means through which the state and employers can redistribute risk to the individual: '"Flexibility" is demanded everywhere – or, in other words, an "employer" should be able to fire "employees" more easily. "Flexibility" also means a redistribution of risks from state and economy to individuals.'

In recent writing on the English skills profile a rather more nuanced analysis has been developed which overcomes some of the determinism that characterized the earlier accounts (see Crouch et al., 1999; Brown et al., 2001). In these analyses the economy is described as embodying a high-skills, low-skills model, with skill shortages existing at intermediate levels – that is to say, at below degree level in, for example, engineering (Green with Sakamoto, 2001: 130). In this case part of the economy, including for example bio-technology and multimedia, is characterized by high skills whereas other sectors are based on low skills. The difficulty here is that the low-skills sector is sufficiently large so that it precludes the development of product markets based on quality rather than price. A large low-skill sector means that wages will be depressed and that therefore consumers will seek out goods on the basis of price. This means that the development of a high-skill economy across sectors will be inhibited as the market for high-quality goods will not be fully developed. Where competition is based on quality rather than price, employers will be given an incentive to invest in the skills of the workforce as these will enhance the quality of products. For writers such as Giddens (1998) and Brown and Lauder (2000; 2001), the high-skills model of the economy will not of itself create high levels of employment and therefore social policies will need to be established to address this issue. For example, Brown and Lauder (2000: 241) call for a social wage that would be sufficiently high to sustain the unemployed for at least a year whilst they upgrade their skills: 'Unemployed people need a relatively high level of compensation so that they can focus on taking the opportunities to retrain rather than be distracted by the question of where the next family meal will come from.' However it is unlikely that New Labour with its mix of 'neo-liberal' and 'social democratic' policies would be in a position to support such a strategy.

Brown et al. (2001), in contradistinction to the earlier post-Fordist arguments, suggest there is no necessary tendency for the economy as a whole to move towards a high-skills model. Rather there would only be an imperative to do so if one is committed to the tenets of social justice, in as much as a high-skills economy can raise wage levels, improve the quality of welfare provision and is better placed to overcome poverty. Thus for Brown and Lauder (2000) the struggle is to fight for and support a form of capitalism that invests in the skills of its workers and mitigates the excesses of American and British shareholder capitalism. However, the difficulties with such an analysis remain. There is a failure to address the antagonistic relations that exist between capital and labour, or indeed to recognize the dynamism and malleability of capitalism. The assumption that we have now moved into a new epoch where previous forms of antagonism between capital and labour have been transcended is deeply problematic and somewhat naive. The logic of capitalism has not changed and remains concerned with the ongoing accumulation of capital by whatever means. There is no necessary commitment either to a high or low-skills model of the economy. However, for those who argue for the development of a post-Fordist high-skills model of the economy the preceding points ignore the varieties of capitalism as well as the distinctive features of the current period. For those writers who follow this argument 'there is no alternative' but to develop a high-skills economy that brings together capitalist and social interests into some sort of equilibrium. It is arguments such as these that underpin the development of the curriculum in post-compulsory education.

Curriculum issues

Better educated and more highly skilled people are more likely to be in work, earn more and contribute more productively to our economy and society. Knowledge and skills provide individuals with their surest route into work and prosperity, helping eradicate the causes of poverty and divisions in society (DfES, 2001: 7).

This section of the chapter has three main objectives. It explores the curriculum in relation to the vocational/academic divide, touches on key skills and finally examines the institutional context in which the curriculum is placed. But, to start with, it is necessary

to recognize long-standing critiques of the post-16 curriculum as
well as the secular patterns of exclusion that have surrounded the
English education system, marked as it is by elitism and mass failure. These latter processes have existed alongside a curriculum that
has been construed, in the case of A-levels, as overly narrow and, in
the case of the vocational, as one of low status, with much that is
set within a restricted notion of competence (Hyland, 1994). Such
curricular patterns operated well with Fordism in as much as mass
educational failure aligned well with the needs of the industrial
system for semi- and unskilled labour. Low participation rates and
disaffection from education held no particular economic costs for
employers. However, in the new conditions we now face this is no
longer considered to be the case. Educational processes and experiences that deter learners are now thought to carry unacceptably
high economic and social costs. Educational underachievement
damages the pursuit of economic competitiveness by undermining
the quality of labour and carries social costs through the creation of
a socially excluded 'underclass'. To be economically successful
requires an inclusive education system, one that supports lifelong
learning (DfEE, 1998). The academic/vocational divide is thought
by many to inhibit the aspiration of creating a learning society
(Young and Spours, 1997; Hodgson and Spours, 1997; 1999; Young,
1993; 1998; 1999). Such analyses lead to arguments that we should
move towards a unified post-16 curriculum – although it should be
noted that, for a number of commentators, 14–19 is a more appropriate framework than post-16 (Hodgson and Spours, 1997).
Underpinning this suggested curricular framework lies a 'high skills'
model of the economy: an economy in which there is rapid social
and technological change and one in which it is necessary constantly to refresh and upgrade skills. This requires that individuals
are committed to lifelong learning and that they contribute to the
continuous improvement of productive processes. The capacity to
learn is crucial and is far more important than the content of what
is learnt because the skills base of the economy is subject to ongoing transformation. The skills of today, it is claimed, will be
redundant tomorrow, whereas the capacity to learn will allow the
individual to reinvent him or herself in a form that will 'guarantee'
employment. If educational processes are to align with the needs of
the economy they need to be able to deliver lifelong learners who
have the skills effectively to participate in the economy. It is at this
juncture that Key Skills have a part to play.

From Dearing to Curriculum 2000

In 1995 Sir Ron Dearing was invited, by the then Conservative Secretary of State for Education, to consider and advise on the way in which the framework for 16–19 qualifications could be strengthened. The subsequent report (Dearing, 1996) proposed a national framework of awards for 16–19-year-olds in which there were four levels and three pathways. This aimed to introduce a level of coherence and clarity to the qualification structure:

	National Award: Advanced level	
AS and A Level;	GNVQ Advanced level;	NVQ Level 3
	National Award: Intermediate level	
GCSE Grades A–C;	GNVQ Intermediate level;	NVQ Level 2
	National Award: Foundation level	
GCSE Grades D–G	GNVQ Foundation Level	NVQ Level 1
	National Award: Entry level	
	common to all pathways three grades A/B/C	

(*Source*: Dearing, 1996: 13).

The three pathways were the academic (GCSE and A-level), applied education (GNVQ) and vocational training (NVQ). Parity of esteem was expected, as was a degree of mobility between pathways:

> I recommend that the distinguishing characteristics appropriate to each pathway should reflect the underlying purpose, as outlined below.
>
> **A Level and GCSE**
> • where the primary purpose is to develop knowledge, understanding and skills associated with a subject or discipline

Applied Education (GNVQ)
- where the primary purpose is to develop and apply knowledge, under-standing and skills relevant to broad areas of employment

Vocational training (NVQ)
- where the primary purpose is to develop and recognise mastery of a trade or profession at the relevant level (Dearing, 1996: 15–16).

The stamp of the then Conservative government on the Dearing Report is reflected in the pathways indicating their desire to retain the 'gold standard' of A-levels. Historically, three or four subject-specific A-levels have been taken by a minority of pupils as an entry qualification for university. Nevertheless the report, by proposing a national framework for qualifications and holding out the possibil-ity of modularity with students working across a number of pathways, offered the potential for more radical curricula. Writers such as Michael Young, Ken Spours and others responded to the Dearing Report seeking to further its radical and progressive poten-tial. Some years earlier, Young (1993), drawing on research on the British Baccalaureate, argued in favour of interdisciplinarity, the integration of the vocational with the academic and the develop-ment of a curriculum marked by connectivity (Finegold et al., 1990, and see the previous section):

> connective specialisation is concerned with the links between combinations of knowledge and skills in the curriculum and wider democratic and social goals. At the individual level it refers to the need for an understanding of the social, cultural, political and economic implications of any knowledge or skill in its context, and how, through such a concept of education, an individual can learn both specific skills and knowledge and the capacity to take initiatives, whatever their specific occupation or position . . .
>   As a curriculum concept it points to the interdependence of the content, processes and organisation. As a definition of educational purpose it aims to transcend the traditional dichotomy of the 'educated person' and the 'competent employee' which define the purpose of the two tracks [academic/vocational] of the divided curriculum (Young, 1993: 218).

For Young, current economic conditions offer the context in which to develop connective specialism. The need for competitiveness is embodied in a call for a curriculum that enhances educational per-formance and develops the skills required by a post-Fordist economy. In addition there is a strong reformist current that rests upon a quasi-technicist response to the failings of English educa-tion. English education has been criticized for its elitism, for neglecting the development of the national pool of talent and for being marked by an anti-intellectualism which marginalizes and devalues the vocational. A national awards framework, given this context, can be understood as a first move towards the creation of a unified qualification structure, a structure anticipated in the British Baccalaureate. Young and Spours (1996) would argue, however, that successful reform of the qualification system requires consensus. Incrementalism could carry such a consensus, one freed from ideology:

> The analysis in this paper suggests that we can move beyond critique and ideologised debate if the Dearing agenda is built upon incrementally . . . If qualification reform is undertaken in an incremental, planned and well-managed way with adequate resourcing at each stage, a consensus for change can be established (ibid.: 17).

Hodgson and Spours (1997: 3) forward a similar position when they write: 'This book argues throughout that the discussion of system changes in England needs to move away from ideological positions and critique towards a strategic debate about the process of change involved in creating a unified system.' Sentiments such as those of Young, Spours and Hodgson reflect a politics that views change in the curricular structure to be simultaneously progressive as well as advantageous to the economy, thereby sustaining capitalist interests. The requirement to overcome the vocational/academic divide is predicated upon a particular reading of economic conditions. By jettisoning the differentiation between the narrowly vocational and academic the curriculum can serve both the educative needs of learners as well as those of the economy:

> Fundamental changes in the economic infrastructure and the structure of occupations have forced increasing parallels to be drawn between vocational education and liberal education or, to use more conventional terms education and training. In essence the argument is straightforward. It is claimed that we have seen the passing, at least in the advanced industrial world, of the sort of semi-permanent occupations which require an easily identifiable set of skills for which training could be designed and given. In the 'post-industrial' world, citizens and workers are required to master an ever widening range of complex information. What is needed it is claimed, is the ability independently to acquire new knowledge and skill, so that learning how to learn becomes increasingly important. People also need to understand the procedural nature of work, to improve their problem solving skills and to be able to move flexibly from one task to another as the situation demands (Jamieson, 1993: 200–1).

In these analyses learning to learn becomes pivotal to individual, social and economic development. The vocational/academic divide loses significance in this context and is ripe for transcendence. The ongoing development of Key Skills is seen within these arguments to play an increasingly important role in the preparation of young people for work and adult life:

> Students need to know that adult life in the twenty-first century will require multiple forms of intelligence . . . Interpersonal skills, emotional intelligence and creativity as well as cognitive intelligence will be required to aid self-reflexivity, to work in teams in learning organisations, as well as to deal with rapid personal and social change (Brown and Lauder, 2001: 244).

Curriculum 2000

In September of that year Curriculum 2000 implemented changes to the qualification framework for 16–19-year-olds. It was to build on the recommendations of the Dearing Report and placed the acquisition of Key Skills in a pivotal position. The aim was to develop an enriched curriculum that supported breadth, depth and flexibility and was a response to critiques that suggested traditional A-levels lacked breadth. Consequently, Key Skills qualifications were introduced. AS-levels were reworked so that they constituted the first year of a two-year programme. As a qualification AS-levels stood between GCSE and A-level. Students were encouraged to take up to four AS-levels together with Key Skills. In the second year of their programme learners would usually study no more than three of their A2 subject choices. The exception to this pattern arose with vocational A-levels. In the case of vocational A-levels the modules studied, whether during the first or second years, were all at the same level, one slightly lower than A2 (QCA, 2001: 17).

As part of an attempt to integrate the vocational with the academic, learners were able to combine modules drawn from across the curriculum. Thus, for example, students could combine AS with vocational modules. In addition learners were encouraged to develop Key Skills.

Key Skills

Six Key Skills have been identified:

1 communication;
2 application of number;

3 information technology;
4 working with others;
5 improving own learning and performance; and
6 problem-solving.

The justification for the development of Key Skills is that they are transferable across different areas – employment and social life as well as education. For more than 25 years employers have frequently criticized young people for their failure to communicate adequately, and for their lack of numeracy as well as their undeveloped social skills (Moore, 1983). In many respects Key Skills is an attempt to address these perceived defects, thereby rendering young people more employable.

The latter three Key Skills (working with others, improving own learning and performance, and problem-solving), address the social dispositions of young people. For example, in its Introduction to Key Skills at Level 3 (working with others), QCA (undated: 2–3) states:

You will agree the objectives for and show you can:

- plan, work and agree responsibilities and working arrangements;
- seek to establish and maintain co-operative relationships agreeing ways to overcome any difficulties;
- review work with others, include factors that influenced the outcome.

The assumption is that such skill development fits well with the demands of work and so if individuals are habituated to working in such a way prior to their entry into the labour market, they will be better placed to possess the dispositions and habits of mind that employers require. A similar process arises in relation to the Key Skill 'improving own learning and performance'. In this case there is a resonance with work-based practices concerned with continuous improvement as well as with processes of performance management. The learner is to agree targets and is to consider the way in which he or she will go about meeting these so as to improve his or her own learning and performance. Problem-solving becomes technicized, the learner is to identify the problem and to come up with solutions. However, problem-solving cannot be really thought of outside the social context in which it takes place. This means we should consider the social processes that lead to the definition of some issues as problems and not others. The very notion of problem-solving implies there is a solution than can be applied.

It then becomes only a matter of diligence and thought to determine an appropriate response and, in this way, problem-solving becomes no more than a technique, a means to an end. In a number of respects Key Skills are Janus-like. They can become a means through which there is an attempt to shape student subjectivity in a manner that aligns it to the economic system. In this way young people will develop the forms of creativity, problem-solving and teamwork that render them self-policing subjects – learners who have acquired forms of identity and subjectivity that sit comfortably with the economic system. However, when pushed to their limits, Key Skills may lead to some difficult questions being asked about the nature of teamwork or problem-solving in capitalist societies – whose interests are being served? And when learners or, for that matter, workers are encouraged to 'improve their own learning and performance', is there an interest here with the formation of labour power that continuously reinvents itself as economic and technological change requires?

Curriculum 2000 has been subject to ongoing review and evaluation which have led to modification of the assessment regime, particularly in the case of Key Skills. However I would like to comment on two issues: first, the relationship between the vocational and academic and, secondly, Key Skills. The incorporation of GNVQs into the curriculum framework as vocational A-levels which are at a lower level than A2s seems to replicate the traditional relationship between the vocational and academic. Indeed, institutionally the privileging of A-levels remains in place and we can perceive a progression route from vocational A-levels on to foundation degrees. It is at these levels that there are concerns about skill shortages (LSC, 2001).

The forms of connectivity Michael Young has called for are far from being realized, although incremental change may bring ongoing reform. However, underpinning Curriculum 2000, as can be seen in the earlier discussion of Key Skills, is a central concern with meeting employer needs and shaping learner subjectivities and dispositions appropriately. It therefore sits well with the 'economizing' of educational relations in the direction encouraged by the competitiveness settlement. But whether or not such a standpoint can seriously address issues concerned with social justice and the further democratizing of society is a moot point.

Institutional arrangements

Conservative education policies led to an increasingly differentiated system, one that was criticized for its tendency to reproduce class inequalities. Although New Labour espouses a concern for the disadvantaged and socially excluded, it, too, accepts and is in the processes of deepening a differentiated education system. Paradoxically, these policies are underpinned by an apparent commitment to equal educational opportunities and the formation of a meritocratic society. However, the likelihood of the economic system being able to create employment structures that would render this aspiration realizable is deeply problematic, unless equal opportunity is transmogrified into employability – being fit for work.

The development of new vocational pathways at 14 plus addresses, at one level, disaffection from the education system and seeks to encourage young people to progress to higher levels (see DfES, 2002). Yet at the same time, as is the case with Curriculum 2000, these new pathways work within the academic/vocational division. *Schools Achieving Success* (DfES, 2001a: 31) states:

> For the first time there will also be the opportunity of a predominantly vocational programme for those with the aptitude, beginning at 14 and going right through to degree level. Such a programme might include a significant element of work related learning from 14, followed by a modern apprenticeship or full time vocational study at college and then a foundation degree for those who have the potential.

Such differentiation within institutions will be matched by a similar process across schools and colleges. New Labour emphasizes its commitment to excellence, and part of this strategy is to encourage, within the secondary system, specialist schools orientated towards particular aspects of the curriculum. This is paralleled in post-compulsory education by the development of Centres of Vocational Excellence in Further Education (COVEs):

> Centres of Vocational Excellence will develop new, and enhance existing, excellent vocational provision which is focused on meeting the skills needs of employers, nationally, sectorally, regionally and locally. They will seek to give a greater number of individuals from all backgrounds access to the high quality vocational training which they need to succeed in a modern economy (LSC, 2001: 3).

COVEs will also reach back into the compulsory sector with a view to enhancing the vocational education of 14–19-year-olds. Learners

will increasingly find themselves confronting a highly differentiated education system through which they will have to steer a
path. It will be those who possess cultural capital who will be in a
position to make best use of such a system. The 'Chinese complexities' to which Gramsci eludes may well serve to reproduce and
sustain class privilege.

Limits and possibilities

> This is not a moment to take intellectual prisoners or to compromise
> with a political project that amounts to the abandonment of any chal-
> lenge to global capitalism (Callinicos, 2001: viii).

The competitiveness settlement ties education to an economic
logic, one which associates economic success with the furtherance
of social justice. This can be seen clearly in the learning and skills
sector and in the dominant position employers hold. The conditions in which we are now located, it is claimed, are characterized
by a coincidence of interests in which there is an affinity between
those of capital and labour. Such a consensual model of society
ignores the antagonistic relations that exist between capital and
labour. However, there are a number of contradictions that surround the current policy context that hold progressive possibilities.
The association of economic success with the development of a
society characterized by social cohesion and inclusion is a potential
source of tension. Workless growth (that is to say, economic development that is not matched by increased levels of employment)
and the polarization that exits within the English skill structure,
provides the basis for the development of an alternative politics
and education strategy.

The call for the upskilling of the population as a whole, together
with the emphasis placed upon the development of people's creativity, similarly generates points of tension. Although these
developments are lodged within a post-Fordist and capitalist framework they will not necessarily be contained within them. It is here
that the conceptual frameworks of both hegemony and settlement
have a part to play in that both are subject to continual reworking
and reorganization. It is this that provides both their strength and
weakness, in as much as the ongoing renegotiation of settlements
constitutes their vulnerability. The failure of the current settlement

to deliver wider economic benefits would be a case in point and is reflected in the increasing sense of insecurity and vulnerability surrounding paid employment (Apple, 2001). The attempt to create a common sense that aligns with capitalist interests may fail and, in doing so, opens up the potential for education processes to address critically the nature of the economy and social structure. Paradoxically, Michael Young's notion of connectivity anticipates such a process.

It could be argued that this chapter has adopted a particular political position which could be set against a more measured analysis of post-compulsory education and training. The point, however, is that lying behind questions of educational effectiveness and issues of what works – a technicist framework – rests a set of assumptions about the structure of society and the role of education within it. These assumptions are not innocent and carry within them a particular standpoint. One of the important questions for education studies is to clarify these assumptions and to draw out their political implications for society, education and social justice. Whether we like it or not educational processes are intimately tied to political struggles, issues of social justice and visions of society.

Student task

Read any recent white/green paper or ministerial speech that addresses post-compulsory education (e.g. DfEE, 1999; DfES, 2002). In the case of white/green papers, these can be accessed through the DfES website, as can the speeches of education ministers and those of the Secretary State for Education. Prime ministerial speeches can be accessed through the Number 10 website.

The task
Examine the following issues:

1 The way the economy is constructed. What is the desired direction for the economy?
2 What role does education play for the individual, society and economy?
3 What model of society is found in the document? Is it based on consensus or conflict?

4 What notion of social justice is used? Is there a view on equal opportunity? How is this understood?
5 Has anything been left out you felt should have been included? If so, what?

Suggested further reading

Avis et al. (1996) address many of the issues raised in this chapter, examining the socio-economic context in which post-compulsory education is located and providing a robust critique of managerialism. Brown and Lauder (2001) discuss the progressive potential that resides within the new conditions facing the economy and education. Halsey et al. (1977) provide an edited text which, while difficult, gives access to key authors in the field. Gray and Griffin's (2000) edited text explores a number of issues surrounding post-compulsory education.

Avis, J., Bloomer, M., Esland, G., Gleeson, D. and Hodkinson, P. (1996) *Knowledge and Nationhood: Education, Politics and Work*. London: Cassell.
Brown, P. and Lauder, H. (2001) *Capitalism and Social Progress: The Future of Society in a Global Economy*. London: Palgrave.
Gray, D., Griffin, C. (2000) *Post-Compulsory Education and the New Millennium*. London: Jessica Kingsley.
Halsey, H.A., Lauder, P., Brown, P. and Wells, A.S. (1997) *Education: Culture, Economy Society*. Oxford: Oxford University Press.

Relevant journals
British Journal of Educational Studies
British Journal of Sociology of Education
Journal of Education Policy
Journal of Education and Work
Journal of Vocational Education and Training

References

Apple, M. (2001) *Educating the 'Right' Way: Markets, Standards, God and Inequality*. London: RoutledgeFalmer.
Avis, J. (1993) A new orthodoxy, old problems: post 16 reforms. *British Journal of Sociology of Education*, 14(3): 245–60.
Avis, J. (1996) The myth of the post-fordist society in Avis, J., et al. (eds) *Knowledge and Nationhood: Education, Politics and Work*. London: Cassell.
Avis, J. (2002) Imaginary friends: managerialism, globalisation and post compulsory education and training in England. *Discourse: Studies in the Cultural Politics of Education* 23(1).

Avis, J., Bloomer, M., Esland, G., Gleeson, D. and Hodkinson, P. (1996) *Knowledge and Nationhood: Education, Politics and Work*. London: Cassell.

Beck, U. (1999) *World Risk Society*. Oxford: Polity Press.

Brown, P., Green, A. and Lauder, H. (2001) *High skills: Globalization, Competitiveness, and Skill Formation*. Oxford, Oxford University Press.

Brown, P. and Lauder, H. (eds) (1992) *Education for Economic Survival: From Fordism to post-Fordism*. London: Routledge.

Brown, P. and Lauder, H. (1996) Education, globalization, and economic development. *Journal of Education policy,* 11: 1–24.

Brown, P. and Lauder, H. (2000) Human capital, social capital, and collective intelligence. In Baron, S. et al. (eds) *Social Capital, Critical Perspectives*. Oxford: University Press.

Brown, P., and Lauder, H. (2001) *Capitalism and Social Progress: The Future of Society in a Global Economy*. Basingstoke: Palgrave.

Callinicos, A. (2001) *Against the Third Way*. Oxford: Polity Press.

Crouch, C., Finegold, D. and Sako, M. (1999) *Are Skills the Answer? The Political Economy of Skill Creation in Advanced Industrial Countries*. New York: Oxford University Press.

Dale, R., Bowe, R., Harris, D., Loveys, M., Moore, R., Shilling, C., Sikes, P., Trevitt, J. and Valsecchi, V. (1990) *The TVEI Story: Policy, Practice and Preparation for the Work Force*. Milton Keynes: Open University Press.

Dearing, R. (1996) *Review of Qualifications from 16–19 Year Olds*. London: SCAA.

DfEE (1998) *The Learning Age: A Renaissance for a New Britain*. London: HMSO.

DfEE (1999) *Learning to Succeed: A New Framework for Post-16 Learning*. London: HMSO.

DfES (2001a) *Schools Achieving Success*. London: DfES.

DfES (2001b) *Education and Skills: Delivering Results: A Strategy to 2006*. London: DfES.

DfES (2002) *14-19: Extending Opportunities, Raising Standards*. London: HMSO.

Du Gay, P. (2000) Representing 'globalisation': notes on the discursive ordering of economic life, in Welfare et al. (eds) *Without Guarantees: in honour of Stuart Hall*. London: Verso.

Education Group (1979) *Unpopular Education Schooling and Social Democracy in England since 1944*. London: Hutchinson.

Education Group II (1991) *Education Limited: Schooling and Training and the New Right since 1979*. London: Unwin Hyman.

Finegold, D., Keep, E., Miliband, D., Raffe, D., Spours, K. and Young, M. (1990) *A British Baccalaureate: Overcoming Divisions between Education and Training*. London: IPPR.

Finegold, D. and Soskice, D. (1988) The failure of training in Britain: analysis and prescription. *Oxford Review of Economic Policy* 4(3): 21–53.

Giddens, A. (1998) *The Third Way: The Renewal of Social Democracy*. Oxford: Polity Press.

Gleeson, D. (ed.) (1988) *TVEI and Secondary Education: A Critical Appraisal*. Milton Keynes: Open University Press.

Gramsci, A. (1971) *Selections from the Prison Notebooks*. London: Lawrence & Wishart.

Green, A. with Sakamoto, A. (2001) Models of high skills in national competition strategies. In P. Brown et al. (eds) *High Skills: Globalization, Competitiveness, and Skill Formation*. Oxford: Oxford University Press.

Hodgson, A. and Spours, K. (eds) (1997) *Dearing and Beyond: 14–19 Qualifications, Frameworks and Systems.* London: Kogan Page.

Hodgson, A. and Spours, K. (1999) *New Labour's Educational Agenda: Issues and Policies for Education and Training from 14+.* London: Kogan Page.

Hutton, W. (1995) *The State we're in.* London: Jonathan Cape.

Hutton, W. (1997) *The State to Come.* London: Vintage.

Hyland, T. (1994) *Competence, Education and NVQs: Dissenting Perspectives.* London: Cassell.

Jamieson, I. (1993) The rise and fall of the work-related curriculum. In J. Wellington (ed.) *The Work Related Curriculum: Challenging the Vocational Imperative,* London: Kogan Page.

Johnson, R. (1998) Sexual emergenc(i)es: cultural theories and contemporary sexual politics. *Key Words* 1: 74–95.

Keep, E. (1997) 'There's no such thing as society': some problems with an individual approach to creating a learning society. *Journal of Education Policy* 12 (6): 457–71.

Kennedy, H. (1997) *Learning Works. Widening Participation in Further Education.* Coventry: Further Education Funding Council.

LSC (2001) *Centres of Vocational Excellence in Further Education: The Way Ahead* (http://www.LSC.gov.uk).

Moore, R. (1983) Further education, pedagogy and production. In D. Gleeson, (ed.) *Youth Training and the Search for Work.* London: Routledge & Kegan Paul.

QCA (2001) QCA's *Review of Curriculum 2000 – Report on Phase Two.* London: QCA.

QCA (undated) *Introduction to Key Skills,* (http://www.qca.org.uk/nq/ks/wor_imp_pro.asp).

Rose, N. (1999) Inventiveness in politics. *Economy and Society* 28(3): 467–93.

Young, M. (1993) A curriculum for the 21st? Towards a new basis for overcoming academic/vocational divisions. *British Journal of Educational Studies* 41: 203–22.

Young, M. (1998) *The Curriculum of the Future: From the 'New Sociology of Education' to a Critical Theory of Learning.* London: Falmer.

Young, M. (1999) *Knowledge, Learning and the Curriculum of the Future: An Inaugural Lecture.* London: Institute of Education.

Young, M. and Spours, K. (1997) Unifying academic and vocational learning and the idea of the learning society. *Journal of Education Policy* 12(6): 527–37.

8

The Expansion of Higher Education: A Consideration of Control, Funding and Quality

Ann-Marie Bathmaker

Since the Robbins Report of 1963, higher education in the UK has undergone major expansion, changing it from an elite to a mass system. This chapter explores the changing socio-economic context in which this transformation has taken place and considers how the expansion of higher education has raised issues of control, quality and funding.

Introduction

The Dearing Report on higher education published in 1997 (NCIHE, 1997) was the first officially sponsored examination of the higher education (HE) system in the UK since the Robbins Report of 1963 (Committee on Higher Education, 1963). Dearing was asked to solve immediate problems and to look ahead to the future. His vision was that HE should contribute to the development of a learning society:

> Over the next 20 years, the United Kingdom must create a society committed to learning throughout life. That commitment will be required from individuals, the state, employers and providers of education and training. Education is life enriching and desirable in its own right. It is fundamental to the achievement of an improved quality of life in the UK (NCIHE, 1997: 1).

However, the immediate problem which the Dearing committee had to deal with, and which is seen to have created the impetus for the inquiry, was the financial crisis in HE of the 1990s, brought about by the combined effects of underfunding and expansion (Watson and Taylor, 1998).

This chapter examines the expansion of HE in the UK and how it has changed from an elite to a mass system. The first part of the chapter considers changes to the socio-economic context and their impact on the role and purpose of HE. The second part of the chapter explores how the HE system has expanded in response to these changes and considers two key issues – funding and quality – which have grown in significance with the expansion of the system. These issues can be seen to highlight the problems of a system with elite instincts and traditions, challenged by an agenda of inclusion and widening participation.

HE in the global knowledge economy

The idea of a university

The traditional image of HE is of an elitist university sector for a minority of academically successful young people, who attended public schools and grammar schools. Although this image is very different from the HE system in the UK today, it reflects traditions on which the modern sense of the university in western cultures is based, with origins reaching back to the Renaissance.

The mediaeval universities were groups of scholars who formed themselves into self-governing guilds. They later became established as formal foundations with designated powers to award degrees. The idea of a university meant a mutual recognition of the members of the guild or association and a common language (Latin). Both masters and students shared the common goal of inquiry (Barnett, 2000: 72). From these origins the university in the nineteenth century came to be seen as a site of universal knowledge, meaning that it should represent an openness towards knowledge. The university was a place for teaching and searching for truth. The purpose was to expose students to the best thinking and knowledge in the world (Smith and Webster, 1997a; 1997b).

The modern sense of the western university has been based on these foundations, drawing on Enlightenment concepts of human reason, including the belief that certain things matter, such as a willingness to search for truth, respect for others, tolerance of rival views, a willingness to be self-critical and a commitment to putting forward new ideas (Barnett, 2000). The pursuit of knowledge and social justice is seen as the basis for a better world, and academic freedom to engage in intellectual inquiry and critique is considered essential.

These foundations have faced strong challenges in recent times. The world in which we now live is 'a disturbing place to be in' (Barnett, 2000: 78), characterized by the breakdown of certainties, a feeling of crisis and a sense of fragmentedness, often defined as the 'postmodern condition' (Bauman, 1997: 20). The university, the knowledge it engages with and the value system on which it is based are more uncertain and subject to question, and are open to challenge and change. Performance, outcomes and standards are presented as 'the new faiths' (Barnett, 2000: 168).

Moreover, HE is no longer the sole domain of long-established universities. Following the Further and Higher Education Act 1992, the university sector includes 'old universities' which existed pre-1992, and 'new universities' which were polytechnics and colleges of HE before the 1992 Act. In addition, HE is provided by colleges of HE, and by further education colleges, which are officially part of the Learning and Skills Sector.

Changes to the socio-economic context

The changing nature of HE reflects wider changes to the social and economic context. The hallmark of the late twentieth century and the beginning of the twenty-first century is rapid economic, technological and social change which has had a major impact on all aspects of people's lives, changing both the nature of work and the way we live. Technological innovation and cheaper transportation costs mean that companies can move production to where costs are cheapest, leading to competition between labour markets across the world (Clarke and Newman, 1997). Whilst Fordist mass production of standardized products still continues, it is widely believed that western capitalist economies need to concentrate on high-value goods produced in low volume in order to remain competitive, which requires an investment in high skills. Furthermore, there is the emergence of what is described as the knowledge economy, based on the production, distribution and use of knowledge and information (Clarke, 2001). In the knowledge economy, increasing numbers of workers need to utilize and be able to respond to changing forms of knowledge (Jarvis, 2000).

There is no doubt that the achievement of competitive advantage has impelled educational expansion (Halsey, 1997). Brown and Lauder (1995: 21) talk of 'global knowledge wars' to describe how knowledge is now seen to be a crucial factor in gaining competitive advantage in a global economy, with education and training forming a central part of economic policy-making. As Ashton and Green (1996: 1) explain:

> Rarely if ever has the education of the large majority of the workforce been seen as the central lever of economic growth. Now, however, as twentieth century capitalism draws to a close, a new consensus is emerging among politicians of many different persuasions, among scholarly writers and among popular feeling, a consensus that the salience of a nation's education and training system is becoming the key item in the struggle for economic superiority.

The changing economic context places new demands on HE. The belief that there is a limited pool of talent is no longer acceptable. Brown and Lauder (1995: 27) suggest that 'education and training systems must be organized on the premise that all rather than a few are capable of significant practical and academic achievements', and they believe that given the right motivation, at least 80 per cent of the population is capable of achieving the intellectual standards required to obtain a university degree.

Changes to the nature of work mean that employers seek new skills and qualities in graduates. There is extensive debate about the changing nature of knowledge. Specific disciplinary knowledge, technical skills and qualifications are not enough; employers want generic personal and interpersonal skills, such as communication, negotiation and teamwork so that employees can work with others and engage in project work. They seek people who can cope with flexibility and change and who are capable of applying knowledge to unfamiliar contexts (McNair, 1997). A long-term career with one employer is no longer typical, and graduates need to be prepared for a portfolio career (Brown and Scase, 1997) comprising a number of different jobs over their working life.

Whilst economic change often appears to dominate debate, HE has wider purposes which go beyond preparing people for employment. Coffield and Williamson (1997: 4) emphasize that HE has 'a role to play in public life, in helping people to understand their world in a critical way and in promoting active debate about democratic values and morality', and Dearing's vision for the future quoted at the beginning of this chapter highlights such broader purposes for HE. Here, too, society has undergone major changes. Globalization and communication technologies have had a major impact on cultural and value systems. With much wider access to other cultures, people are confronted with different value systems, which challenge 'our notions of who we are, and where the boundaries are around our own identity' (McNair, 1997: 101).

The complexities and uncertainties which people now face are often defined in terms of risk and individualization, drawing on the work of Giddens (1991) and Beck (1992). For both Giddens and Beck the certainties of the industrial era are at an end, and scientific knowledge is no longer trusted as the basis for progress – the only certainty is uncertainty. There are new kinds of risk, particularly risks associated with scientific and technological developments.

The increasing complexity of the world means that individuals have to cope with a surfeit of knowledge and information. This is not just within their immediate environment. Individuals now have to understand the wider context in which they live and work, and this means dealing with multiple frames of reference over and beyond their immediate situation. Giddens (1994: 7) explains this by saying that 'individuals more or less have to engage with the wider world if they are to survive in it'. They have to become more reflexive about their own lives, and actively plan and develop their own biographies.

The risks and uncertainty inherent in the changing social context create further demands on HE. The development of knowledge and of personal qualities such as breadth of mind, self-reliance, flexibility and adaptability needs to be understood in the new circumstances in which we live. Barnett (2000) sees the role of HE in this context as enabling students to handle uncertainty in such a way that they are able to act effectively.

The expansion of HE in the UK: changes to structure and funding

Expansion to the HE system in the UK needs to be understood against this backdrop. The changes which have taken place since the Robbins Report of 1963 (Committee on Higher Education, 1963) are connected to the increasing demands made on higher education to be responsive to social and economic pressures, challenging the autonomy and self-determination which universities may have enjoyed in the past (Kogan, 1993). The expansion of the system has brought with it major concerns related to funding and quality. Underlying both these concerns are issues related to control of HE. This second part of the chapter outlines the expansion and restructuring of the UK HE system since Robbins and considers how the tensions in creating a more widely accessible and inclusive system can be seen clearly in questions relating to funding and quality.

From an elite to a mass system of HE

Following Trow (1973), a HE system can be defined as elite, mass or universal. An elite system serves the purpose of reproducing leading positions in society, whereas mass or universal systems are intended to provide a much broader supply of white-collar professionals and technically qualified staff. For Trow, a HE system ceases to be elite when more than 15 per cent of the eligible population participate. It is considered to be mass when 15–40 per cent participate, and it becomes universal when more than 40 per cent is enrolled. Trow uses this formula to argue that expansion of the system forces it to change. This does not mean that it changes uniformly. Elite and exclusive institutions may continue to exist in a diversified mass system, but on their own they cannot sustain mass forms of HE.

By the beginning of the 1990s, all three major political parties in the UK (Labour, Conservative and Liberal Democrats) shared the view that a mass system of HE was inevitable for the twenty-first century (Halsey, 1997). However, this was not reflected in coherent policy in the period between the Robbins and Dearing Reports for, despite the economic and social imperatives creating a more significant role for HE in the past 40 years, expansion of the system in the UK has been uneven and has not been systematically planned (Walford, 1991).

Until the Robbins Report of 1963 (Committee on Higher Education, 1963), HE in the UK was geared towards educating a small elite of the population. The defining features were academic subjects, didactic teaching and independent research agendas. Students were young, on full-time courses and predominantly male and middle class. In the 1960s, this elite model faced a number of criticisms. It did not respond to the emerging needs of the economy and the need for applied research and it was seen as socially exclusive (Coffield and Williamson, 1997). The social democratic ideals of the postwar years offered a vision of social mobility and greater social equality through wider access to educational opportunities, including HE. The Robbins Report reflected these ideals, with a commitment to make a place available for all who were qualified by ability and attainment to pursue HE and wished to do so.

Following the Robbins Report, the number of students roughly doubled in the UK between 1963 and 1970 (Walford, 1991), though the system remained elite as defined by Trow (1973). The economic crisis in the 1970s, and the policies of the Conservatives in the 1980s which aimed to reduce government spending, led to a levelling off of expansion which lasted until the end of the 1980s. Then in 1989, Kenneth Baker, Conservative Secretary of State for Education, called for an increase in student numbers, leading to a rapid rise between 1988 and 1992. By 1992, participation had reached 30 per cent of school-leavers.

Following this period of expansion, the Conservative government placed a cap on further growth in publicly funded full-time undergraduate student numbers (NCIHE, 1997), and participation remained at around 33 per cent for the rest of the 1990s. Nevertheless, the rise in student numbers between 1987 and 1997, from 17 per cent to 33 per cent participation, meant that in only a decade the British HE system moved from being an elite to a mass system (see Figure 8.1).

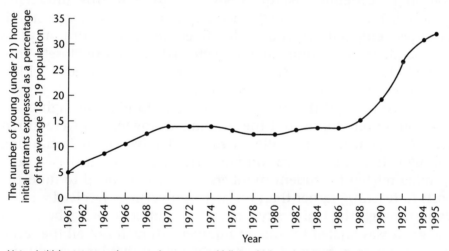

Notes: Intitial entrants are those entering a course of full-time higher education for the first time.
1961 figure estimated using Robbins Report App 2A Table 3 (Percentage of the population of each age receiving higher education GB Oct 1961).
Due to minor change in definition, the year 1961 to 1970 indusive are not strictly comparable with later years.
Due to minor change in definition, years from 1980 onwards are not stricly comparable with earlier years.

Figure 8.1 *HE age participation index (API) – GB institutions*

Source: National Committee of Inquiry into Higher Education (1997: para. 3.9)

The vision of the Labour government in 2001 was that participation should rise still further to 50 per cent participation by 2010 (HEFCE, 2001). However, it should be noted that this goal involves a redefinition of participation. Labour proposes that 50 per cent of those aged 18–30 should participate in some form of HE rather than focusing on participation by young people.

From a binary to a unified system

The expansion of HE following Robbins was achieved through the creation of what is referred to as a binary system, meaning that it was divided into two sectors. It consisted of universities on the one hand and polytechnics and colleges on the other. Universities were legally independent and able to appoint their own vice-chancellors and staff, construct courses, award their own degrees and select students. Polytechnics and HE colleges were part of the public sector under the control of local education authorities (and sometimes religious foundations). Degrees were awarded by the Council for National Academic Awards (CNAA) or by a nearby university (Walford, 1991). They were defined as public sector HE. Whilst universities enjoyed considerable freedom and autonomy as independent institutions, public sector HE was more closely controlled. The latter was supposed to relate to the needs of local economies and offer more applied courses.

The two parts of the binary system were funded through grant aid from public funds, but the funding arrangements were different. Polytechnics and colleges received most of their funding through their local education authority. Funding was based on a formula related to student numbers and was intended to fund the costs of teaching rather than research. Universities received a block grant through the University Grants Committee (UGC). The size of the grant was related to student numbers, though not all the funding was intended for teaching. It was expected that between 30 and 40 per cent would be spent on research. Thus, although the two halves were defined by government as 'different, but of equal status' (Walford, 1991: 167), the way they were funded clearly differentiated between research-led institutions and teaching-led institutions. Furthermore, the UGC allowed universities to maintain considerable independence from government, whereas Walford believes that, in creating the binary system, it was hoped that the polytechnic and college half would be cheaper to run, more open to public control and more responsive to the needs of industry.

Expansion post-Robbins was quite generously funded and, although funding was reduced during the 1970s in the wake of the economic crisis, it was the election of a Conservative government in 1979 which was to have the next major impact on HE (Walford, 1991; Brennan and Shah, 1993). The Conservatives were committed to reducing government expenditure on education, increasing efficiency and making the education system more responsive to the perceived needs of industry. There were major cuts to university funding in 1981, resulting in reductions in academic staff and extensive reorganization. The UGC was reluctant to reduce the unit of resource and protected as far as possible the amount of money spent on each student. Expansion came to a halt in the university sector in the 1980s but continued in polytechnics and colleges, despite restrictions made by central government on the amount which local authorities could spend on HE.

The Education Reform Act 1988 (ERA) brought further changes to the sector. The Act freed polytechnics and HE colleges of local authority control and created a new funding body, the Polytechnics and Colleges Funding Council (PCFC). ERA also wound up the UGC which funded universities and created the Universities Funding Council (UFC) in its place. In order to increase efficiency and promote expansion, the government shifted a proportion of block grant core funding across to the tuition fees paid by local education authorities for each student. Institutions could increase student numbers but would receive tuition fees only for their increased numbers. The response of the two parts of the sector was different. Whilst universities tried to protect their unit of resource and avoided expansion, the polytechnic and college sector was prepared to increase recruitment of students for whom they received only tuition fees (Green, 1994). As a result, the expansion of student numbers between 1988 and 1992 took place largely in polytechnics and colleges of HE, and was achieved with lower per capita funding.

The differing response to expansion was the impetus for the unification of the system four years later. Universities were not achieving the efficiency goals the Conservative government wanted. Abolishing the binary line was seen as a means of facilitating greater competition between institutions and ensuring expansion at reduced costs. The Further and Higher Education Act 1992 gave polytechnics and large HE colleges full autonomy with degree-awarding powers and the right to use the title university. To fund all institutions in the new unified system, higher education funding councils for England, Scotland and Wales were introduced.

Following unification, funding became an increasingly serious concern in the 1990s. There has been a constantly shrinking unit of resource allocated by the government. Institutions have been required to make year-on-year efficiency gains through a consistent reduction in core funding so that in the 20 years leading up to the Dearing inquiry the unit of funding per student fell by 40 per cent (NCIHE, 1997). Individual students have also faced increasing hardship, with a growing burden placed on them to pay the cost of their study. In 1990, access to the maintenance grant for students was capped. Student loans were introduced and a Student Loans Company founded to take responsibility for issuing loans and for the recovery of debt. Between 1990 and 1999, maintenance grants were progressively reduced and loans increased. From 1999, all new students have had access only to a student loan. Regular reports in the national press highlight the impact of these measures on students – participating in HE means poverty and debt, reflected in headlines such as 'Students would be better off on benefit' (Woodward, 2002).

By the mid-1990s the university system was in financial crisis. Vice-chancellors threatened to take the law into their own hands and proposed to charge top-up fees to students. Anticipating a general election, the opposition Labour Party and the Conservative government agreed to set up a national committee of inquiry – the Dearing Committee – to address the problem. Dearing was set the task of ensuring that fees paid by the state would in future be paid by students and their families, but in the run-up to the general election this remit was kept out of the public eye and the inquiry was used as a means of parking the problem until the election was over (Parry, 1999).

The Dearing Report was published after the 1997 general election, and the importance of funding is demonstrated in the prominence given to financial issues in the final report, which fill most of the second half (Longden, 2001). Dearing proposed that the block grant to universities should be replaced by a system of funding which followed the student and put forward proposals for how students should finance their study. Yet although Dearing offered detailed and carefully researched proposals, the Labour government introduced their own policy solutions, which were not based on the ideas in the Dearing Report. In doing so they have perpetuated rather than resolved the funding problems facing both institutions and students, and this has precipitated a further financial crisis in 2002, with a £1 billion funding gap identified between funding needs and provision. The burden of cost to universities who widen access to non-traditional students has led to proposals to oppose further expansion (NATFHE, 2002).

The expansion of HE has thus brought with it major questions in relation to funding. Whereas developments following the Robbins Report were well funded, the New Right Conservative government of the 1980s challenged the belief that the system should be financed by the state and based expansion on market-led reform (Brown and Lauder, 1995). In what Halsey (1997: 640) refers to as 'the decade of the market', reflecting the goals of the Thatcher government elected in 1979, consumer choice and competition between institutions were seen as the way to achieve greater efficiency and to bring down costs. Allied to this was the belief that individuals should increasingly bear the cost as they would gain most benefit from HE. The impact of the market philosophy on both students and institutions since then has been a serious and increasing problem of underfunding. The central dilemma of who pays has been replaced with the question of what is a reasonable balance between state and student (Longden, 2001), and this remains highly contested.

The pursuit of quality and standards

The problems and issues involved in funding the system have been accompanied by increasing concern with quality and standards. The central policy dilemma is the need to expand student numbers with shrinking public funds, without loss to the quality of teaching and research (Coffield and Williamson, 1997; McNair, 1997; Winter, 1999). Even if not in decline, quality may be different in the current mass, unified system of HE compared with the past (Brennan and Shah, 1993). As a result, what is meant by quality is the subject of extensive debate and has resulted in what Watson and Taylor (1998: 74) refer to as 'quality wars'.

There are tensions between the internal world of the university, concerned with the status quo, quality, status and tradition, and an external world concerned with optimizing resources, value for money and extending access to HE for all those capable of benefiting from the experience (Longden, 2000). Brennan et al. (1997: 175) suggest that current changes are seen by some as 'a lack of trust in universities to be responsive to the economic needs of the country', particularly as the burgeoning of quality assessment and audit procedures has coincided with the shift from an elite to a mass system of HE.

Systems of quality audit and assessment

The various quality systems which have been introduced (see Table 8.1) cover a range of different aspects of provision in HE. The assessment of research through the Research Assessment Exercise and of teaching quality through the Quality Assurance Agency subject review are perhaps the most widely known. These systems of review are carried out by peers who are considered to be experts. The outcomes are reported with a numerical score, which allows comparisons to be made between departments and institutions and for league tables to be published. Institutional audits examine the systems an institution has in place for managing its work – its quality assurance procedures – and how these are put into practice. These include procedures related to the provision of courses, the management and development of staff, communication structures and responsiveness to feedback from students, external examiners and external bodies such as employers.

A further development in addressing quality has been the publication of national benchmark standards for undergraduate programmes in response to a recommendation put forward in the Dearing Report. They identify key outcomes which are intended to form explicit threshold standards across all provision. By 2000, these were published in 22 subject areas, with a further 24 to be published in 2002. They are intended to provide institutions with a framework for developing and specifying the intended learning outcomes of programmes and to assist peer reviewers, including external examiners, with a point of reference, amongst others, for making judgements about the appropriateness of standards. They are also intended to ensure public and employer confidence that HE awards, especially at first-degree level, are recognized nationally and understood widely. In this way, Watson and Taylor (1998) believe that benchmarking reflects a shift in attention from examining the quality of the student experience in individual institutions to the confirmation of standards across provision.

Table 8.1 *Examples of quality audit and assessment in HE*

Form of quality procedure	Description	System in UK
Teaching quality assessment	Subject assessment of teaching and learning by academic peers, using a prescribed procedure to measure quality (currently with a numerical score)	Quality Assurance Agency subject review (introduced 1997)
Research assessment exercise	Assessment of research output by subject and elite peers. Numerical outcomes linked to funding	Research assessment exercise (introduced 1986)
Quality audit	Institutional-level audits of quality processes mainly by managerial peers	Individual institutions arrange own procedures
Undergraduate benchmarking	Qualifications framework and subject-by-subject benchmarks of graduate outcomes. Used for reporting on overall subject quality in institutions by subject specialists	National benchmark standards. Institutional programme specifications related to standards. First 22 subject benchmark standards published 2000
Accreditation of teaching staff	Accreditation of individual teachers in HE by a national Institute for Learning and Teaching	Institute for Learning and Teaching (Introduced 1999)
External examining	Monitoring and moderation of examining procedures for each course carried out by peers from other institutions	External examiners appointed by university departments for a period of 3 years at a time

Source: Adapted from Jary (1999: 45)

What is meant by quality?

Whilst all these systems claim to evaluate quality, there is no one single agreed definition of what quality means. Green (1994) provides a useful overview of how definitions of quality vary. She explains that the concept of quality has traditionally been associated with providing a product or service that is distinctive or special. It implies exclusivity and something that is out of reach of the majority of the population. Alternatively, quality can mean conformance to specifications or standards. Standards here mean the characteristics and criteria used to measure a product or service. Achieving quality then depends on the criteria set to define standards. Although this definition allows for a wider application of the notion of quality, it raises a number of problems. If the standards used do not reflect perceptions of what is significant, there may be disagreement about what counts as a quality product or service. There are concerns that identifying suitable criteria encourages a definition of quality in terms of standards that are easily measurable, and this may not be straightforward in education. It may avoid important purposes which are difficult to measure.

Furthermore, the term 'standard' is often associated with a different meaning in HE with standard meaning excellence or a high standard of academic achievement. This definition is inherent in concerns about the dilution of the quality of the intake. Whereas Robbins perpetuated an elite system, based around full-time study often away from home for 18–21-year-olds (Watson and Taylor, 1998), the expansion of HE in the 1990s has brought changes to the nature of the student cohort. Although many students still enter university at the age of 18 or 19, there are increasing numbers of mature students in HE (McNair, 1997). There has been a steady growth in part-time undergraduate numbers and a huge expansion of post-graduate study on taught programmes (Watson and Taylor, 1998). Furthermore, whilst the majority of students have continued to come from middle-class backgrounds (Kogan, 1993; Longden, 2000), the focus of expansion in the Dearing Report is on widening participation of under-represented groups, and the report emphasizes the need to promote progression to HE through projects which address low expectations and achievement. As students enter HE with a wider range of educational attainment, and with a variety of qualifications rather than simply A-levels, there is a fear that standards of excellence in academic achievement may be reduced (Green, 1994).

A further definition of quality is fitness for purpose, where quality is judged according to whether a product or service meets its stated intention. This raises questions about who defines the purpose. Whereas academics have traditionally played a major role in defining the meaning of HE, there is increasing pressure to define fitness for purpose as meeting customer requirements. This raises a further question of who the customer is – the state, employers, students and their families all have an interest in HE. Moreover, in an increasingly differentiated mass HE system, purposes may not be the same across provision. One approach to addressing this issue is to measure quality according to how institutions define their goals and purposes. In a differentiated system, this allows institutions to be measured against their own quality goals. Yet this approach tacitly acknowledges that the system is not just differentiated but stratified, despite its overt appearance as a unified system, with a hierarchy of esteem allowing an elitist model of what constitutes HE to be retained in certain institutions and departments (Coffield and Williamson, 1997).

The impact of quality procedures on HE

There is a great deal of concern about the impact of the quality procedures which have been implemented in the British HE system in the past ten years. The rise to prominence of the quality agenda has coincided with cuts in spending on HE, and audit and subject review have been attacked for being expensive and intrusive (Watson and Taylor, 1998). For many commentators, the introduction of systems of quality audit and assessment relate to the market philosophy introduced by the Conservative government (Walford, 1991; Brennan and Shah, 1993). For the market to operate effectively, the various 'customers' of HE require assurances that they are getting a suitable product. The government wants assurance that institutions are producing the graduates the country needs. Employers want to be sure of the consistency of academic and professional competence. Students want to know they are getting a qualification which is recognized and valued by the outside world and in the labour market.

The drive to increase efficiency and to get more value for less money creates a tension between questions of efficiency and quality. There is a fear that quality is being traded for efficiency so that, for example, changes in approaches to teaching and learning respond to demands for greater efficiency rather than higher-quality learning (Green, 1994). Within HE institutions there are concerns about the impact of overcrowding and the effect of pressures on staff-student ratios and resources on academic standards. For Halsey (1997: 645) the overall emphasis on efficiency means that it is only realistic to interpret the impact of expansion as a 'levelling down of standards'.

Autonomy and accountability in HE

Surrounding discussions of systems of quality assurance are major debates about autonomy, accountability and responsibility. Even if the principle of institutional autonomy has been maintained within HE (Watson and Taylor, 1998), the boundaries around such autonomy are much more tightly defined, with the introduction of ever more precise specifications of what HE should do and how it should do it, albeit in the name of accountability and quality assurance.

The spread of quality systems is believed to have far-reaching consequences for HE. The discourse of quality audit, the way it defines what people do and the language used to define it mean that audit is not neutral. As Woodhouse (1998: 264) argues: 'Audits do as much to construct definitions of quality and performance as to monitor them.' In this way, audit can structure how those working in HE behave and discipline HE into certain ways of working. The emphasis on efficiency, financial viability and accountability encourages what is called performativity (Jary, 1999), so that those working in HE become orientated to a management discourse of performance indicators, competition, comparison and responsiveness.

Amidst worries concerning the impact of managerialism and performativity, it is easy to lose sight of legitimate demands for democratic accountability. Democratic forms of accountability would be responsive to a range of stakeholders. However, many of those currently defined as stakeholders in HE, including the state, industry, students and their families, are currently immersed in a discourse of the market. They are encouraged to see themselves as customers who should seek compensation if the product they are receiving fails them. Democratic accountability poses challenges to old forms of academic autonomy. But it also challenges understandings of stakeholders in HE, both in terms of who the stakeholders are and how their role is defined. As HE continues to expand, the need to address these questions becomes more pressing.

There is a key role for academics here, as Coffield and Williamson (1997: 5) argue:

> Academics have no right to impose a particular model, but they do have a responsibility to ensure that debates about it are informed, critical and open. They have a responsibility to develop different visions of their own future which can be evaluated in public debate so that public choices in this major area of policy are well informed.

Equally, there is an important contribution to be made by the wider community. Their views should not replace the visions of the academic community but would work with these visions to contribute to future understandings of HE.

Conclusion

Around 34 per cent of young people now pursue HE, and an increasing number of people do so as adults. The widening of participation reflects changes to the social and economic context, changes in government policy and the changing aspirations of individuals. Whilst the opening up of HE to a wider audience may be welcomed, it brings with it pressures and challenges. There are competing tensions between the national requirement for a well educated workforce and the cost of providing such a workforce; between the desire by HE to retain autonomy of purpose whilst being driven towards greater accountability and dependence through funding; and between the move towards a mass and possibly universal HE system set against the desire to retain the qualities and intimacy of an elite system (Longden, 2000).

The changes which have taken place represent important challenges to the former elite system, which are welcomed by many commentators. However, the form these changes have taken has faced wide-ranging critiques. The concern is not just with particular aspects of reform but the underlying direction of reform. The emphasis on meeting economic need and achieving greater efficiency is seen as drawing attention away from more fundamental concerns.

Barnett (2000) proposes that 'higher' education should refer to a genuine higher learning, where students are enabled to understand and confront the complexities they face. This means that there

needs to be a democratic imperative, not just an economic imperative (Coffield and Williamson, 1997). A democratic imperative
'argues that a learning society worthy of the name ought to deliver
social cohesion and social justice as well as economic prosperity to
all its citizens' (ibid.: 3). Coffield and Williamson argue further that
'A viable model for higher education is inseparable from one for
society as a whole' (ibid.: 5).

The Dearing Report appears to respond to these concerns. The
report identifies four main purposes for HE. These are, first, to
enable individuals to achieve their highest potential, to equip them
for work, to enable them to contribute to society and to achieve
personal fulfilment; secondly, to increase knowledge and understanding for their own sake and to foster their application for the
economy and society; thirdly, to meet the needs of an 'adaptable,
sustainable, knowledge-based economy' at local, regional and
national level; and, fourthly, to play a major role in shaping a
'democratic, civilised, inclusive society' (NCIHE, 1997: 5).

Yet the daily business of HE often appears to remain dominated by
agendas concerned with efficiency and meeting the need to educate
and train a suitable workforce. It is tempting to see the expansion of
HE as exacerbating these pressures rather than opening up the potential for wider access to broader understandings of a genuine higher
learning. Yet if universities are to be key agencies in developing a
more egalitarian, participatory and socially just society (Watson and
Taylor, 1998), then such tensions need to be addressed.

This chapter has aimed to:

- contextualize the role of HE in a modern knowledge economy;
- provide an overview of the way that the HE system in the UK has
  changed and expanded since the Robbins Report of 1963;
- discuss the problems of funding a mass system which has developed out of elite traditions;
- explore changing understandings of quality and standards in HE;
  and
- consider the challenges of maintaining a broad, democratic
  vision of HE in the face of economic imperatives.

In an age of risk and uncertainty, there will be no certain solutions,
for as Beck (1992) suggests, in modern times, the only certainty is
uncertainty.

Student tasks

1 The principal goal of HE is the nurturing of a critical understanding amongst students in whatever discipline they study (Barnett, 2000). How does this claim match up with your reasons for entering HE, and your experience of studying in HE?
2 Has the expansion of HE widened participation to a broader population?
3 Find and discuss data on participation by class, gender, ethnic origin and age in your own institution and compare this with the national picture.
4 Look up the benchmark standards for your area of study on the QAA website (look under benchmarking at qaa.org.uk). How are they reflected in your course of study?

Suggested further reading

Coffield, F. and Williamson, B. (eds) (1997) *Repositioning Higher Education*. Buckingham: Society for Research into Higher Education and Open University Press. This edited book considers the role of HE in modern society. There are chapters on quality, the curriculum, qualification frameworks and social justice. All chapters put forward visions for the future which are intended to provoke debate.
Kogan, M. and Hanney, S. (2000) *Reforming Higher Education*. London: Jessica Kingsley. This book looks at HE policy over the last 30 years and examines the relationship between HE policy and the state.
Scott, P. (ed.) (2000) *Higher Education Re-formed*. London: Falmer. This edited volume discusses the challenges facing HE and how it will be reformed in the new millennium, from a range of perspectives. Different chapters look at the history, management and organization of universities and at the nature of knowledge in HE.
The three main journals in the UK which focus on HE are:
Higher Education Quarterly
Higher Education Review
Studies in Higher Education

References

Ashton, D. and Green, F. (1996) *Education, Training and the Global Economy*. Cheltenham: Edward Elgar.
Barnett, R. (2000) *Realizing the University in an Age of Supercomplexity*. Buckingham: Society for Research into Higher Education and Open University Press.

Bauman, Z. (1997) *Universities: old, new and different*. In A. Smith, and F. Webster, (eds) *The Postmodern University? Contested Visions of Higher Education in Society*. Buckingham: Society for Research into Higher Education and Open University Press, pp. 17–26.

Beck, U. (1992) *Risk Society: Towards a New Modernity*. Newbury Park, CA: Sage.

Brennan, J. and Shah, T. (1993) Higher education policy in the United Kingdom. In Goedegebuure et al. (eds) *Higher Education Policy. An International Comparative Perspective*. Oxford: Pergamon Press, pp. 290–314.

Brennan, J., Williams, R., Harris, R. and McNamara, D. (1997) An institutional approach to quality audit. *Studies in Higher Education,* 22(2): 173–86.

Brown, P. and Lauder, H. (1995) Post-Fordist possibilities: education, training and national development. In L. Bash and A. Green (eds) *Youth, Education and Work. World Yearbook of Education 1995*. London: Kogan Page, pp. 19–32.

Brown, P. and Scase, R. (1997) Universities and employers: rhetoric and reality. In A. Smith and F. Webster (eds) *The Postmodern University? Contested Visions of Higher Education in Society*. Buckingham: Society for Research into Higher Education and Open University Press, pp. 85–98.

Clarke, J. and Newman, J. (1997) *The Managerial State*, London: Sage.

Clarke, T. (2001) The knowledge economy. *Education + Training,* 43(4/5): 189–96.

Coffield, F. and Williamson, B. (1997) The challenges facing higher education. In F. Coffield and B. Williamson (eds) *Repositioning Higher Education*. Buckingham: Society for Research into Higher Education and Open University Press, pp. 1–26.

Committee on Higher Education (1963) *Higher Education. Report of the Committee on Higher Education (the Robbins Report)*. London: HMSO.

Giddens, A. (1991) *Modernity and Self-Identity: Self and Identity in the Late Modern Age*. Oxford: Polity Press.

Giddens, A. (1994) *Beyond Left and Right. The Future of Radical Politics*. Oxford: Polity Press.

Green, D. (1994) What is quality in higher education? Concepts, policy and practice. In D. Green (ed.) *What is Quality in Higher Education?*. Buckingham: Society for Research into Higher Education and Open University Press, pp. 3–20.

Halsey, A.H. (1997) Trends in access and equity in higher education: Britain in international perspective. In A. Halsey et al. (eds) *Education, Culture, Economy and Society*. Oxford: Oxford University Press, pp. 638–645.

HEFCE (2001) *Partnerships for progression* (www.hefce.ac.uk/pubs/hefce/2001/01_73.htm).

Jarvis, P. (2000) The corporate university. In J. Field and M. Leicester (eds) *Lifelong Learning. Education across the Lifespan*. London: Routledge Falmer, pp. 43–55.

Jary, D. (1999) The implications of the audit society? The case of higher education. In M. Dent et al. (eds) *Professionals, New Public Management and the European Welfare Sate*. Stafford: Staffordshire University Press, pp. 29–52.

Kogan, M. (1993) The end of the dual system? The blurring of boundaries in the British tertiary education system. In C. Gellert (ed.) *Higher Education in Europe*. London: Jessica Kingsley, pp. 48–58.

Longden, B. (2000) Elitism to inclusion – some developmental tension. *Educational Studies*, 26(4): 455–74.

Longden, B. (2001) Funding policy in higher education: contested terrain. *Research Papers in Education*, 16(2):161–82.

McNair, S. (1997) Changing frameworks and qualifications. In F. Coffield and B. Williamson (eds) *Repositioning Higher Education*. Buckingham: Society for Research into Higher Education and Open University Press, pp. 100–15.

National Association of Teachers in Further and Higher Education (2002) *Core Funding Must Tackle University Basic Needs: Building and Teaching*. NATFHE Press Release, 20 May (http://www.natfhe.org.uk/says/rels2002/2002pr39.shtml Accessed 10 June 2002).

National Committee of Inquiry into *Higher Education (1997) Higher Education in the Learning Society* (the Dearing Report). London: HMSO.

Parry, G. (1999) Education, research and policy-making in higher education: the case of Dearing. *Journal of Education Policy*, 14(3): 225–41.

Smith, A. and Webster, F. (eds) (1997a) *The postmodern university? Contested visions of higher education in society*. Buckingham: Society for Research into Higher Education and Open University Press.

Smith, A. and Webster, F. (1997b) Changing ideas of the university. In A. Smith and F. Webster (eds) *The Postmodern University? Contested Visions of Higher Education in Society*. Buckingham: Society for Research into Higher Education and Open University Press, pp. 1–14.

Trow, M. (1973) *Problems in the Transition from Elite to Mass Higher Education*. Berkeley, CA: Carnegie Commission on Higher Education.

Walford, G. (1991) The Changing relationship between government and higher education in Britain. In G. Neave and F. A. Van Vught (eds) *The Changing Relationship Between Government and Higher Education in Western Europe*. Oxford: Pergamon Press, pp. 165–83.

Watson, D. and Taylor, D. (1998) *Lifelong Learning and the University: A Post-Dearing Agenda*. London: Falmer Press.

Winter, R. (1999) The University of Life plc: the 'industrialization' of higher education? In J. Ahier and G. Esland (eds) *Education, Training and the Future of Work. Volume 1. Social, Political and Economic Contexts of Policy Development*. London: Routledge and the Open University, pp. 186–98.

Woodhouse, D. (1998) Quality assurance in higher education: the next 25 years. *Quality in Higher Education*, 4(3): 257–73.

Woodward, W. (2002) Students 'would be better off on benefit'. *Guardian* 20 February: 9.

9

Education for Lifelong Learning

Steve Bartlett

This chapter examines the ideological underpinnings of the term 'lifelong learning'. Global pressures which have led to the international development of policies in this area are outlined and then the increasing importance lifelong learning has assumed in England is considered. The chapter concludes by questioning whether the process of lifelong learning is really about the self-fulfilment of the individual or if it is part of the continuing adaptation and development of education as a form of social control.

Lifelong learning is very closely linked with many of the other issues explored in this volume. The term 'lifelong' suggests that learning begins at birth, progresses through early childhood into compulsory then post-compulsory education and on through the rest of life. Lifelong learning involves all types of student and can therefore be identified as inclusive. It has a role in the development of citizenship, social justice and democracy and can be seen as being driven by global forces. The repercussions of the introduction of policies of lifelong learning will be felt not just in industrial and post-industrial societies but also in those societies that may be variously labelled as 'developing'.

Defining lifelong learning

Lifelong learning is a term which has become prominent in education discourse in recent years. For many of those involved in debates on educational issues the term was not really used even as recently as ten years ago. Many of us first became aware of lifelong learning during recent election campaigns with politicians making speeches about inclusion, opportunity and standards of living. It was only, in fact, after the general election of 1997 that the first Minister for Lifelong Learning was appointed by the Labour government. Lifelong learning is presented almost as a new approach to living, not linked exclusively to the left or the right in political terms and thus providing a third way.

All aspects of education, however, are ideologically shaped in some way (see Bartlett et al., 2001) and this is also the case when analysing the meanings and policies associated with lifelong learning. For instance, a progressive view of lifelong learning sees the needs and wishes of the learners as being central. Learning is viewed in its broadest sense, being both informal as well as formal and as happening in all areas of life. Alternatively, an instrumentalist standpoint tends to view lifelong learning as taking place after the compulsory phase of education has been passed through by the learner. This learning is closely associated with the career development of the individual and the updating of the skills and capabilities of the workforce as a whole. There is a tendency here to emphasize a planned approach to learning which is monitored and accredited. Many accounts of lifelong learning use aspects of both these ideological approaches, perhaps emphasizing one and then the other at different times.

What, then, does the expression lifelong learning mean? Learning is something we do all the time. We learn from birth, through childhood, at school, in the workplace. We have learnt how to live in society and we are the product of our own learning. We have learnt how to communicate with others and how to interact with them in a multitude of situations. We have learnt how to 'earn' a living and all the other things we need to do to survive. We learn continually as our lives change from one phase to another. We pass through childhood, adolescence and into adulthood. Thus we are learning into our old age, though we may forget a great deal on the way and even become absent minded. The learning process takes many forms and there are a multitude of theories which attempt to explain how it happens but, certainly, it takes place throughout our lives. The term, 'lifelong learning' presented in this way may seem self-explanatory and obvious. Taking this view one can understand why it was never a separate and clearly identified aspect of education policy in the past. We could be excused for wondering what all the fuss is about and why the concept of life-long learning should now become so significant.

It could be assumed that education policy and planning take into account learning throughout life. However, traditionally, formal education which has taken place in institutions of some form has been concentrated upon young people aged from about 5 years old into their mid-teens, though this span has in fact much expanded in industrial nations in recent years. Lifelong learning has now appeared as a high-profile topic for politicians and also, perhaps as a result of this, for educationalists. The term now appears in policy documents concerned with all levels of educational provision. Thus universities claim to embrace the concept, colleges of further educa-tion see themselves as heavily involved and schools promote a desire for lifelong learning within their pupils. Even continuing profes-sional development (CPD) for teachers fosters a belief in the lifelong learning of these professionals (DfEE, 2001). Why has the term come to be used so much and why does it carry such importance?

The terms 'learning society' and 'learning organization' are now also used as signifying some modern new approach to life/educa-tion/work in which we should all be involved. These concepts seem to be closely linked to and at times interchangeable with lifelong learning. Tight (1999), in fact, sees a trinity of lifelong learning: the learning organization and the learning society as articulating the importance of continual learning at different levels stretching from the individual to the whole society. Unfortunately their meanings remain somewhat unclear (see Ranson, 1998, for a discussion of the learning society).

The second report of the Labour government's National Advisory Group for Continuing Education and Lifelong Learning (NAGCELL – Fryer, 1999) stated that the breadth of the field of lifelong learning constituted its attraction and also its potential weakness. Lifelong learning can include a range of highly formalized, structured educa-tional settings as well as very informal learning situations. It can cover all levels, purposes, contents and outcomes of learning. Different learning styles and approaches to learning are incorporated, and Fryer (ibid.) suggested that in this way diversity is celebrated. However, the report also recognized that this all-inclusiveness may inhibit sharpness of focus. Thus: 'Strategy to promote lifelong learn-ing may easily become so multi-stranded that it prevents the development of a clear sense of priority' (ibid.: 4).

Kogan (2000: 343), in noting how lifelong learning appears in a number of ways in both the literature and also the political discourse, suggests that it includes 'Those novel forms of teaching and learning that equip students (learners, individuals) to encounter with competence and confidence the full range of working, learning and life experiences'. Different strands of lifelong learning have existed for some time under a variety of different titles such as liberal education, adult education, continuing education, continuing vocational education, and continuing professional development. Kogan (ibid.) suggests that current proponents of lifelong learning would argue that this term now goes further in that it should be universal in terms of the age and educational abilities of those involved, it should include a wide range of providers and also other stakeholders in the community and society.

We discussed earlier how the term lifelong learning can be interpreted ideologically in different ways. The individual and his or her wider development may be seen as central; lifelong learning is part of attaining self-fulfillment and individuals should explore life in their own way following their own interests. Thus a progressive approach to lifelong learning covers all kinds of learning and may actually stress the informal and unintentional. An important element of this process is the involvement of learners and their willingness to go further in their learning. Much of this learning, though personally rewarding to learners, may not benefit them or the wider society economically. Qualifications are not considered as significant because the inner satisfaction and achievement of the learner do not have to be proved or measured by others.

Alternatively, an instrumental approach stresses how lifelong learning can bring tangible benefits to the individual and also to the wider society. Here the learning is not an end in itself but it is done for the economic benefits it brings. This view looks at how certain forms of learning may enhance employability and add to productivity. As such it is concerned with learning outcomes which are often linked to some form of qualification. Thus measuring levels of attainment becomes important.

These views can co-exist. International literature on lifelong learning and government publications contain both ideologies, talking of individual fulfilment and also the need to update skills for economic development. However, the resulting policy invariably has an instrumental emphasis. Thus, when investigating the promotion of lifelong learning by different governments, we see that they focus on planned learning – that is, preferably accredited in some way, usually at post-compulsory level (it may also be work based or linked to employment). The emphasis is on adult learners who are potential or existing members of the labour force.

Smith and Spurling (1999: 9) consider the concept of lifelong learning as having a two-part framework:

> At the empirical level – lifelong learning is intended and planned learning, which goes on more or less continually over the lifespan...there is some room for informal learning within the idea of lifelong learning, but the latter must be built on a good solid backbone of intentional and planned learning if an individual or organization is to claim to be a lifelong learner. At the moral level – lifelong learners will additionally live by four basic moral principles: personal commitment to learning; social commitment to learning; respect for others' learning; and respect for truth.

Thus a lifelong learner practises learning continually. He or she shows a personal and social commitment to learning and respects the learning of others. Significantly, the learning should be planned. This emphasis on lifelong learning being intended and planned leads us to focus upon clearly identified, more formalized learning with measurable outcomes such as qualifications. This certainly begins to narrow the field, and the more informal, spontaneous and accidental aspects, a broader view of lifelong learning incorporates are likely to be 'dropped' due to difficulties in identification and measurement.

The international development of lifelong learning

Lifelong learning has become important at an international level as a result of what have been perceived as global economic and social developments. One of the first of a number of significant international documents on lifelong learning was a United Nations Educational, Social and Cultural Organization (UNESCO) report, *Learning to be* (Faure, 1972). This report was based on the traditions of liberal educationalists, regarding education as a means of developing the human condition, leading to individual fulfilment.

In proposing the development of what it called lifelong education, *Learning to Be* called for the vertical and horizontal integration of education and also for its democratization. By vertical integration was meant an education system which allowed individuals to opt into formal education at any stage in their lives. This, of course, would involve removing psychological and social barriers to learning as well as the structural economic ones, as creating access alone does not in itself ensure greater participation. Horizontal integration was perceived as the fostering of education in a multitude of non-formal as well as formal settings. Democratization referred to a greater involvement of learners in the design and management of their learning (see Boshier, 1998, for discussion of these concepts). These three developments would combine in the creation of learning societies where greater access to and involvement in learning creates increasingly democratic societies. Thus lifelong learning, or lifelong education as it was called in this report, was felt to be a liberating force.

The Organization for Economic Co-operation and Development (OECD) produced its report, *Recurrent Education: A Strategy for Lifelong Learning*, in 1973. The OECD was concerned with what it termed 'recurrent education', which was basically ways of extending formal education and training to more of the industrial populations. It was interested in ways of developing economic potential in the workforce, seen as human capital, in order to improve standards of living which would ultimately strengthen democracy. The OECD's concern with lifelong learning was in finding practical ways of expanding education for those in work.

In these two significant publications exist the beginnings of different approaches to lifelong learning. The Faure Report had, essentially, a liberal vision of developing education in its broadest sense. Education was valuable, whether formal or informal, and encompassed far more than economic utilitarian considerations. Individual fulfilment through education would lead to a more enlightened and thus a more open and democratic society. The OECD was also concerned with these ideals but chose to be pragmatic in its approach concentrating on how to expand existing adult education and on the economic priorities of training. Thus from this point in time the ideals of true learning could be said to have been hijacked and harnessed instead to economic gain. Boshier (1998) sees a shift from a socialist, Utopian, template for reform embodied in the Faure Report to a neo-liberal view arising from the interests of global capitalism. Governments and industrialists are using the ideals of liberal education for their own ends of increasing production and wealth.

Field (2000) points out that concern by politicians and industrialists for lifelong learning declined in the 1980s as many governments worldwide were preoccupied with economic problems of recession and that tackling the issue of unemployment became their priority. However, during the 1990s, at international and national policy level, lifelong learning became an umbrella term covering all of what had earlier been referred to as 'lifelong education', 'recurrent education', 'popular education', 'adult education' and 'post-initial education and training'. Hodgson (2000: 4) suggests that the term 'lifelong learning' was useful to policy-makers because it was so all encompassing and could be tailored to fit the requirements desired:

> If, in the 1990s the term 'lifelong learning' became, in some senses, meaningless, because of its many and varied translations at the policy level, its existence as a concept or vision remained very powerful at the level of rhetoric. Lifelong learning was the 1990s response to, or even defence against, a changing, frightening and unknown technological, economic, social and political environment – it became a concept as slippery and multifaceted as the environment in which it exists.

Thus lifelong learning came once again to the fore in international and individual governmental policy. This is seen as the result of certain economic, technological and social developments which had been growing throughout the preceding decades. Two factors are regarded as particularly important: the effect of globalization on world trade and the increasing impact of information and communication technology (ICT). These meant not just rapid communications speeding up economic activity but also continual changes in terms of production and the skills required from those employed. Many 'advanced' industrial nations were also facing an ageing workforce as life expectancy increased whilst birth rates had been in decline over a number of years. Thus there were pressing issues about the future skills which would be needed by the workforce, how quickly current skills were becoming obsolete and the need for workers to be flexible, continually learning and retraining. It was important to lure those already in employment back into learning to review and update their skills.

Beck (1992) took these as changes in the very nature of society, a transformation from modernity to what he called reflexive modernity. This reflexive modernity can be characterized as 'the risk society' due to its uncertain nature when we can no longer be sure of our social structures, such as the family, work or even the government itself, as they are in a state of constant flux. Market forces, which are beyond individual or state control, are perceived to have increasing power; in tandem with this is the stronger emphasis on individualization. Beck notes a growing variation in the ability of individuals to manage their positions in this risk society. Some sections of the population benefit from greater choice, wealthier life-styles and the latest technology. For others, those who do not have the marketable skills required for regular employment, this increasing choice brings the risk of them losing out even more, resulting in widening social division.

For these reasons lifelong learning has become increasingly important as part of an international agenda. Whilst the issues have been discussed at European and also world summit level, it is up to individual countries to make their own local response. Consequently different countries have interpreted the significance of lifelong learning in the light of their own particular circumstances and have developed their national policies accordingly. It now becomes appropriate to examine the development of lifelong learning in England.

Lifelong learning: the English experience

In the light of the discussion above, Ball (1999) suggests that Labour's education policies do not belong specifically to Labour at all but are rather local manifestations of global policy paradigms. The Labour government, on coming to office in 1997, set up a National Advisory Group for Continuing and Lifelong Learning (NAGCELL) which issued its first report, *Learning for the Twenty-first Century* (Fryer, 1997). This report takes the seismic economic changes we are currently living through and their enormous effect upon our society as its starting point:

> As we approach the twenty first century, the people of this country, in common with those of many others, face a bewildering mixture of uncertainty, risk, insecurity, division and yet opportunity. The challenges of rapid change are evident all around. They can be seen in radical shifts in the organization of industry and labour markets. They are apparent in rapid changes in occupations and the demand for skills. They are occurring in the structure of communities and in the family forms, roles and relationships. They manifest themselves in new technologies and patterns of

communication. They impact upon individual identities, produce new
opportunities for active citizenship and affect even the nature and form
of knowledge itself (ibid.: 11).

The Fryer Report sees these challenges as being at least partly met
by moving towards a learning culture though it does not view this
development as a substitute for other political and economic
action. The claim is not that lifelong learning will solve all economic and social problems but that it will better equip us to do so.

Lifelong learning is a process which can prepare people for, and
help them to navigate around, the many risks and uncertainties
involved in daily life. Fryer does note that many individuals are
unable, for a variety of different reasons, to participate in this society. Lifelong learning may be a way of developing their skills and
confidence, enabling them to become part of this new social order.
Thus it can help people to participate in and to construct the
changing society rather than being its possible victims. If, however,
something does not happen to intervene, a large group of socially
excluded and dispossessed people will evolve, which will in turn
lead to an increasingly unstable society. Unfortunately, as Fryer
(1999) noted, those most able to benefit from lifelong learning are
the ones who currently find themselves excluded from it.

The report points out the growing influences of global economic
forces on our everyday life and that a policy of total economic iso-
lationism is no longer possible. There are also internal changes in
the structure of the labour force as more women remain in or re-
enter work, as part-time employment opportunities are created
rather than full-time careers, and as the labour force ages. The
report also notes changes in employment through the introduction
of new work practices, the application of new technologies, the
production and delivery of new products and services, and the
reduced size of workplaces (Fryer, 1997: 11). These changes have
significant effects upon the type of worker required and it is suggested that in the future there will be diminishing opportunities for
unskilled and semi-skilled employment and those with only 'one
industry' or task-specific skills will be increasingly at risk. Thus we
are in the midst of changes in the time, location and forms which
work takes.

Fryer (ibid.) drew attention to how these economic changes
impacted upon communities differently. Some people live in
'employment-rich' households and communities. They are educated,

possess the modern skills which are needed, they are adaptable, enterprising and able to take new opportunities as they arise. However many others find themselves in a different position. They are in 'employment-poor households'. Often concentrated in particular neighbourhoods or communities, they have experience of periods of unemployment and there is the constant threat of redundancy.

This widening of social and economic inequality has been a particularly disturbing development resulting from the changes in employment over recent years. Whilst many groups in society have benefited from economic change and material development, others have fared less well and suffer from increased poverty, social exclusion and reduced life chances. These inequalities affect all aspects of life and are interlinked. Those who make up the poorer sections of society tend to suffer inequality in a number of areas such as income, housing, employment, health, education, training and transport. Thus, Fryer suggests, we have the emergence of sections of society suffering from compound forms of exclusion, on the one hand, and a virtual 'super class' of privilege on the other.

The Dearing (NCIHE, 1997) and Kennedy (FEFC, 1997) reports join Fryer in pointing out that, whilst there has been recent expansion in numbers of students in both FE and HE, there still exists what has been referred to as 'a learning divide'. Those from unskilled, manual, working-class backgrounds are far less likely to be involved in any form of education or training: 'On the one hand, there are those who are already well qualified and who continue to be learners throughout life. On the other, there are those who either leave education largely unqualified or who neither engage in learning as adults, nor intend to do so in the future' (Fryer, 1997: 15). There are certain groups which have been identified as under-represented across the whole range of post-school education: unskilled manual workers, part-time workers, temporary workers, the unemployed, older adults, ethnic minority groups, people with learning difficulties including numeracy and literacy, ex-offenders, disaffected young men, single mothers and women on low incomes. It is suggested that these are the groups that need to be actively encouraged to become involved if a true culture of learning is to develop.

These points were illustrated by Marks (2000) in an investigation into the attitudes of working-class men from Merseyside towards education. He noted the traditional working-class anti-educational culture which denies the value and significance of education. He suggested that these traditional views were reinforced by 'lived experiences of structural unemployment, "bogus" training courses, a sense of individual powerlessness in the face of global capitalism and, ultimately, a hostility or ambivalence to the world of work in general' (ibid.: 304). What was regarded as important was an ability to live off one's own wits. This view had evolved as a result of the region's history of casualization in employment. Marks indicated that this rejection of, or lack of interest in, education shown by these working-class men had not been there from the start of their educational career but had developed as a form of bravado or a defensive explanation for their early failure to achieve what, as pupils, they had initially hoped for.

Changes in society, as noted in *Learning for the Twenty First Century* (Fryer, 1997), are not just confined to employment. There are also changes in interpersonal relationships as reflected in the statistics for divorce rates, second marriages, co-habiting couples and single-parent families. Also noted is the changing nature of political activity and the importance of lifelong learning in helping to maintain, strengthen and develop democracy in the future. Lifelong learning, in being able to reach all sections of the population, has a significant role to play in the creation of the active citizen contributing to the good of society (see Chapter 5). Thus as the economy changes and new opportunities present themselves, the role of a culture of lifelong learning for all is 'to open up those avenues and opportunities for many more people in our society' (ibid.: 12).

In response to the Fryer Report, the Labour government published their green paper on lifelong learning, *The Learning Age: A Renaissance for a New Britain* (DfEE, 1998). Lifelong learning was taken to mean 'the continuous development of the skills, knowledge and understanding that are essential for employability and fulfilment' (ibid.: Introduction, s. 3: 1). In the Introduction, David Blunkett, then Secretary of State for Education, suggested that 'Learning is the key to prosperity – for each of us as individuals, as well as for the nation as a whole. Investment in human capital will be the foundation of success in the knowledge-based global economy of the twenty-first century' (ibid.: 1). The first section of this green paper reiterates current European views and those of Fryer that we are in a new age of information and of global competition. Having no choice we must prepare for this age in which 'the key to success will be the continuous education and development of the human mind and imagination' (DfEE, 1998: Introduction, s. 1: 1). Once again the theme is on the development of human capital. The green paper talks of the old industrial revolution being based upon plant, machinery and physical skills, whereas this new revolution is information and knowledge based. The greatest challenge for the country is the requirement to equip ourselves with new skills, knowledge and understanding.

The green paper goes on to show how the creating of the learning age forms part of the broader Labour strategy and that the vision is wider than just employment: 'The development of a culture of learning will help to build a united society, assist in the creation of personal independence, and encourage our creativity and innovation' (ibid.: Introduction, s. 2: 8). Thus lifelong learning and the creation of a learning culture are part of the wider process whereby individuals work together in forging a better and more inclusive society. In *The Learning Age* the importance of learning is outlined for individuals, businesses, communities and the nation. Thus we hear resonances, once again, of learning organizations and a learning society in the context of lifelong learning. The green paper flags up the need to overcome inequality in education and training and to erase the 'learning divide' which produces a vicious cycle of exclusion.

Labour policy, in response to the development of a 'risk society', is one of widening participation, inclusion and working in partnership. In this way broader social and economic regeneration strategies, such as the Excellence in Cities initiative, link clearly to education policies and in particular to the development of lifelong learning. Thus inner-city regeneration involves a strategy for business and enterprise, housing development, improvement of schools and incentives for encouraging adults back into learning and skills acquisition. The New Labour administration portrays this as the development of 'joined-up government'. A key aim as part of this policy is the modernization of public services, most notably the health service and education. The feeling is that, for the education system to be more responsive to the needs of the economy, the compulsory sector needs to be 'put right'. A poor initial experience was after all why many young people left school at the earliest opportunity never to return to education as adults.

The Labour government has placed education as a central plank in their policy of modernization. In the compulsory education sector they initially laid out their plans in the white paper, *Excellence in Schools* (DfEE, 1997). Here Blunkett stated that their policy was 'as much about equipping the people of this country for the challenge of the future as . . . about the Government's core commitment to equality of opportunity and high standards for all' (ibid.: 3). Once again the rhetoric was about developing talents to enable us to compete in a global economy and live in a civilized society. There was a need to build on existing strengths and also to overcome the spiral of disadvantage whereby 'alienation from, or failure within, the education system is passed on from generation to generation' (ibid.). Thus the importance of education, both in the compulsory years and throughout life, was stressed. Labour was, as it had done in the 1970s, talking about the importance of investing in human capital.

This need to increase opportunity and raise educational standards is reflected in the monitoring of achievement via pupil assessment, the compiling of performance tables, regular school inspection and the setting of targets which show annual improvement and increased 'value for money' in schools. There have been many other developments across the compulsory sector, such as guidance on effective ways of subject teaching, the introduction of the literacy and numeracy strategies, the identification of 'beacon' schools which will share their good practice with others, the expansion of nursery education, the publication of guidelines on good nursery practice and the creation of specialist schools. Citizenship, which emphasizes the role of these future pupils in a democratic society, is also currently being developed throughout the curriculum (see www.dfes.gov.uk/citizenship for an update). A stated aim of these policies is the raising of standards and a reduction in the failure and alienation of certain historically underachieving groups of pupils. It is argued that these policies will lead to a generation of school-leavers better equipped to take their place in society and possessing a desire to carry on the learning which will be required throughout their working lives. Certainly the success of such policies, which involve increasing direction from the centre whilst championing individual choice, in creating a more open learning society remains to be seen. Already the influence of the education action zones, created by the government to be innovative and raise achievement in deprived areas, has been called into question.

A criticism of education policies in the past has been that the different sectors of education are seen as separate and that the continuing development of people as learners throughout their lives has never really been taken on board. The historical experience was that children went to school to receive their education. They left for employment and became young adults never to return to education. This issue now appears to be under consideration by politicians. The Labour government, on being returned for a second period of office, stated its aims as being to create a society that is both inclusive and prosperous (DfES, 2001). In order to do this, raising standards in education was again placed as 'number one priority.' In *Education and Skills: Delivering Results. A Strategy to 2006* (DfES, 2001), using what may now seem familiar language, the then newly appointed Secretary of State for Education, Estelle Morris, stated:

> There is now wide acceptance that to build an economy that will continue our success in the global market place we will need an even better educated and more highly skilled workforce. Equally importantly, to build a fair and inclusive society everyone must have the opportunity to realize their full potential (ibid.: 2).

To achieve these aims the DfES 'proposes to create opportunities, release potential and achieve excellence' (ibid.). The objectives are to:

- Give children an excellent start in education so that they have a better foundation for future learning.
- Enable all young people to develop and equip themselves with the skills, knowledge and personal qualities needed for life and work.
- Encourage and enable adults to learn, improve their skills and enrich their lives (ibid.: 4).

This policy document goes on to outline targets and strategy to achieve these objectives. What is significant is not so much the individual targets, which are a continuation of the policy of the previous Labour administration, but the acceptance of the importance of linking different parts of the education system together with overarching aims and objectives. The Learning Skills Council (LSC) has, for instance, been created to co-ordinate post-16 developments. This brings under one umbrella sixth-form colleges, school sixth-forms, FE colleges, other post-16 trainers and education provision (not HE). The local LSCs are, according to the government, 'central to the Learning Partnerships being developed to plan and develop coherence in post-16 provision'. In terms of a policy of promoting lifelong learning, the thrust is to encourage greater cohesion between the different education sectors and wider participation in FE and HE (the areas of FE and HE are looked at in Chapters 7 and 8).

The website for lifelong learning (www.lifelonglearning.dfee.gov.uk) outlines the broader strategies for learning that the government has been developing. Key learning themes are identified along with details of the initiatives which they embrace. Many of these initiatives are linked and overlap the different themes. For instance, under the theme of 'basic skills' are listed: the report of the working group on English for speakers of other languages (*Breaking the Language Barriers*), the report of the working group looking into the basic skills needs of adults with learning difficulties and disabilities (*Freedom to Learn*), the report on post-school basic skills (*A Fresh Start*) and *Better Basic Skills*, the government response. There are links to the Basic Skills Agency and the Adult Basic Skills Strategy Unit which are responsible for the implementation of the national strategy to improve literacy and numeracy skills. Several of these, specifically disability and race, also appear under the theme of equal opportunities. Strategies for tackling age discrimination and promoting age diversity in the workplace are also outlined under equal opportunities as well as being addressed under a specific theme of older workers.

Within the theme of communities there are concerns to widen participation in learning and improve standards of basic skills, particularly for those in disadvantaged neighbourhoods. This also ties in with other government initiatives on neighbourhood renewal. The theme of family learning encourages parents to be more involved in their children's education and to work alongside them. Also the development of other skills, such as parenting and financial management, is increasingly being seen as important. Interestingly, the National Childcare Strategy has been developed as a means of 'meeting the needs and enhancing the opportunities of children and their families'. This would appear to be a way also of enabling parents, mothers in particular, to return to work.

There are, then, on the UK government website a wide range of initiatives promoting lifelong learning. For those in work and also the unemployed the aim is to retrain and to update their skills. This involves the development of more flexible learning opportunities to cater for differing needs and lifestyles. It is also seen as important to involve those who have been traditionally excluded from learning. Thus certain groups are specifically targeted, such as young offenders, the unemployed, single parents and those with low levels of literacy and numeracy.

The fact that more of an overview on education policy is now being taken by politicians may be an indication of progress in the promotion of a culture of lifelong learning. However the approach of the Labour government to education generally, and lifelong learning in particular, remains largely instrumentalist in orientation.

Critiques of lifelong learning policy

As noted earlier in this chapter, the policy of upskilling the workforce is a development of human capital theory. This theory underpinned the post Second World War expansion of primary and secondary education in England up to the 1970s and was based on the assumption that improving the quality of the workforce led to higher levels of production, more efficiencey and greater economic competitiveness in world markets (see Bartlett et al., 2001). Conversely, from the same viewpoint, poor economic performance results from a low-quality workforce. In this way the education system can take some of the blame for economic problems along with the workforce itself for not retraining. Thus the capitalist system of production is able to shift responsibility for poverty and unemployment on to the individual.

Human capital theory draws attention away from the structural inequalities which exist in terms of access to education and the possession of social capital. Thus factors which influence achievement in education such as the ability to pay for tuition, gender, race and the support of family and peers are played down. Human capital theory also fails to address the increasing differentials in terms of income and wealth both nationally and internationally. Similarly, the increasing proportion of poorly paid, untrained, part-time and temporary jobs in the labour market is ignored. Emphasis is placed upon individuals taking charge of their own learning and it becomes their responsibility to improve themselves and to enrol on educational and training programmes, preferably in their own time and at their own expense (Minter, 2001). Thus an element of compulsion emerges as, whilst the political rhetoric may be enabling and inclusive, the practical content of lifelong learning emphasizes formal, accredited and vocational provision aimed at those in the labour force. Individual responsibility to take part is stressed with the threat of economic and social exclusion hanging over those who do not (Tight, 1999).

The relationship between economic production and levels of education, which the human capital theory assumes, certainly remains in doubt and it is the strength of such questionable beliefs which have led Hughes and Tight (1998) to regard much of the discourse surrounding lifelong learning to be in the nature of social mythology. The productivity myth, asserting the need to increase productivity, and the change myth, claiming that we are living in a period of unprecedented change, lead to a second layer of myths. Here the lifelong education myth proposes that education and training should carry on throughout our lifespan. The learning organization myth suggests that only those (work) organizations which involve all members, as individuals and groups, in continual learning activities and processes will survive. Hughes and Tight (ibid.) suggest that these four myths interconnect to create the learning society myth. This is an image of a society where individuals as part of social groups are involved in learning throughout their lives. This learning benefits themselves, their social groups and the society as a whole.

They are not suggesting that the concerns about productivity and change are completely unfounded nor that lifelong learning, learning organizations or learning societies do not or cannot exist but that the rhetoric surrounding these areas goes far beyond any reality. This is because these myths serve to maintain a false consciousness about the structural position of labour and capital. For instance, the learning society myth, by suggesting that there are opportunities available to all, places the blame on the unemployed for their failure to find a decent job. In this way the myths help to ensure that the powerful and privileged groups in society maintain their position. We can all think of individuals who have 'made it' in society by their talent and enterprise and this draws attention away from the fact that these are the exceptions rather than the norm. Also Gorard et al. (2002) suggest that the government strategies for the retraining and upskilling of the workforce have, so far, had very little impact in England at all in spite of all the media hype which has surrounded them. Myths such as the learning society draw together disparate power groups. In this case there is an alliance between the interests of educators, employers and politicians. They each have different interpretations but all benefit from promoting the myth. Thus Hughes and Tight (1998: 188) suggest that the learning society myth provides 'a convenient and palatable rationale and packaging for the current and future policies of different power groups within society'.

So despite its shortcomings the human capital approach, which stresses the importance of lifelong learning, remains popular with politicians for a number of reasons. It offers an easy solution to economic problems whilst providing politicians with a forum (education and training) in which they can take action. By increasing expenditure on education and at the same time appearing to be tough, using the rhetoric of increasing efficiency and value for money, they are seen to be decisive and in control. It avoids public realization of structural inequalities which are much more difficult to tackle and are often beyond the influence of governments. Bourn (2001) states that, for many British government departments, lifelong learning is a convenient and fashionable cover for poorly thought-out policies that look no further than current industry skill needs. Thus whilst there may be no real movement towards a learning society or lifelong learning these concepts make current policies appear new and more interesting and help to create a feeling that things are improving.

A more extreme view would portray policies of lifelong learning as no more than aspects of social control with lifelong learning being a process which is used to socialize workers to the demands of government and employers. Terms such as empowerment, employability and flexibility ignore the reality of intensification of work, increasing job insecurity and periodic unemployment. Lifelong learning helps to mask the conflicting interests of employers and employees and gives the false impression that all are operating on the same 'team'.

In looking at current government initiatives, Hodson and Spours (2000) suggest that they are fragmented and based on a 'deficit model', being largely targeted at those who have not traditionally taken part in post-compulsory education or training for a variety of reasons. This is a piecemeal approach rather than system building for all and they argue for the development of a 'strong framework' approach which would provide a clear vision of a lifelong learning system. It would involve the building of common structures that support individual empowerment and a planned approach to lifelong learning at local, regional and national levels. They argue for the concept of 'all-throughness' in lifelong learning based on three basic dimensions: 'a vision of a holistic, all-through system, the creation of an infrastructure for lifelong learning and the development of personal capacities for learning within the compulsory education system' (ibid.: 200). They see the importance of an education system that does not treat older and younger learners differently. Thus the 'compulsory' education sector should be about preparing young people for a lifetime of learning rather than being focused upon their leaving exams. Compulsory education could then become more relevant to the needs of the learners and not preoccupied with indicators of performance which serve to demotivate pupils. It should be possible for learners to return to formal education at different stages of their lives and, for this to happen, barriers to access need to be removed. It would seem that even today the proposals of Faure still have resonance.

Conclusions

Where has this discussion taken us in terms of the meaning of lifelong learning, how it interacts with society currently and where it is likely to lead in the future? The term is open to varying interpretations and can be used in different ways. A broad, progressive approach considers all aspects of learning throughout life. It wishes to see individuals achieving self-fulfilment through the opportunities which should be available in our technologically advanced societies. An instrumentalist approach is more focused upon intended, planned learning related to the career advancement of the individual. A central concern of the instrumentalist is the rate of economic change and the need constantly to upskill the labour force in order to remain competitive internationally. In reality both ideological stances are in operation. They are able to co-exist for much of the time and both can be identified in policy statements. There is, however, an important difference in their emphasis and eventual outcomes.

The policy of successive UK and European governments has overwhelmingly emphasized the instrumental approach. Lifelong learning is still assumed to be something which happens after, and is separate from, compulsory education though compulsory education itself may be increasingly viewed from an instrumentalist standpoint. As lifelong learning benefits individuals it becomes their responsibility to update their skills and so an element of compulsion is incorporated into policy and blame is attached to a failure to remain employable. Worries are expressed by politicians about certain social groups who exist on the periphery of society and who remain marginalized. Casual, part-time and older workers are less likely to be involved in company training schemes which focus upon employees with already high levels of training and who offer the greatest potential benefit for the company. Those with the lowest levels of literacy, numeracy and basic skills will have the most difficulty in 'upskilling'. It is on improving the basic skills of these groups, under the auspices of social inclusion, that government policy of lifelong learning tends to be focused.

There have been questions raised in Britain about how effective policies for lifelong learning have been initially. For example, the adult literacy stratategy does not seem to have had a major impact so far. By devising lifelong learning strategies politicians appear to be showing concern for those who are excluded and powerless and also for the lifestyles of the population as a whole. They appear to be taking decisive action whereas, in reality, it may be that nothing is being radically altered and the old structural inequalities remain.

Many would like more consideration to be given to the pedagogical aspects of lifelong learning with questions of what it involves, how it takes place and the role of the learner being addressed more fully. They call for a wider approach to lifelong learning with its purposes being seen from a much broader perspective. Tight (1999) suggests that, whilst the dominant view portrays lifelong learning as being closely associated with and embedded in work, other forms of learning remain marginal and unconsidered. It will be interesting to see in this new millennium if the preoccupation of governments and educationalists with lifelong learning heralds the beginning of a new dawn of learning or if it is simply a further evolution of employment-focused training.

Student tasks

1 Analyse *The Learning Age: A Renaissance for a New Britain* (DfEE, 1998) in terms of progressive and instrumental educational ideologies.

How would you describe the government's approach to lifelong learning?
2 Choose one of the following groups: unmarried teenage mothers, young prisoners, the over 50s, adults with learning difficulties in literacy and numeracy, children living in areas of relative economic deprivation. Investigate current national initiatives which are targeted at the chosen group. Find out what support is being offered, how much this is costing and how effective these initiatives have been.

Suggested further reading

Field, J. and Leicester, M. (eds) (2000) *Lifeling Learning. Education across the Lifespan*. London: RoutledgeFalmer. This volume starts from the perspective that lifelong learning encompasses all ages rather than being concerned solely with post-compulsory education and training. The issues are examined in four sections: 'Theoretical perspectives'; 'Curriculum'; 'International perspectives', and 'Widening participation'. This collection is very useful in developing the issues outlined in this book.

Hodgson, A. (ed.) (2000) *Policies, Politics and the Future of Lifelong Learning*. London: Kogan Page. This edited volume offers the perspectives of several authors. They present a historical background to lifelong learning and place it in the European and then the UK context before considering policy under New Labour.

References

Ball, S.J. (1999) Labour, learning and the economy: a 'policy sociology' perspective. *Cambridge Journal of Education,* 29(2): 195–206.

Bartlett, S., Burton, D. and, Peim, N. (2001) *Introduction to Education Studies*. London: Paul Chapman Publishing.

Beck, U. (1992) *Risk Society. Towards a New Modernity*. London: Sage.

Boshier, R. (1998) Edgar Faure after 25 years: down but not out. In J.Holford et al. (eds) *International Perspectives on Lifelong Learning*. London: Kogan Page.

Bourn, D. (2001) Global perspectives in lifelong learning. *Research in Post-compulsory Education, 6* (3): 325–38.

Coffield, F. (1999) Breaking the consensus: lifelong learning as social control. *British Educational Research Journal* 25(4): 479–99.

DfEE (1997) *Excellence in Schools*. London: HMSO.

DfEE (1998) *The Learning Age: A Renaissance for a New Britain*. London: HMSO.

DfEE (2001) *Schools. Building on Success*. Norwich: HMSO.

DfES (2001) *Education and Skills: Delivering Results. A Strategy to 2006*. Sudbury: DfES Publications.

Faure, E. (1972) *Learning to Be: The World of Education Today and Tomorrow*. Paris: UNESCO.

Field, J. (2000) *Lifelong Learning and the New Educational Order*. Stoke-on-Trent: Trentham Books.

Fryer, R. (1997) *Learning for the Twenty-first Century: First Report of the National Advisory Group for Continuing Education and Lifelong Learning*. London: NAGCELL.

Fryer, R. (1999) *Creating Learning Cultures: Next Steps in Achieveing the Learning Age*. London: NAGCELL.

Further Education Funding Council (FEFC) (1997) *Learning Works. Widening Participation in Further Education (the Kennedy Report)*. Coventry: FEFC.

Gorard, S., Rees, G. and Selwyn, N. (2002) The 'conveyor belt effect': a re-assessment of the impact of national targets for lifelong learning. *Oxford Review of Education* 28(1): 75–89.

Hake, B. (1998) Lifelong learning and the European Union: a critique from a 'risk society' perspective. In J. Holford et al. (eds) *International Perspectives on Lifelong Learning*. London: Kogan Page.

Hodgson, A. (ed.) (2000) *Policies, Politics and the Future of Lifelong Learning*. London: Kogan Page.

Hodgson, A. and Spours, K. (2000) Building a lifelong learning system for the future. In A. Hodgson (ed.) *Policies, Politics and the Future of Lifelong Learning*. London: Kogan Page.

Hughes, C. and Tight, M. (1998) The myth of the learning society. In S. Ransen (ed.) *Inside the Learning Society*. London: Cassell.

Kogan, M. (2000) Lifelong learning in the UK. *European Journal of Education*, 35(3): 343–59.

Marks, A. (2000) Lifelong learning and the 'breadwinner ideology': addressing the problems of lack of participation by adult, working-class males in higher education on Merseyside. *Educational Studies*, 26(3): 303–19.

MINTER, C. (2001) Some flaws in the common theory of widening participation. *Research in Post-compulsory Education*, 6(3): 245–59.

National Committee of Inquiry into Higher Education (NCIHE) (1997) *Higher Education in the Learning Society (the Dearing Report)*. London: HMSO.

OECD (1973) *Recurrent Education: A Strategy for Lifelong Learning*. Paris: OECD.

Ranson, S. (ed.) (1998) *Inside the Learning Society*. London: Cassell.

Smith, J. and Spurling, A. (1999) *Lifelong Learning. Riding the Tiger*. London: Cassell.

Tight, M. (1999) Lifelong learning: opportunity or compulsion? *British Journal of Educational Studies*, 46(3): 251–63.

10

Education for Development

Tim Wright

This chapter considers the concept of 'development', reviewing its claim to be a movement for the good of humankind. In particular, the chapter explores whether education has played a positive role in the development process, or whether 'exporting' knowledge has led to the domination of certain ideology and knowledge systems. A question posed throughout is whether so-called education has been used to maintain the old colonial status quo or whether it has been used to promote a liberating agenda.

Introduction

Currently, millions of people in the world are starving and the lives of countless others are blighted by disease. Wars and natural disasters place intolerable burdens on individuals and nations. Around 1.3 billion people (approximately a quarter of the world's population) live in extreme poverty, and access to health and education is severely restricted. Some 125 million children (of whom two thirds are girls) receive no education at primary level (Oxfam, 2002); 12 million children die each year (Watkins, 2000).

Such problems are of immense proportions and demonstrate the complex interconnectedness of peoples, states, politics and economics, to name but a few 'players' in what amounts to a macabre game of life. The quality of individual lives is seemingly determined by factors beyond individual control. Life chances are, perhaps more than ever, the accidents of birth and the struggles appear unequal. Poverty, chronic disease and lack of education do not affect all people; some live lives of comparative affluence, supported by a seemingly unequal access to resources. The study of 'development' examines these issues.

Education is inextricably bound up with development. Indeed, so important is education now viewed that a target for universal primary education has been set for 2015 (see for example, the Jomtien World Conference, 1990, the white paper on international development, 1997, and the World Education Forum in Dakar, 2000). However, approaches to development are hotly contested as, despite half a century or so of action and certain successes, many of the apparently fundamental problems of the world community still persist.

This chapter seeks to chart the way in which the concept of 'development' has arisen and to explore how it has been interpreted in action. Although the discussion strays into 'global' considerations, a detailed analysis of globalization and education will be found in the next chapter.[1]

What is development?

Development is a contested term and what follows are two contrasting perspectives, culled from many. Firstly, one might consider development as a concept implying a process that is natural – *a function of growth*. For example, one talks of a baby developing, implying that it will move through a certain set of recognizable stages (physical, intellectual or whatever), each one apparently a necessary prerequisite in ensuring the next step towards maturity and the realization of potential. If the baby does not develop in the way most babies develop (and thus in a way that is seen as 'normal'), it is considered to be defective in some measure, in need of 'help', perhaps. The potential of the 'ideal' child is not attained. Such an analogy might also be applied to states, the belief being that there is an underlying historical momentum that, given sufficient time, will lead inexorably to the attainment of potential. However, as Rist (1997) points out, the evidence disputes this. For example, at a simplistic level, there is no proof that every village is '*destined* to become a big town' (ibid.: 27, emphasis added). Nor is every state *destined* to be economically successful.

A further implication of the analogy is that the process of development it describes would create potentially mutually destructive pressures. For example, would development apply to individuals, families, local communities, regions, nation-states or the whole world, as the realization of the potential of one of these might be at the expense of another? To continue the biological analogy, a food chain implies clear winners and losers in the 'game of life'; if a comparable approach were to be taken to development it would be necessary to decide whether it was morally right to apply such a hierarchical, 'predatory' process to our fellow human beings – the world might not be able to accommodate all of us in a 'developed' state (see Hardin, in Sterba, 1994).

Secondly, one might consider development as a *deliberate intervention in order to gain improvement.* Indeed, much of the self-styled 'development' of the past 50 or so years has legitimized itself by ostensibly espousing this aim. It seems entirely reasonable to enhance and share the good things of human existence and to alleviate the ills of our condition wherever possible. Surely it would be progress if no people in the world were starving, if all people had access to 'good' health care, if all children were educated, if all people were free from war and poverty? Yet what counts as an ideal social condition is not viewed in the same way by everyone, nor are the means by which it might be achieved. For example, despite such apparently self-evident rhetoric regarding the desirability of certain 'end conditions' relating to poverty, health care and peace, wars *are* fought, and the protagonists may well argue the *necessity* of conflict. Health care for all is fine, but if my child needs treatment I will probably use whatever pressure is at my disposal to get to the head of the queue; and the satisfaction of your child's hunger is fine, provided my child does not go hungry.

It is helpful here to examine a critique of development considered by Sutcliffe (1999) – namely, that of a journey in which it is necessary to consider the starting point, the nature of the journey itself and the end point. Let us consider the implications of this. If we use the terms 'developed' and 'developing' to apply to the conditions of human beings and if it is proposed to undertake some kind of intervention in order to help those human beings change from a state of what we see as 'developing' to 'developed', this implies that we have a view as to what constitutes the differences between the two states. In this model, 'developed' is the goal of 'developing'. All those people seeking to develop must, by definition, start in one condition and aim to finish in another condition which is seen as preferable. At best there is, perhaps, an element of the patronizing in this line of thinking – namely, that the starting point is seen as primitive, backward or deficient in some way and that developing societies need to 'catch up' with those that are developed.

Sutcliffe (1999) also notes that such a line of reasoning would require all societies to develop from some sort of roughly similar place, no matter how 'developed' they might be at the moment. Thus the Europe of several hundred years ago would apparently equate to an underdeveloped country of today. Thus one has the irony that 'Societies that deviate from the European techno-economic standards are designated as "traditional" or "primitive" despite the fact that they are contemporaneous with those who label them as such' (Tucker, 1999: 8). And herein lies a fundamental point, namely, that 'developed' has been (and still is) often taken to mean developed in a particular way, namely, in the style of a modern northern state. The reasons for this are many but relate to the fact that northern states have tended, over a long period of time, to be in a position of power relative to southern states, this power arising from resources, military strength, technology, dominance in economic policies (e.g. the spread of capitalism) and access to and the *definition* of knowledge.

The person (or state) who has knowledge has power, and one of the key influences on the development of nations has been the way in which they have been able or not to increase their so-called 'knowledge capital'. However, the knowledge required to participate on today's global economic playing field is not necessarily the knowledge that enabled one's ancestors to hunt successfully. What constitutes 'important' and 'valuable' knowledge changes as societal conditions change. Knowledge is not neutral (see, for example, Meighan and Siraj-Blatchford, 1997). Furthermore, as Watkins (2000: 53) points out, the world, in its efforts to accumulate wealth, has moved from one dominated by physical factors of production to one 'dominated by knowledge' – knowing how to use ICT may be more valued than knowing how to smelt steel or, rather, having the *capacity* to maximize the economic effects of ICT may be more valuable than the *capacity* to smelt steel.

Be that as it may, the access to knowledge as related to the accumulation of wealth has been uneven across the peoples of the world; some peoples have 'the knowledge' and lead lives of comparative

ease and others do not, and lead lives of poverty. Access to knowledge is in part determined by mass education systems, and the
uneven global distribution of access to 'knowledge capital' is in no
small measure derived from the ways in which western powers have
defined, exported and imposed knowledge through the domination
of colonialization and through post-colonial development policies.
In the event, one set of societies (loosely referred to as western/north-
ern) has thus been able to determine not only what it means to be
developed but also to determine the route to take in order to become
developed – namely, by 'imitating' the 'forward or progressive ones'
and thereby . . . 'taste too of the same fruits of progress' (Wallerstein,
1991: 53). How has this situation arisen?

The beginnings of development

The beginning of the 'development age' is often located at the end
of the Second World War, this period coinciding with the creation
of the United Nations, The Declaration of Human Rights (1948)
and a speech by President Truman of the USA (the so-called 'Point
Four Speech') which urged a 'bold new programme for the . . .
improvements and growth of underdeveloped areas' (Public Papers
of the Presidents, pp. 114–15, cited in Rist, 1997: 71). However,
although the early articulation of 'development' as a currently used
(even if disputed) concept might reasonably be located in the late
1940s, the philosophy, the opportunities and the interactions
between states which shaped its present form lie further back in
recorded history. In order to appreciate something of the current
relationships between developed and developing countries, it is
necessary to chart three processes. Firstly, it is necessary to examine
one of the major influences on the shaping of western knowledge,
namely, the 'Enlightenment'. Secondly, it is necessary to see how
this 'modern' western knowledge was first 'exported' from Europe.
Thirdly, it is necessary to consider how such knowledge has been
embedded and sustained in education systems in developing countries and is still prevalent today as a dominant and determining
global force.

The age of the Enlightenment and the definition of western knowledge

The age of Enlightenment in Europe (a period corresponding *approximately* to the eighteenth century) was a time which was marked by a keen interest in rationality, particularly that apparently underpinned or so-called 'proved' by science. Science seemed to offer an approach to a truth that was beyond superstition and beyond the vagaries of the interpretation of individual people. The truth appeared to be attainable, identifiable. Scientific method appeared to make certain knowledge uncontestable. Instead of relying on the handed-down knowledge of the 'ancients', a new role for reason itself was proposed and it was felt that the people living in that age could build on the knowledge of their predecessors – 'We are dwarfs perched on the shoulders of giants' (Rist, 1997: 35, quoting Bernard of Chartres). There was a growing belief in progress and in the normality of change as part of that progress. The world would not be as it had always been; it would move forward if assisted by rational thought and the application of science. Human beings were not inevitably trapped in a particular condition; they had the power and the ability to transcend a given context. As Larrain (1994) points out, the ills and unhappiness of humankind came to be seen as related to ignorance and prejudice, such a condition being amenable to the application of rational thinking (and the liberating effects of education) and science (Coulby and Jones, 1995). Enlightenment thinking favoured human beings and protected them from the onslaughts of 'Nature'. Its subscription to reason (as exemplified by the scientific approach) offered a way of freeing humankind from the vicissitudes of existence. Progress became assured and was given a clear direction; the goal became one of 'emancipation' (Larrain, 1994).

'Enlightenment' thinking thus offered a framework by which a European of the time might 'analyse' a person from a non-European culture. Such a non-European might be seen as 'backward', 'primitive', 'irrational', 'uneducated' because he or she did not have access to the latest knowledge (apparently, worthwhile, proven and rational). Indeed, the theory of 'social evolutionism' would have provided confirmatory legitimization of this perspective of development. This theory proposed that there were essential stages through which every society had to pass:

that all nations travel the same road; and all do not advance at the same speed as Western society, which therefore has an indisputable 'lead' because of the greater size of its production, the dominant role that reason plays within it, and the scale of its scientific and technological discoveries (Rist, 1997: 40).

In this way, the Europeans of the time were able to define what it was to be civilized. They were also able to define what was seen as important and worthwhile knowledge and they could point to a variety of apparent improvements in support of their claims (in medicine, for example). They felt they had a justification to claim that their way of interpreting the world was the right one and that their 'modernist' knowledge was of benefit to humanity. Indeed, the philosophy and methodologies of the age came to be seen as the sine qua non for any country seeking to improve. (Of course, an obvious flaw in the claim that the Europeans made regarding what it means to be civilized is that it was based only on *their* view as to what constituted civilization. Any group can achieve this. For such a view to be implemented, however, it has to be linked to power.)

The export of western knowledge

An obvious mechanism by which western knowledge was exported was via colonialization and, although colonial expansion has a long history, it is perhaps reasonable to single out the nineteenth century as a time when colonial rule was consolidated (Bernstein, 2000). Whatever any particular state's motives for expansion (e.g. trade, secure military bases, access to resources, etc.), the motives of the people involved in colonialization were complex and varied. For some of those involved, colonialization was seen as a duty; for others, as an opportunity. However, no matter what the motivation of individuals, many peoples of the so-called 'Third World' found themselves, by the nineteenth century, being ruled by a European state. And these European states had a confidence that they (the Europeans) were civilized, had a knowledge of what was true and what constituted the ideal ordering of society; a confidence that could trace its lineage to the ideas spawned in the Enlightenment.

The nineteenth century also saw a resurgence in missionary activity: in 1792 the Baptist Missionary Society had been formed, in 1795 the London Missionary Society was founded, followed by the

Church Missionary Society in 1799 and the Wesleyan Missionary Society in 1813 (Smith, 1998). So, by the time of the upsurge in colonial activity in the 1800s, many missionary groups became involved with the expansionist endeavour, seeing an obvious opportunity and/or duty to evangelize and to convert. As Comby (1992: 118) points out, French bishops at the opening of the First Vatican Council in 1869 observed: 'Never since the foundation of the church has such a broad and easy way opened for the conversion of the infidels, or so wide a door, as in our time.' In other words, missionaries came to see European expansion as providential.

Colonizing states (and the people who were the colonizers) would presumably have appeared certain in the values and knowledge of their own societies and therefore did not question such values, in public at least. They therefore created a view of the colonized people as perhaps inferior, degenerate, savage and in need of improvement. Indeed, their own literature would have reaffirmed these beliefs and stereotypes; Robinson Crusoe merely dubs the 'native' he befriends as 'Friday', with no overt respect for 'Friday's' own perceptions of his name (Fleck, 1998). Myths of the 'White Man's Burden' would grow and reinforce the legitimizing sense of duty. As Mangan (1993) comments, 'Britain and Africa . . . [represented] opposite poles of a single system of values variously phrased as light opposed to darkness, civilisation to savagery, good to evil'; an opposition of the 'best way' of knowing the world against an 'inferior and imperfect' way of knowing the world. To all intents and purposes, this was truth versus falsehood.

If such was the view of colonial powers, how might the 'backward heathens' be brought to an appreciation of the truth? Clearly an obvious way would be through the education of children, and that is precisely what happened. Missionaries were deeply (though not exclusively) involved in this process. Although, as has been noted above, the motivation of many missionaries might have been one of conversion to the 'true' faith, the nature of the knowledge they were able to 'impose' on indigenous peoples via the education systems they established would also have suited the ambitions of the colonizing state, both by creating useful 'servants' of that state (i.e. equipping indigenous peoples to undertake useful administrative/functional duties on behalf of the colonizing state) and by reinforcing values that would also be useful (e.g. respect for authority). Indeed, Comby (1992) comes to the conclusion that missionaries were also often nationalists and came to be seen by indigenous peoples as being engaged on the same task as the soldiers and administrators of the ruling power.

Here it would be timely to sound a note of caution: firstly, it is very easy with the benefit of hindsight to criticize the actions of others and to ascribe motives to them which cannot be verified in any absolute way; and, secondly, it is easy to fall into the trap of considering a group of people to be homogeneous and to begin to attribute the same motives and beliefs to all members of the group. Patently, that is a nonsense. When considering the group 'missionaries', for example, although we might expect them all to be devout, well meaning people we cannot say it with any certainty. Equally, we cannot consider them all to be bigoted fanatics. Nor can all 'indigenous people' be seen as homogeneous, nor all 'colonizers', 'women', 'teachers' and so on. Thirdly, although the discussion will consider the nature of 'colonial education', that too will have varied widely, not only from place to place but in time as well.

Education for development

What, then, and how did children learn under the colonial regime? In particular, what was the nature of the knowledge it valued and imparted? Although there is evidence that, in the nineteenth century, missionaries often made a concerted effort to get to know local languages (see, for example, Comby, 1992: 123), it is also the case that for many children the language of instruction was that of the colonizing power. Thus, during the time of Bentinck (Governor General of India 1828–35), it was decided that English was to be the language of instruction in schools in India. Indeed, Bentinck also declared that the 'great object' of British rule in India was to be the 'promotion of European literature and science' (Smith, 1998: p. 51 citing Metcalf, Aftermath of Revolt, p. 22). And the domination of the English language in British colonies began with children of a young age. Focusing on Uganda between 1894 and 1939, for example, Okoth (1993) notes that English was the compulsory language to be used within the school bounds even for children of nursery age (indeed, English became the official language of Uganda). In other colonial countries, the official language of schools, of the law and of government became Spanish, French, Portuguese and so on.

Commenting on African missions as late as 1930, Comby (1992: 153) notes that in the Belgian Congo 'the church had a virtual monopoly on public teaching' and that 'Education was a universal preoccupation; the administrations encouraged it, requiring the language of the colonizing country to be taught'.

Commenting on Malayan education, Watson (1993) notes that the textbooks used portrayed British rulers as benefactors (a useful 'hegemonic ploy'; see later) and that traditional Malay society might be idyllic but was in reality backward. Watson (ibid.) also notes the apparent claims by some colonizers concerning Africans/Asians that they had no logic, no real religions and that there were links between the challenge of the climate and the absence of civilization. Children would also be taught the European names of the geographical features of their countries. Indeed, they would be taught that their countries had been 'discovered' by the Europeans, their mountains conquered, their rivers tamed. It was as if there had been no knowledge of the country before the colonial power took control; there was no real history before the advent of the Europeans.

Lessons on the gospels would have emphasized Christian ideals, beliefs and customs and it can be imagined that they would have given little consideration to prevailing indigenous religions (Mangan, 1993: 113). For example, the religious practices of the Africans in Kenya might well have appeared immoral to western eyes and would not be acknowledged as of worth: 'Such practice included polygamy, female circumcision, and what was seen as 'lewd' dancing during traditional ceremonies' (Natsoulos and Natsoulos, 1993: 112). And when considering education provision in the Indian state of Travancore, Kawashima (1998: 84) comments that the missionaries 'dominated in the area of western education in Travancore'. He continues to note that, in the 1860s, the missionaries considered their educational activities as an important means of proselytizing. One LMS (London Missionary Society) missionary of the time, a Mr Newport, wrote:

> The Heathen children at first stoutly refused to learn any Scripture Lessons like other children. They are however obliged to do so by the rules of the school . . . Very soon, they became much interested in the lessons and now learn them with as much zest as the Christian themselves and in some cases have even greater knowledge of the Christian religion than those who profess it (cited in ibid.: 88).

Samuel Mateer, another LMS missionary, stated in 1871:

> Education is thus spreading in a remarkable degree in this interesting country, and must inevitably bring with it, by the blessing of God, the downfall of superstition, error, and oppression, and be a means of introducing an era of national enlightenment, progress and freedom (cited in ibid.: 92).

Textbooks might well have set problems within colonial rather than indigenous contexts. Imagine the children of Kenya approaching this one: This example, cited in Natsoulos and Natsoulos is from: Bishop, 1990. 'The escalator at Holborn tube station is 156 feet long and makes the ascent in 65 seconds. Find the speed in miles per hour' (cited in Natsoulos and Natsoulos, 1993: 113). Okoth (1993: 145) talks of the central part that music played in the daily lives of Ugandan people prior to colonialization and how 'the teaching of African music was prohibited because the missionaries claimed that it was part of "paganism"'.

And so we might continue to cite a wealth of other examples to demonstrate how the influence of the colonial power via the education systems of the colonized countries appeared to act in such a way as to over-ride the indigenous culture and to put in its place a western view of the world and what *it* considered to be worthwhile, 'correct' knowledge. Many readers considering the examples cited would conclude that they demonstrated the actions of bigots and racists. The curriculum would be seen as little more than the imposition of one society's norms on to another for selfish reasons through an abuse of power. Would that be a fair criticism? What was the purpose of the education offered to indigenous peoples under colonial rule?

A kindly view would conclude that the purpose was to bring about improvement. It was merely an expression of one human being wishing to assist another in coming to understand a useful body of knowledge. This was powerful knowledge that could save lives, control pain, increase agricultural production and enhance the quality of human existence. If one believes one has access to a beneficial truth, is it not reasonable to share that knowledge? Indeed, would it not be reprehensible *not* to share it? However, so-called 'modern' knowledge has had a chequered history. It has been used to support arguments which so-called 'proved' the inferiority of Jews, racial links between intelligence and race and so on. Its position as somehow 'true' is open to huge challenges.

A less kindly, yet still reasonably benevolent, view would conclude that the purpose was to bring a heathen people to the knowledge of an all-powerful, all-loving God. Again, this could be interpreted as the action of a caring person and, again, it is easy to see how people firmly believing in a faith would respond. If a person honestly felt he or she was being ordered by God to take a particular action (so-called 'Divine Command Theory'; see, for example, Holmes, 1993) then he or she would be literally 'duty bound' to undertake that action. Again, should he or she deny such a call, believing it to be true?

A less sanguine view would conclude that the education provided was there in order to provide a level of skill and knowledge in those indigenous peoples necessary to meet the administrative demands of the ruling state. Thus, it would be necessary to educate certain selected people to assume relatively low-level positions of authority in order to ensure the smooth running of the bureaucracy of colonialization. A purpose of colonial education would have been the creation of a class of people fitted for, as an example, the colonial civil service of the imperial power. And these were to be people not only skilled in the application of particular knowledge but also people who could be trusted because, as in Macauley's minute of 1835 to the Board of Directors of the East India Company: '. . . we must at present do our best to form a class who may be interpreters between us and the millions we govern – a class of persons Indian in blood and colour but English in tastes, opinions, in morals and in intellect' (Watson, 1993: 155). A sterner view would be that the ruling elite would use education to prove that they were, by right and by rational argument, in an unassailable position of power and authority compared to those they ruled. Bauman (1993) provides another comment on the way in which such 'otherness' is perceived. He muses that time stands for a kind of hierarchy in which 'later' becomes identified with 'better'. Such a view he considers to have fitted well 'the need to legitimise the conquest and subordination of different lands and cultures, and that of presenting the growth and spread of knowledge as the principal mechanism not just of change, but of change to the better – of *improvement*' (ibid.: 38–9; see also Sutcliffe, 1999).

Other authors would point to the patriarchal nature of the knowledge imparted by colonial education: 'The central figure of Western humanist and Enlightenment discourse, the humane, knowing subject now stands revealed as a white, *male* colonialist' (Loomba, 1998: 66, emphasis added; see also Visvanathan et al., 1997). Or they would point to its ability to reinforce social or ethnic divides already present.[2] Yet others would point out the tension in status between procedural knowledge (knowledge *how*) and propositional knowledge (knowledge *that*) and how the latter might be afforded higher status (see, for example, Gould, 1993: 118).

Take as an example of this tension the contentious nature of 'vocational' knowledge. As Natsoulos and Natsoulos (1993) point out with regard to 'colonial Kenya', certain so-called 'industrial schools' offered a technical training which consisted of 'carpentry, masonry work, agriculture, saddlery, coach and wagon building, brick and tile works, general building, telegraphy, hospital dressers, tailoring, printing, gardening and road construction'. Surely, this could be seen as an attempt to match education to the needs of students? Not all students would be suited (so runs the argument) to an academic career. Why not teach them useful crafts and trades, a 'technical education'? (See, for example, Iber Der Thiam, 1984, for an impassioned advocacy of this approach.) Yet such vocational education could also be interpreted as a way of subjugating others by denying them access to knowledge which was in any way linked to power, and that schools might thus merely 'reproduce' the structures and hierarchies of society (see, for example, Apple, 1979). Vocational education, so runs this side of the argument, would merely keep people in their places, no matter what the well intentioned motives of the teachers who provided it. However, it is salutary to note that Ghandi advocated a return to the traditional skills of Indian village life as part of his drive for independence (Woodcock, 1972; James, 1997). Nothing, it seems, is straightforward.

Knowledge and political independence

Whatever the rights and wrongs, an obvious result of the colonial system was that, over a number of years, certain indigenous peoples became, finally, imbued with 'western knowledge' whilst still (at the level of a 'whole culture'), perhaps, retaining some elements of the original knowledge of their own societies. Generations of children, wishing to be considered 'educated' and wishing to attain the apparent benefits accruing from such an education (and their parents, wishing the best for their children or, vicariously, for themselves), would have participated in the colonial education being offered. Nevertheless, as might be expected, the mere fact of participating in the colonial education on offer, for all its attempts to impose the dominant ideologies of the colonizing power, would not bar pupils/students from considering the imposition of that power and its ideologies as an injustice. Thus, over time, elements of this 'western' knowledge were adopted, embraced and improved upon in their turn by certain pupils who were indigenous. Although perhaps originally intended to have a training sufficient only to enter the colonial civil service (e.g. as clerks, teachers, medical assistants) in order to support the efficient running of empire, these former pupils, aided by acquiring literacy in western languages to a level beyond that intended by their teachers, were able to take western knowledge and principles and use them in argument against the colonial power (Bernstein, 2000): 'They were able to articulate their resistance to foreign domination through turning principles of democracy and justice (and sometimes the vocabulary of socialism) against their colonial masters' (ibid.: 267).

In addition, those arguing for independence might well have been versed in Christian teaching and could thus use arguments relating to Christian belief – e.g. how the notion of Christian love required all people to be seen as of equal worth in the eyes of God and that a fundamental tenet was the relief of suffering (ibid.). One might also note the effects of the dissatisfaction of indigenous people who, although supposedly educated, were denied the highest posts in the civil service or education or the army of the colonial power. Watson (1993) comments on this circumstance as causing discontent between educated Indians and the Raj. Such pressures were a spur to the rise of nationalist movements and the drive towards independence.

It is perhaps simplistic to observe that no nation has a monopoly on thought, and that thought cannot be entirely constrained and shaped by the blandishments of teachers and others in positions of power. History demonstrates that there are people who, although virtually indoctrinated into one way of thinking, are able to liberate themselves from such shackles and to think in creative ways that differ from the 'required' norms of an education system. Thus was born a challenge to the old rhetoric of colonialism; the appearance of a generation of *indigenous* thinkers, reformers, surgeons, politicians or whatever; individuals who were every bit as accomplished in using western modernist knowledge as the colonial masters themselves; and people who could play the old leaders at their own game and show themselves to be, at least, equal.

The reasons for the 'granting' and 'gaining' of political independence are complex. However, it is apparent that the articulation of arguments against colonial rule and in favour of independence would require the advocacy of people well versed in the knowledge systems of the colonial power; thus the moves to independence were aided by the very education system that had sought to retain the colonial status quo. The very system which had required its pupils to adopt a western epistemology and method of argument had furnished those same pupils with the only armaments to which the western view was vulnerable – i.e. its own. Indeed, it is, perhaps, the supreme irony that it was western education which encouraged such accomplishment in western thought processes which led eventually to the rejection and overthrow of direct western rule. One wonders how Livingstone would have regarded such events had he been alive: 'As far as I am myself concerned, the opening of the new central country is a matter for congratulation only in so far as it opens up a prospect for the elevation of the inhabitants' (Comby, 1992: 120, citing Livingstone, 1857).

In the event, by the late 1960s, most previously colonized countries had become politically independent. Yet for all that they were politically independent, they were not ideologically free as they found themselves operating in a world system of capitalism in many ways controlled not by themselves but rather by their former colonial masters/mistresses. This 'post-colonial' power of the western/northern states had been maintained in a variety of ways. For example, in 1944 the Bretton Woods agreement was reached. This was an attempt to restructure the world economy but, as Hewitt (2000: 291) points out, of the 44 nations represented, most of the developing countries were from Latin America and the event was dominated by the USA and Britain. This was hardly a true representation of the international community.

Two of the institutions set up by the Bretton Woods agreement included the International Bank for Reconstruction and Development (later to be called the World Bank) and the International Monetary Fund. Through these institutions, the 'financial, economic and political workings of the world were to be regulated and monitored' (ibid.). It is the case that the President of the World Bank, according to its constitution, should be a US citizen (Allen and Thomas, 2000: 204). Bretton Woods can thus be seen to have been more favourable to the 'continued dominant position in the world economy of those developed countries which later formed the OECD' (Hewitt, 2000: 291).[3] The world cake, it would seem, was still being carved according to northern wishes.

Newly independent countries were thus required to operate in a system which continued to value northern knowledge, which required participation in northern trading systems and which saw 'development' as being the promotion of modernity achieved largely through economic growth. And economic growth meant capitalism if for no other reason than that this was the accepted orthodoxy of the societies *defining* the orthodoxy: 'The key to prosperity and happiness was increased production' (Rist, 1997: 76; see also Rostow, 1960; and Easterly, 2001, for a current view of a World Bank employee).

If a developing country were to wish to participate successfully in the world economic system, it is clear that the education systems of that country would have to prepare its citizens for such participation. If a developing country was to receive so-called 'development funding' it would be necessary for it to toe the orthodox economic line as defined by those offering the funding. One can recognize that a probable effect on education would be to maintain the predominance of the old colonial values (after all, the old colonial states were providing the money for development and making the conditions for its deployment) achieved through a curriculum and a pedagogy which owed their shape to the imposition of norms on pupils which had been essentially determined by colonial power. (These 'global' issues are considered in the next chapter but see, for example, commentary on the effects of 'structural adjustment' in Rist, 1997; Allen and Thomas, 2000.)

The legacy

One might note the legacy of the colonial system of education. At a technical level, as Watkins (2000: 3) points out, some of that legacy includes 'top-down educational planning, irrelevant curricula, inappropriate languages of instruction, and an undue emphasis on rote learning'. Yet the legacy goes beyond technical considerations. It has shaped the philosophy of education and nowhere more so than in the debate as to what constitutes worthwhile knowledge. Knowledge is a commodity, and its possession is a route to power, and especially the power, currently, of the economy[4] and, although one might value traditional knowledge, one's own language, one's own rituals, art, modes of thought, and might wish to preserve and honour them, if they do not contribute to the global position of the state, they are unlikely to be prioritized, valued, promoted and paid for via the education system of a state operating, willingly or otherwise, on a global stage.

Much of the preceding discussion has been focused on mass education systems. Yet mass education systems, although usually controlled by the state for its own ends (otherwise, why fund a mass education system?), are experienced by individuals. Is it therefore possible to identify apparent benefits of such education systems that *most* people, no matter what their geographical, social or economic location, might agree to be benefits? Are there benefits of education, not at global or national level, but at a level at which most individuals might see it as a positive event?

Firstly, one might point out the possible benefits of science, though even here, as Coulby and Jones (1995: 32) wryly comment, 'After the destruction of Hiroshima and Nagasaki, the benevolence of the Enlightenment would never again receive unhesitating endorsement'. Nevertheless, it is perhaps reasonable to assume that most people would prefer surgical procedures to be completed with, rather than without, an anaesthetic, and education in the ways of 'modern' science would have contributed to the necessary understanding and skill. In addition, apart from teaching the actual technology of 'modern' medicine, education apparently offers (currently) potentially huge health benefits. For example, in almost all developing countries, 'death rates are inversely related to the level of maternal education' (Watkins, 2000: 29). Levels of, in particular, literacy amongst mothers are, it seems, strongly linked to the health of children in developing countries. Then again, despite the arguments concerning the 'best' ways to distribute the world's wealth, education *can* offer a way out of poverty for some, and the opportunity to participate on a more equal footing in the world's markets. It can provide the language and, to some extent, the confidence necessary to challenge other views and opinions.

In short, it would seem that education *can* enhance the empowerment of peoples to influence the policies and institutions which affect their lives. However, whether this is 'improvement' in any absolute sense is again open to all the questions raised previously and even these few paragraphs assume that there is a consensus as to what constitutes 'benefit'. It is so easy to fall into the trap of thinking everyone else is the same as oneself, with the same value systems and aspirations. Who can say *with certainty* that anaesthetics are a 'good thing'? Nevertheless, whatever one's personal vision of what constitutes important knowledge and the purposes to which it can be put, education has been and still is inextricably bound up with the process of the construction and dissemination of knowledge. Thus education has played a significant part in creating the power relations in the world today and, although there may have been benefits to indigenous peoples themselves through the introduction of 'modern' knowledge, there may also have been costs, as part of gaining a new culture is the losing of at least part of an old one.

Prior to this point in the chapter, there has been no acknowledgement that 'education' is, itself, a contested term. However, it is important to note that the 'aims' of education are not necessarily the same as the 'purposes' to which education is put (see Bartlett et al., 2001, for further discussion). Thus one might describe the aims of education in terms designed to be value neutral (e.g. 'the pursuit of truth') yet the *purposes* to which such a process is put might be far from value free (as, indeed, might be the *processes* by which the determination of truth might be conducted and analysed). In addition, the word 'education' has often been used throughout the colonial and post-colonial periods (and not just in the developing world) to mean something *less* than education and often *nothing more* than training or even indoctrination. Yet, education is surely far more than 'solemn pronouncements of the needs of future citizens' (Walsh, 1993: 90); it is about challenge, liberation and choice. A so-called education that deliberately restricts cannot be considered truly educative, as the end point of education is unknown whereas that of training *is* known (for a discussion, see, for example, Hamm, 1989). The self-styled 'education' that has been offered as part of 'development' might therefore not be *education* at all, but a variant of training or indoctrination, offering a restricted access to certain knowledge. How might such a process be accomplished?

How can *ideologies* be transmitted through the channel of so-called *education* and still find themselves embedded in the minds of others? Going to school is clearly *not* the same as becoming educated.

Analysis of hegemony

A possible model of the hegemony of education is shown in Figure 10.1. Readers are invited to consider its applicability to the control of knowledge as applied to developing countries, such application resulting from either the political regimes internal to a country or as a result of external pressure arising from other states supplying development funding or both.

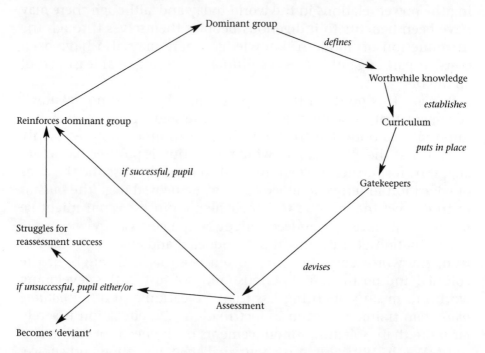

Figure 10.1 *How education systems can be used to maintain power relations in a society*

Firstly, it is necessary to recognize that the 'dominant group' is not necessarily the same as the government. Governments are in power because someone else either encourages them or allows them to be in power. Even a despot has to have supporters in order to survive. The dominant group of one state may be dominated by other groups from other states, of course, but in the event the dominant group can determine (as a result of its power) what is worthwhile knowledge. Interestingly, any one society is unlikely to reach consensus as to what constitutes worthwhile knowledge (one has only to look at the letters page of a local newspaper to see that the debates still rage) and despite the best efforts of philosophers to determine if there is a fundamental core of knowledge, absolute, universally applicable and free of values (see, for example, the work of Phenix, 1964; Hirst, 1965), the dominant group can impose its will by virtue, self-evidently, of its dominance.

For the missionaries working in the nineteenth century and for the colonial powers of that time, the content of their education systems and the apparent right to impose it were defined and legitimized by firstly, modernity, the 'glamorous, fashionable' knowledge of its time and, secondly, Christian faith; this view *was* imposed on more than one generation of children. In 1988, the Education Reform Act in the UK *did* impose a view of worthwhile knowledge; the study of the subjects of the National Curriculum is required by law. In 1967, President Nyereyre *did* impose his view as to what was necessary to achieve 'self-reliance'. In 2002, the dominant group in the UK *is still* imposing its will (e.g. Key Stage 3 numeracy and literacy strategies, notions of what constitutes 'good citizenship') and inspection and funding ensure accountability vis-à-vis the views of the dominant group. Domination of education is not an event limited solely to developing countries. Knowledge is power and whoever wishes to have power must control knowledge, both its definition and its supposed attainment.

The content of a 'mass education' curriculum will reflect the content of what is considered to be the worthwhile knowledge as defined/agreed by the dominant group. In addition, it will enshrine an approach to learning about that knowledge, a pedagogy. At one extreme of the pedagogy there will be the transmission model the so-called 'empty vessel' model and at the other extreme a 'constructivist' model. The former model favours didactic teaching because, by its tenets, the teacher literally knows best whereas the constructivist model tends to promote a pedagogy that values inquiry and challenge (see, for example, Pollard, 1997).

In this context, it is interesting to note the work of Paulo Freire, who wrote extensively on the role of pedagogy, notably in relation to 'the oppressed'. Freire opposed what he called 'banking concept education' (at its simplest, the transmission model referred to above) to 'problem-posing education'. Freire viewed the former as a virtual insult to human rights, reducing people to mere receivers of information who did not have the opportunity to question – 'For apart from inquiry . . . individuals cannot be truly human' (Freire, in Freire and Macedo, 1998: 68) – whereas the latter approach was a way in which people might 'fight for their emancipation' (ibid.: 79). The nub of his argument was that it was possible to devise a *pedagogy* that stimulated a sense of worth and capability in those taught, empowering them, in effect. In Freire's work in South America and elsewhere the *pedagogy itself* was seen as being a liberating force; 'true' education, he argued, could be used to challenge the political status quo. It is interesting to speculate what would happen if a teacher in the UK offered a series of lessons which taught children *how* to challenge the status quo of the current UK political system.

Knowledge is not the sole gift of teachers: textbooks, too, are potent transmitters and shapers of knowledge. And not just books per se; distance-learning packages, software and the Internet can also be considered in this category. The content can reflect any view the author likes but because textbooks/ICT packages/the web (as used by educational establishments) are constrained by finance and, in order to sell, must dance (or at least resonate) to the power base of the day, content is likely to reflect/define acceptable/dominant attitudes and values, is likely to reinforce notions of 'worthwhile knowledge' and is likely to use existing arguments (no challenge to the status quo). Textbooks (and other such resources) epitomize the concern that when we think and communicate, we have less autonomy than we often claim because we use the rules of thinking (e.g. what counts as significant, what rules of evidence we will adopt) that have been devised by the people who precede us (Cherryholme, 1988, musing on the work of Foucault; see also Wolfreys, 1998).

Such resources might also determine *how* the teacher teaches and yet, surely, such decisions are rightly the province of the professional *teacher* as being, at the very least, an informed guide between 'the message' and 'education' and 'the pupil'. Yet in the absence of trained teachers, what else is available as a source of apparent 'authority'? In 1991, Lockhead and Verspoors said of developing countries: 'Teachers lack not only text books but also the teacher guides that supplement text books' (p. 53) and, in 2000, Watkins (with a specific focus on Uganda) commented on the potentially prohibitive cost of textbooks to poor households, and the 'serious problems . . . in the delivery of books to schools'. Uganda has adopted a target of 'one book per child for each subject by 2003' (p. 300). Thus, textbooks (and electronic sources) are recognized as having a potentially important role to play yet, before they have even entered the field, they are seen to be constrained and thus might often be far removed from the notion of freedom and choice, which is, arguably, education.

At the next stage in the hegemonic cycle, teachers (amongst others) stand as gatekeepers, deciding who shall enter the citadel and who shall not, those who pass and those who fail. Yet what is it that pupils are passing or failing? It is clear that teachers themselves are versed in the ideologies of the dominant group through their initial teacher training, continuing professional development and promotion criteria and are thus likely to reinforce the dominant group's view of worthwhile knowledge. But who has determined the *worth* of the knowledge, let alone the reliability and validity of the test? The assessment of knowledge is also problematic and culturally influenced (see, for example, Gipps and Murphy, 1994). The argument goes round and round but the hegemony is maintained.

Conclusion

That is it, then. Education is no more than the control of one group of people by another for selfish ends, and the world might as well accept injustice, disease, poverty, inequity and ignorance. Not necessarily. Although education systems and 'schooling' are susceptible to political hijack, education itself is not. Indeed, paradoxically, education per se is probably the most powerful route by which the *manipulation* of learning can be recognized and challenged. Education incorporates the open, free consideration of the human condition, a consideration that transcends political or selfish control and is sensitive to cultural differences and similarities. It has the power to recognize and expose hegemony, the power to make equable decisions, the power to transform lives.

Despite several thousand years of practice, however, education as actively practised across the world is in its infancy. There are still huge issues to confront, methods to debate and purposes to clarify. Yet, fallible as the attempts to 'educate' might be, they seem to be worthwhile. At one level, this 'worthwhileness' is at a limited, utilitarian stage. However, why should a utilitarian approach be derided if a result is that many parents are now able to read the instructions on a medical advice leaflet and so prevent the unnecessary deaths of their children? Yet the potential of education extends beyond the utilitarian. It extends to the empowerment of people; it enables people to have the tools to consider choices and to guide, challenge, judge and then promote or reject those decisions which affect their lives and the lives of others. Imperfect as current approaches might be, development policies are beginning to recognize the part that education can play in the achievement of such goals. Thus UNICEF includes as a desired outcome for children that they should learn 'to respect diversity, practise equality, and resolve differences without violence' (UNICEF, 2002: 2) and Oxfam (2002: 2) comments 'Education is important above all because it empowers people to take more control of their lives . . .'.

The aspirations of education might become perverted on the world stage, and it is necessary that one is alert to the processes by which such perversion might be accomplished. Nevertheless, it is also important to recognize and celebrate the potential of education. Knowledge may well be power but education is *liberation*.

Student tasks

1 Some of the people who became involved in colonialization did so because they truly believed they were doing the right thing and that their actions would improve the lives of others. Within such a context of 'development', how should anyone decide if he or she is 'doing the right thing' and how should he or she subsequently behave if convinced of that 'rightness'?

2 Identify what you judge to be a current human injustice created through what you consider to be an abuse of power in the past. How would you set it right?

Suggested further reading

Allen, T. and Thomas, A. (eds) (2000) *Poverty and Development: Into the 21st Century*. Oxford: Oxford University Press. Although often adopting an ultimately economic perspective, this book offers a good, general introduction to development issues, including their historical roots.

Rist, G. (1997) *The History of Development: From Western Origins to Global Faith*. London: Zed Books. A rather more challenging read, which provides an excellent overview of the history of development combined with an intellectually provocative commentary.

Watkins, K. (2000) *The Oxfam Education Report*. Oxford: Oxfam. Any analysis of development issues requires the reader to have some comprehension of current affairs. This book provides a cogent report on the state of educational provision in the developing world at the time of writing.

Notes

1 The term 'western' is taken to mean equating to western Europe and is used in the text to denote a locus of 'modernist' knowledge prior to the formation of the USA. The term 'northern' is taken to mean a later 'modernist-derived' power base that includes as a minimum western Europe and the USA; the terminology builds on the findings of the Brandt Report (1980). The term 'indigenous' is taken to refer to any society that might reasonably claim that a certain geographical location is where that society lives and has lived beyond the memory of direct, personal experience and might justifiably claim as having been 'home', prior to any period of European expansion. 'Nation' and 'state' are used interchangeably and mean an amalgamation of societies which results in an overall homogeneity of interest or some other commonality. This does not ignore ethnic or political minorities within such a configuration. It is recognized that these terms are in themselves contentious and loosely applied.

2 It is useful to recognize that the education offered to 'indigenous' peoples would have mirrored the education offered to the 'people at home'. Curricula for the growing mass domestic consumption, for example, would doubtless have cast women in the same light, as well as reinforcing notions of social class.

3 The OECD, formed in 1961, stands for Organization for Economic Co-operation and Development. Its membership of 25 developed countries is drawn largely from Western Europe and North America, but includes Japan, New Zealand and Australia (see Hewitt, 2000: 291).

4 'Economy' is only a current fashion. Tomorrow, it might be health, or the rights of men, or the sustainability of the environment. Knowledge can serve them all.

References

Allen, T. and Thomas, A. (eds) (2000) *Poverty and Development: Into the 21st Century*. Oxford: Oxford University Press.

Apple, M. (1979) *Ideology and Curriculum*. London: Routledge & Keegan Paul.

Bartlett, S., Burton, D. and Peim, N. (2001) *Introduction to Education Studies*. London: Paul Chapman Publishing.

Bauman, Z. (1993) *Postmodern Ethics*. Oxford: Blackwell.

Bernstein, H. (2000) Colonialism, capitalism, development. In T. Allen, and A. Thomas (eds) *Poverty and Development: Into the 21st Century*. Oxford: Oxford University Press, pp. 241–70.

Brandt, W. (1980) *North–South: A Programme for Survival. Report of the Independent Commission on International Development* (the Brandt Report). London: Pan Books.

Bishop, A.J. 'Western mathematics: the secret weapon of cultural imperialism' *Race and class* (1990), 32(2): 53.

Cherryholme, C. (1988) An exploration of meanings and the dialogue between textbooks and teaching. *Journal of Curriculum Studies*, 20(1): 1–21.

Comby, J. (1992 trans. J. Bowden 1996) *How to Understand the History of Christian Mission*. London: SCM Press.

Coulby, D. and Jones, C. (1995) *Postmodernity and European Education Systems*. Stoke-on-Trent: Trentham Books.

DFID (2001) *The challenge of universal primary education*. London: DFID.

Easterly, W. (2001) *The Elusive Quest for Growth: Economists' Adventures and Misadventures in the Tropics*. London: MIT Press.

Fleck, A. (1998) Crusoe's shadow: Christianity, colonization and the Other. In J.C. Hawley (ed.) *Historicizing Christian Encounters with the Other*. Basingstoke: Macmillan pp. 74–89.

Freire, P. (1972a) *Pedagogy of the Oppressed*. Harmondsworth: Penguin Books.

Freire, P. (1972b) *Cultural Action for Freedom*. Harmondsworth: Penguin Books.

Freire, A.M.A. and Macedo, D. (eds) (1998) *The Paulo Freire Reader*. New York: Continuum.

Gipps, C. and Murphy, P. (1994) *A Fair Test? Assessment, Achievement and Equity*. Buckingham: Open University Press.

Gould, W.T.S (1993) *People and Education in the Third World*. Harlow: Longman.

Hamm, C.M. Philosophical issues in education: an introduction. London: Falmer Press.

Hardin, G. (1994) Lifeboat ethics: the case against helping the poor. In J.P. Sterbe (ed.) *Morality in Practice* (4th edn). Belmont, CA: Wadsworth, pp. 81–9.

Hawley, J.C. (ed.) (1998) *Historicizing Christian Encounters with the Other*. Basingstoke: Macmillan.

Hewitt, T. (2000) Half a century of development. In T. Allen and A. Thomas (eds) *Poverty and Development: Into the 21st Century*. Oxford: Oxford University Press, pp. 289–308.

Hirst, P.H. (1965) Liberal education and the nature of knowledge. Reprinted in *Knowledge and the Curriculum* (1974). London: Routledge & Kegan Paul.

Holmes, R.L. (1993) *Basic Moral Philosophy*. Belmont, CA: Wadsworth.

Iber Der Thiam (1984) In *Education Priorities and Aid Responses in Sub-Saharan Africa. ODA/University of London Institute of Education Conference Report.* London: HMSO, pp. 23–6.

James, L. (1997) *Raj: The Making and Unmaking of British India.* London: Abacus.

Kawashima, K. (1998) *Missionaries and a Hindu State: Travancore, 1858–1936.* Oxford: Oxford University Press.

Larrain, J. (1994) *Ideology and Cultural Identity: Modernity and the Third World Presence.* Oxford: Blackwell.

Lochead, M.E. and Verspoor, A.M. (with associates) (1991) *Improving Primary Education in Developing Countries.* Oxford: Oxford University Press for the World Bank.

Loomba, A. (1998) *Colonialism/Postcolonialism.* London: Routledge.

Mangan, J.A. (1993) *The Imperial Curriculum: Racial Images and Education in the British Colonial Experience.* London: Routledge.

Meighan, R. and Siraj-Blatchford, I. (1997) *A Sociology of Educating.* London: Cassell Education.

Munck, R. and O'Hearn, D. (eds) (1999) *Critical Development Theory: Contributions to a New Paradigm.* London: Zed Books.

Natsoulos, A. and Natsoulos T. (1993) Racism, the school and African education in colonial Kenya. In J.A. Mangan (ed.) *The Imperial Curriculum: Racial Images and Education in the British Colonial Experience.* London: Routledge, pp. 108–34.

Okoth, P.G. (1993) The creation of a dependent culture: the imperial school curriculum in Uganda. In J.A. Mangan (ed.) *The Imperial Curriculum: Racial Images and Education in the British Colonial Experience.* London: Routledge, pp. 135–46.

Oxfam (2002) *Education and Poverty* (http://www.oxfam.org.uk/educationnow /poverty.htm. Accessed 18 May 2002).

Phenix, P.H. (1964) *Realms of Meaning.* New York: McGraw-Hill.

Pollard, A. (1997) *Reflective Teaching in the Primary School* (3rd edn). London: Cassell Education.

Rist, G. (1997) *The History of Development: From Western Origins to Global Faith.* London: Zed Books.

Rostow, W.W. (1960) *The Stages of Economic Growth: A non-communist Manifesto.* Cambridge: Cambridge University Press.

Smith, S. (1998) *British Imperialism 1750–1970.* Cambridge: Cambridge University Press.

Stanley, B. (1990) *The Bible and the Flag: Protestant Missions and British Imperialism in the Nineteenth and Twentieth Centuries.* Leicester: Apollos, Inter-Varsity Press.

Sterbe, J.P. (ed.) (1994) *Morality in Practice* (4th edn). Belmont, CA: Wadsworth.

Sutcliffe, B. (1999) The place of development in theories of imperialism and globalization. In R. Munck and D. O'Hearn (eds) *Critical Development Theory: Contributions to a New Paradigm.* London: Zed Books, pp. 135–54.

Tucker, V. (1999) The myth of development: a critique of a Eurocentric discourse. In R. Munck and D. O'Hearn (eds) *Critical Development Theory: Contributions to a New Paradigm.* London: Zed Books, pp. 1–26.

UNICEF (2002) *Education is a Right* (http://www.unicef.org/pdeduc/education/policy/htm. Accessed 18 May 2002).

Visvanathan, N. et al. (eds) (1997) *The Women, Gender and Development Reader*. London: Zed Books.

Wallerstein, I. (1991) *Unthinking Social Science: The Limits of Nineteenth Century Paradigms*. Cambridge and Oxford: Polity Press with Blackwell.

Walsh, P. (1993) *Education and Meaning: Philosophy in Practice*. London: Cassell Education.

Watkins, K. (2000) *The Oxfam Education Report*. Oxford: Oxfam.

Watson, K. (1993) Rulers and ruled: racial perceptions, curriculum and schooling in colonial Malaya and Singapore. In J.A. Mangan (ed.) *The Imperial Curriculum: Racial Images and Education in the British Colonial Experience*. London: Routledge, pp. 147–74.

Wolfreys, J. (1998) *Deconstruction: Derrida*. Basingstoke: Macmillan.

Woodcock, G. (1972) *Gandhi*. London: Fontana.

11

Contemporary Globalization and Education

John Robinson

This chapter considers the various debates relating to contemporary global-ization as a social, cultural, economic and political combination of processes. The relationship between globalization and education is explored through a selected group of issues that refer to knowledge production and curriculum change, the internationalizing of education, the role of the Internet in creat-ing online communities and debates concerning feminism. The chapter then goes on to explore the inter-relationship between globalization, social justice and environmental justice, and argues that environmental justice is social justice and that educational institutions can have a negative and a positive impact in this arena. The chapter then focuses on a case study of one UK sec-ondary school to try to understand the complex relationship between contemporary globalization and teaching and learning. Finally, the negative impacts of contemporary globalization are juxtaposed with the rhetorical nature of the Utopian claims for contemporary globalization.

Introduction

There can be no doubt that *globalization* is a process and a product that affects all our lives in some way – whether it be through the consequences of what happened on 11 September[1] or whether it concerns the products we consume at home. For some, globaliza-tion is about the emergence of supranational institutions whose decisions shape and constrain policy options for any particular nation-state. For others, it means the overwhelming impact of global economic processes of production, consumption, trade, capital flow and monetary independence. For others still, it signals the rise of economic liberalism as a dominant policy discourse. For some, it is about changing cultural forms, communications technologies, the shaping and reshaping of identities and interactions within and between cultures. For others globalization is a product, the construction of policy-makers responding to the demands of organizations such as the World Bank (WB), the International Monetary Fund (IMF) and the World Trade Organization (WTO) which leave governments with 'no choice' but to play by a complex set of global rules, rules not of their making. Whether one adopts a process or a product philosophy regarding globalization it is possible to see globalization as having a dark side or a light side – like fire – which has both its supporters and its detractors. In this chapter I am going to explore some of these issues in relation to education and globalization, to examine the light and the shade of this relationship and to focus on the nature of the impact of globalization on the central issues of social and environmental justice.

What is or might globalization be?

Globalization, in some shape or form, has been a fact of human exchange for a significant part of our histories. What we are concerned with here, though, is what might be referred to as *contemporary globalization* that some commentators place as having its origins in the world petroleum crisis between 1971 and 1973.

From the 1970s onwards, significant changes in the nature of global economic patterns and structures have been experienced. This restructuring had several significant elements:

- A new international division of labour and the economic integration of national economies such as through emerging common markets (such as the European Union) and trade agreements.
- New economic exchange relations between and amongst nation-states and amongst classes and social sectors within countries where information exchange and service industries are seen to be more important than manufacturing industries, particularly in less developed countries (LDCs).

- An increasing internationalization of trade and connectivity of markets which is based on the spread of multinational or transnational corporations (TNCs) who control 25 per cent of the world economy and 80 per cent of world trade and who can move 'capital' between and within countries by moving it within the corporation.
- A restructuring of labour markets, with 'hourly pay'/salaried service being replaced by piecework, unions undermined and short-term temporary contracting of labour.
- A decrease in labour conflicts (largely because of the surplus and mobility of labour) and an increase in competition, decreasing profit margins and less protective labour agreements.
- An increasing flexibility of the labour force, labour processes and labour markets with a decline in the costs of labour and an increase in the speed of movement of products and information from one locale to another.
- Changes in the means and forces of production with the impact of new technologies, particularly robotics within a context of a high-tech information society.
- An increasing importance of capital-intensive production resulting from deskilling or redundancies on a wide scale in large, traditional sections of the workforce, which led to a polarized labour market with a small, highly skilled, well paid and relatively well protected sector and a large, low-skilled, low-paid, unprotected sector.
- An increase in part-time working, female labour and home-working (Burbules and Torres, 2000).

These changes went hand in hand with the adoption of neo-liberal economic policies by many nation-states. At the same time global economic downturns have put increasing pressure on the financial demands of the welfare state in many nations, with the funding of social services, health services, housing and education all being affected, one of the consequences of which was an increasing privatization of these welfare services. Thus the relationship between the state and its workers changed – probably irrevocably. Two types of citizens were created – those protected or included by the state who have access to jobs and enhanced life chances and those unprotected or excluded from employment with reduced life chances, with the latter group being the larger group, often comprising women living in poverty in both advanced industrialized nations (AINs) and LDCs (Offe, 1985; Harvey, 1989). The consequences of these changes have been a unification of capital on a global scale, under the ownership of the TNCs , with workers and other subordinate groups being fragmented, divided and deskilled.

A further consequence of these changes has been an increasing reliance on 'the market' to solve the problems which the unification of capital has brought about – a lessening of environmental quality and a decrease in social justice. In education the privatization of parts of the service has been sold as an increase in consumer choice, with the market forcing up standards as 'consumers' become more choosy about the products they wish to 'purchase'. It is argued that the WB, the IMF and the WTO had contributed to a decline in the power of national governments. National governments are largely concerned with national issues and many have shown a lack of political will to deal with the negative consequences of globalization. Global businesses have a global constituency. Consequently global businesses are well placed to fill the vacuum left by this apparent lack of political will to deal with the negative consequences of globalization (Robinson, M2002). This development gives capital (and capitalists) considerable leverage over nation-states, although this leverage is often exercised indirectly. Intellectual leaders (that is, leaders of large corporations who have become established as business gurus) set the limits of policy options for nation-states (Korten, 1995), allowing the AINs to 'control' the LDCs under the banner of contemporary globalization which, as we shall see later, can be regarded as a contemporary form of imperialism or colonialism. An increasingly borderless world limits and delimits the powers of nation-states to control their own economies. Globalization, then, or contemporary globalization, refers to a set of technological, economic and cultural changes. Globalization has become a regime of truth of the 1990s, 'imbued with its own rationality and self-fulfilling logic' (Blackmore, 2000: 131).

Whilst it is difficult to dispute these changes, what is debatable are the extent and the consequences of globalization. The history of the changes that we characterize as globalization has meant that the changes have not been uniform in their manner, their spread nor their impact. Furthermore, the future of globalization is equally difficult to be certain about. There are several, competing stories of globalization's future – from the saviour of humankind to the end of the world Utopias and dystopias – and like any story of the future they can come true and they might not.

Globalization and the internationalizing of education

The foregoing summary of contemporary globalization gives rise to a consideration of several different issues as they relate to the relationship between education and globalization. These issues include changes to and within the processes of knowledge production and curriculum formulation, pedagogy, the internationalization of education, the creation of digital education communities and the consequential digital divide (which means that some sectors have ready access to advanced communications technologies whereas others are excluded from the benefits of those technologies) and the impact of alternative standpoints or ideologies, particularly, but not exclusively, feminism, on educational policies and practices. These developments have taken place within a context of what Ginsburg (1991) refers to as ideological and social struggles working themselves out against a backdrop of contradictory economic, political and cultural dynamics. Collectively, Ritzer (1993) argues that these changes in educational policy and practice amount to attempts by various agencies of reform operating at state level to achieve efficiency, calculability, predictability and control over the formal and informal systems of education. Ritzer refers to this process as 'the McDonaldization of society' which ultimately leads to a 'dehumanisation of education, the elimination of a human teacher and of human interaction between teacher and student' (ibid.: 142). These changes in educational policies and practices can be seen as a clear manifestation of the globalization of culture, part of which has included the spread of European-American notions of things such as freedom, sovereignty, representation and democracy and the dissipation of the internal coherence of these images as they have spread throughout the world (Appadurai, 1990).

Knowledge production and curriculum formulation

One of the clearest indicators of the impact of globalization, particularly the hegemony of capitalism and neo-liberalist economic discourses on educational policy and practice in relation to knowledge production and curriculum formulation, is to be found in the changes which took place in the English public (i.e. state) school sector from the 1970s onwards. They culminated in the level of curriculum prescription which dominates the English school system at the beginning of the twenty-first century. The often (too often?) quoted signifier of this shift in othordoxy in the English school system is the speech of the then Prime Minister, James Callaghan, in October 1976 at Ruskin College, Oxford. In this speech he signalled a shift towards public accountability of the system in the light of the significant public expenditure on education – education had to show greater 'value for money'. The current manifestation has developed through an ideology of the English National Curriculum heralded by the Education Reform Act 1988. This placed the contribution of subject knowledge to the economic performance of the nation at the forefront of curriculum statute. At the present time it manifests itself, in primary schools at least, in circumstances in which teaching is circumscribed by National Numeracy and Literacy Strategies and the Information and Communications Technologies Strategy and, additionally in secondary schools by the Key Stage 3 strategy. During the same period the marketization of education, set out in the Education Reform Act 1988, with a predominant ideology of producers, consumers and customers and different types of schools competing for diminishing resources, further heightened the globalizing influences on the English public school system. These changes were not unique to England, however. Amongst many such commentaries Angus (1995), for example, refers to reforms in the governance of schools in Australia, Wylie (1995) notes the changes towards school-based management systems in schools in New Zealand, Steffy and English (1995) and Neubert (1995) track similar changes in the USA, and Ben-Peretz (1995) has indicated that similar processes have operated in Israel. What these changes can be seen to amounting to is the harmonization on a large scale of ways of thinking about the processes of schooling, what counts as knowledge and the shape of the school curriculum. The school sector is not unique, either, with similar processes being tracked in higher education systems on a global scale. For a significant part of the twentieth century education was understood by sociologists to be a significant agency of the socialization of young people into the culture of the communities in which they lived. At the beginning of the twenty-first

century it might be seen that what young people are being social-
ized into is a new global, and predominantly western, culture.

A second major consequence of the impact of globalization on
education is the renewed interest in issues relating to cultural identity and citizenship education. In the UK as a response to the
critique of the political Right, in Australia as a response to republicanism, in a fragmented post-Communist Europe, in the Balkans,
in Korea, in a politically reunified Germany, in the emerging political, economic and social restructuring of the European Union
identity politics and the responses of education systems can be
seen. These debates can be seen as a response to the 'new individualism' constructed by a globalized capitalism. They raise questions
about the nature of knowledge and the ownership and control of
that knowledge. 'Globalization requires new understandings about
citizenship vis-à-vis the nation-state in order to address the severe
tensions between citizenship and the market, which pit materialism
against spirituality, rationality against emotion, selfishness against
altruism, atomism against solidarity, and wants against needs'
(Blackmore, 2000: 150). These contradictions develop as the 'needs'
of contemporary globalized capitalism – materialism, markets,
rationality, selfishness, atomism and wants – come up against the
needs of a growing number of individuals who seek 'new age' or
different solutions to living in the twenty-first century – increasing
recognition of emotional and spiritual intelligences (Goleman,
1998; Zohar and Marshall, 2000) which give rise to a more altruistic
worldview. So the market both draws citizens in – as producers and
consumers – and alienates them as citizens at the same time.

The internationalizing of education

A significant element of the features of contemporary globalization
summarized above included the mobility of labour. Similar changes
can be seen within education, with nation-states and supranational
organizations such as the European Union actively promoting the
exchange of scholars – both students and their teachers – through
various mobility systems. Such exchanges, however, are not without their problems. In any human exchange, where parties are new
to each other, there is a negotiation of meaning, status and significance. In an account of one such exchange, Burton (1997) and
Burton and Robinson (1999) describe how a TEMPUS (Trans

European Mobility Programme for University Staff)[2] can be read as an example of the westernization of Eastern European university curricula. Part of the fundamental motivation of the TEMPUS mobility scheme was the democratization of eastern Europe. What Burton and Robinson argue is that by exporting curriculum knowledge through TEMPUS schemes the European Union is asserting ownership over and legitimation of the university curricula.

TEMPUS works through a series of processes involving the transfer of ideas and their borrowings and is intended to promote economic growth.[3] TEMPUS can be seen as an example of how agencies of economic development operate without an apparent awareness of their own underlying values and assumptions that silently but powerfully guide their decisions and their judgements. The globalization of educational policy and practice is bringing about an almost exclusive dominance of a western paradigm of what constitutes good practice (Lynch, 1996), one of the consequences of which is the neglect of indigenous knowledge systems and the implicit and explicit denigration of local culture. As Berger (1995) has suggested, the future is in the hands of those who grasp the market and the market is regulated not by governments but by the WB, the IMF and the WTO. These regulatory organizations insist on westernization in the guise of democratization as part of the package (Lynch, 1996). In internationalizing education those who have grasped the market are the universities who have lead such inter-university mobility actions such as TEMPUS. Part of the consequence of this is that TEMPUS allows eastern Europe to 'let in the fresh air after half a century of closed windows . . . overcoming the negative inheritance of their recent past . . . in order to rejoin the free world' (Absolom, 1993: 127). Or, as Mitter (1992) has put it, 'removing the indoctrinatory pressure' to 'overcome the socialist past' (Kaser and Phillips, 1992).

Whilst we may not yet live in a 'single world society' (Archer, 1990), a major aspect of social reality points to the emergence of a globalized, world economy, what Wallerstein (1990) referred to as the 'real world of the capitalist world-economy'. This has involved the establishment of global financial systems and globalized technological innovation and change through telematic developments. These changes have been extensively documented (Lash and Urry, 1987; Castells, 1989; Harvey, 1989; Oliver and Heater, 1994; Rheingold, 1994). As Heidegger (1971) remarked, there is a process of the 'complete Europeanization of earth and man' and part of the process is the exportation of European curricula, pedagogies and educational ideologies, which is both the precursor of and an obvious adjunct to the development of a capitalistic economic system at the heart of the emerging eastern European nation-states. Part of that process can be found in the underpinnings of TEMPUS. The manifestations of statehood – culture, politics and the economy – operate alongside each other and are directly related to each other: a process of westernization underscored by the fact that mobilities such as TEMPUS operate within a language of communication which is predominantly English (Fine, 2002). Furthermore, the westernization of educational systems and practices is not restricted to what is happening through the sorts of projects supported by the EU in eastern Europe. In many states in southeast Asia and the Pacific Rim, in Africa and in central and Latin America similar processes can be observed. Contemporary colonialism is not limited by any particular geographical boundaries (see, for example, Mebrahtu et al., 2000, for examples of similar processes of the westernization of educational systems and practices from Europe, Africa, central and Latin America and southeast Asia).

Digital educational communities

It is often claimed that information and communications technologies, particularly the Internet, are one of the main drivers of the globalization of education. This claim, however, needs to be considered very closely. In order to establish whether the Internet can or does constitute a global educational community requires us to examine what we mean by the term 'community'. The idea of community can be seen to rest on two sets of values: the idea of co-operation and shared responsibility in order to accomplish shared goals; and, secondly, close ties and affiliations (Burbules, 2000). This ends-orientated way of conceptualizing community makes community, as a concept, a flexible and pragmatic ideological construct, open to different ways of discourse in different manifestations. Such a conceptualization of community, however, no longer stands up to scrutiny. Such a view of community is a mediated view, an idealized view, and certainly a western view. Community is not a given but a claim, delimited by the conditions and practices which dominate in the societies which have given rise to the claim. Community is not an idea; rather, it is an ideal. Furthermore, as a social construct, community is subject to change as a consequence of being subject to competing social forces. In these circumstances Burbules (ibid.) asks whether, under three sets of conditions – mediating conditions, political conditions and the conditions of space and place – online communities can be seen to be educational communities.

In respect of the first set of conditions Burbules argues that all social interactions are mediated, even face-to-face interactions, by the varieties of performance, gestures and rituals which circumscribe the interactions. In this sense online interactions are not different in degree from other forms of interaction, but different in kind. Just as any other form of interaction both reveals and conceals (perhaps, even, in equal measure), so, too, do online interactions. The medium of the interaction frames the mediation. Burbules also suggests that the language of communication mediates the interaction within and between communities. The 'modes of address' (Ellsworth, 1997), he suggests, should not be seen as privileging any particular form of address. Finally, Burbules considers that the communities of practice/s which online communications engender allow individuals to play out multiple and changing identities in a dynamic way.[4] In relation to the political conditions pertaining to digital communities, Burbules (2000: 331) notes that 'political factors are rarely determinative in any simple sense and that these conditions . . . take on a differing significance depending on persons' and groups' responses to them'. In this context the Internet is not politically neutral. Whilst it appears to be *at first* – because you only need to reveal about yourself what you want to reveal – an inescapable truth about the Internet as political is that it is a divisive, socially exclusive rather than inclusive, technology. The digital communication systems which are built around the Internet are built around a rare, in many communities, commodity – electricity.

The Internet also reveals a further aspect of the globalizing of culture which, it was argued earlier, is one of the key elements of contemporary globalization. 'Travelling' around the Internet inevitably brings the 'surfer' into direct contact with many of the emblems of the McDonaldization of culture – Microsoft, MSN and so on – the instantly recognizable logos of globalized capitalism, logos which lie at the heart of Klein's (2000) critique of the structural changes in capitalist economies which have accompanied globalization, as outlined earlier. Klein argues that social space has been 'branded' as consumers are more and more influenced by the branding of consumables – from companies such as Virgin, Starbucks, Gap and Nike who operate largely from a small physical central base with a large, satellized production and delivery system. These changes, Klein suggests, further sharpen the citizenship/market culture clash referred to earlier. The conditions which operate in these spaces and places and their impact on identity are of central concern to an understanding of contemporary globalization. Commentators such as Lefebvre (1991), Harvey (2000), and Soja (1996; 2000) consider many western urban spaces to be the manifestations of hyper-modernity, with no space being very much different from any other. Hyperspace – online space – may be just that – hyper-modern space. Burbules (2000: 345) asks 'where are you when you are online?'. The architecture of the online space Internet users inhabit, albeit temporarily, like any other architecture, anticipates and directs the social interactions which take place within the space. Furthermore, on (in?) the Internet the characteristics of the environment and the means used to represent them are inextricably intertwined. Paths of movement – hypertext links – are, Burbules argues, also, *at the same time* ways of making meaning. 'Being on line is both a place and a process', Burbules comments. As both pathways for and objects of learning the Internet illustrates the way in which it is no longer possible to distinguish what is learnt from the way it is learnt.

Online communities, or virtual communities, are a significant consequence of the spread of advanced communications technologies which have been both responsible for and the consequence of the processes of contemporary globalization. So does the Internet create an online (educational) community? The foregoing analysis would suggest that, first, the Internet cannot be considered to be a community – it is too diverse. Burbules concludes that it would be better to consider the Internet as a meta-community, an overarching set of communities and a set of conditions that make communications possible. He also concludes that the sorts of communities which the Internet can support call into question whether the Internet can be considered to be *a* community – that is, a single community. The possibility for a wide range of communities to co-exist in the space that is the Internet allows for individuals to become or be members of several different communities *at the same time*. The earlier view that the concept of community gains its strength from its flexibility may well be stretched beyond the limits of its usefulness in the context of the plurality and diversity of the meta-community of the Internet. However, what can be concluded is that the Internet gives rise to many – often competing, often complementary – communities that may or may not be educational. It is not the community that is educational, it is the members' responses to membership which make the interactions educational or otherwise. In this sense, then, whilst the Internet as a by-product of contemporary globalization gives rise to the conditions which would allow for globalized educational communities to develop, the presence of the Internet is not a sufficient condition, on its own, for such educational communities to develop.

Globalization as a gender-inflected regime of truth

In this section I want to address an example of how globalization may work in the sense of impacting on a particular social group. To do so I want to consider one of the many virtual communities which occupy part of the space of contemporary globalization – the 'women's movement'.[5] This is not an arbitrary choice. Earlier in this chapter, when we were considering the sorts of social, economic and political processes which exemplify contemporary globalization – particularly in terms of changes to the labour market and social exclusion – it was suggested that women are significantly more likely to feel the negative consequences of these processes than men. In this sense, globalization is gender inflected. By this I mean that the processes and consequences of contemporary globalization are generally and routinely modulated by gender – falling unevenly on women. In this context Blackmore (2000) asks whether globalization is a concept that is useful to or for feminism – theoretically or strategically. Educational policy has changed in response to the sorts of social, economic and political changes which were outlined above as being characteristic of globalization. This has meant that educational policy has become more closely linked to economic needs and productivity gains. Along the way many stakeholders, including educators and feminists, have been excluded from the process of policy formation. Blackmore notes that, as the radical changes in social relations that have been linked to globalization have gathered pace, the paradox is that gender relations have become more of a feature of globalization but remain largely absent from mainstream discussions about globalization. The gender-inflected nature of contemporary globalization impinges on all aspects of education. As workplaces educational institutions exhibit gendered differentiation. As organizations with governing bodies educational institutions are gendered. As marketplaces educational institutions are gendered. As arenas for knowledge production, as an interface between the private sphere of the home and the public sphere, as a conduit for conceptions of citizenry and citizenship, in every aspect of the social, cultural, economic and political lives of educational institutions they are influenced by gender. In all these contexts globalization has destabilized our understandings of the individual, the community and the state. This, Blackmore argues, has caused feminists to be engaged in thinking through what the new social relations mean for women and for men. This may involve recognizing that different discourses about these things are appropriate in different countries. What contemporary globalization does, ironically, is to open up the space for a homogeneous financial ideology of neoliberalism and at the same time open up the space for a response to the domination of capitalism which is diverse, fractured and contested. In that space feminism or feminisms have more to say, not less. Blackmore (2000: 151, citing Mahony and Hextall, 1997) concludes that the 'issue for feminists is to understand better how these new formations [of contemporary globalization] and relationships are gendered and to consider how we need to "develop anti-imperialist curricula and transnational feminist practice"'.

Globalization and environmental and social justice

Commentaries on social justice in education may seek to identify theoretical concerns, such as power, action, autonomy, control, social change, terminology, or policy or practice or some combination of these. Approaching the nature of social justice is often best undertaken by establishing what it is not. Describing injustice which occurs along lines of fracture and difference associated with any of gender, ethnicity, culture, social class, geographical location, religion, sexuality or (dis)ability is both theoretically and empirically easier than describing what a just world organized around these lines of bonding and similarity would be, for our experiences are almost always bound up with fracture and difference rather than bonding and similarity. The idea of starting from where we are rather than where we want to be is not, necessarily, a bad thing. The problem lies in translating this starting point into the basis of social action. Rather than moving towards something that is defined and circumscribed, social justice, we are attempting to move away from what we know and have experienced, social injustice. Social justice cannot be defined in any consensual way but we must continue to strive for it, because the alternative – accepting injustice – is unacceptable. The problem here is in knowing when something has been achieved.

Rather than describing social justice by what it is not, can we picture a socially just world? What contemporary globalization does here is to open up the possibilities of this description. Earlier I discussed the question of digital virtual communities. One of the consequences of the rapid spread of new communications technologies is the increasing availability of knowledge to a larger number of people. We, in the western world, are far more knowledgeable about what is going on elsewhere than ever before. New commentaries on social justice are using that knowledge base to redefine social justice to include environmental justice. Camacho (1998), for example, provides a framework for analysing the connections between social and environmental justice based on a political process model, drawing on the central concepts and assumptions, the theoretical perspectives and the factors which support successful political insurgency in environmental movements. Bath et al. (1998), Berry (1998), Clarke and Gerlack (1998), Sandweiss (1998) and White (1998) all provide plenty of evidence of the ways in which the state and the prevailing capitalist, marketized system systematically work against marginalized groups further to deprive them of the resources to improve their life chances, such as access to clean water. In the USA, for example, a mapping of pollution hot-spots shows a strong relationship to the distribution of socially and economically marginalized groups. Lipman (2002), in a study of policy and the law relating to hazardous waste disposal, shows how LDCs provide an economically attractive disposal option for the AINs. For example, the cost for hazardous waste incineration in the USA in 1991 was US$2,600 per ton, whereas in some African countries the average was US$50 per ton (Kummer, 1995: 5–6). The exporting of hazardous waste to LDCs from the AINs is not in keeping with any principle of environmental justice, she argues, and is a significant example of how globalization can result in environmental injustice. What contemporary commentators argue is that this relationship is not an accidental one but one rooted in the ways in which 'othered' social groups are conceptualized, marginalized and commodified. Otherizing is the social, cultural and mental (both cognitive and emotive) process of 'seeing someone or something as different from me – as unconnected'. Often this involves seeing that someone or something as inferior. In environmental terms it suggests that the natural world and its non-human inhabitants are of less consequence, less value than humans. In social relations, it often means that we see other groups from other places as inferior. This social otherizing can be along lines of fracture to do with gender, ethnicity, disability, sexual orientation, religion, culture, language, geography and so on. In the context of the disposal of toxic waste what it means is that the west can export toxins to LDCs with a clear conscience – because the impact does not matter so much (as I will illustrate later).

The implications of these connections of social and environmental injustice lie in the fact that places of learning (schools and universities) are vital elements in the reproduction of difference, the antithesis of social and environmental justice (as I will try to illustrate in the next section). But it may also be that they can become equally powerful agents in the processes of combating and reversing difference. To do so traditionalist modes of knowledge and its transmission which predominate at the moment will need to be guarded against. Traditionalist modes of knowledge production tend to privilege certain forms of knowledge or ways of understanding over others. For example, western science tends to be seen, in the west, as having made a more significant contribution to human development than other forms of science. This is clearly a highly contestable worldview. To continue to privilege one form of knowledge construction over others will only serve to reinforce division. New forms of curriculum and instruction which centre pluralism and contest are needed to deal with the complexity of twenty-first-century life. One of the most significant difficulties which faces us in that complexity is the global socio-ecological crisis as represented by the depletion of finite resources, pollution, global warming, the viability of life-forms and pharmaceutical exhaustion. The social and the ecological are inextricably bound up in one system of social justice. What contemporary globalization throws up is the realization that there is not one thing called social justice and another called environmental justice. Environmental justice *is* social justice. The natural environment is a social space. Environmental despoilation is social despoilation too. The opportunities afforded by the social, cultural and political consequences of contemporary globalization bring social and environmental justice into a sharp focus. The sorts of practices which are illustrative of social and environmental injustice, such as toxic waste disposal, no longer have any hiding place.

To close this section I want to give an illustration of how such a view of the link between social and environmental (in)justice works. Take, as an example, the despoilation of the forest environment in Indonesia by logging companies as both an environmental and a social problem. The social justice dimension of this environmental problem lies in the illegality of the logging companies whose actions can only continue in an atmosphere of corruption. Corruption continues in an atmosphere of despotism. Despotism signifies the absence of democracy. The rights of the indigenous forest dwellers are eroded and the forest is further depleted (Robinson, 2001). This cycle is supported by the capitalist system in which the international trade in tropical hardwoods operates. Here the economic power of organized capitalism over-rides the rights of individuals to social justice. The point is that in contemporary globalization the social and the environmental are inextricably bonded to each other. Furthermore, as Immanuel Kant argued, when the rights of people are violated anywhere, this affects everybody, everywhere. Here in the UK, as I write this piece, I am not immune from being implicated in these violations of social justice on the other side of the world. In social justice terms the world has no sides. This is the consequence of globalization, and its force. I want to illustrate this idea with a lengthy quotation – about which I am not going to comment:

> Lawrence Summers, who was the World Bank's chief economist, was responsible for the 1992 World Development Report which was devoted to the economics of the environment. This actually suggested that it made economic sense to transfer high-pollution industries to the Third World [sic] countries. In a memo dated 12 December 1991 to senior

World Bank staff, the Chief Economist wrote: 'Just between you and me, shouldn't the World Bank be encouraging more migration of dirty industries to the LDCs?' Summers justified the economic logic of increasing pollution in the Third World on three grounds.

First, since wages are low in the Third World, the economic costs of pollution arising from increased illness and death are lowest in the poorest countries. According to Summers, 'the logic of relocation of pollutants in the lowest wage countries is inescapable and we should face up to that'.

Second, since in large parts of the Third World pollution is still low, it made economic sense to Summers to introduce pollution. 'I've always thought', he wrote, 'that countries in Africa are vastly underpolluted; their air quality is probably vastly, inefficiently high compared to Los Angeles or Mexico City.'

Finally, since the poor are poor, they cannot possibly worry about environmental problems. 'The concern over an agent that causes a one-in-a-million chance of prostate cancer is obviously going to be much higher in a country where people survive to get prostate cancer, than in a country where the under-five mortality is 200 per thousand' (Shiva, 2000: 113–14).[6]

The flip side of this example of how social and environmental injustice operates – in which the thought processes of otherizing are clear – is that social and environmental justice would start by erasing the difference assumed through otherizing. It means erasing the differences based on a hierarchical view of the social and natural worlds and a hierarchical view within the social world. Human beings – all human beings – can only take their place in the world when they take responsibility for that place. This means seeing all things as being connected to all things. The processes of contemporary globalization can make space for such a view. In the next section I want to focus on a case study of one UK school where there is a commitment to move someway to this sort of view.

Contemporary globalization in a school context

So how do the issues explored in this chapter impinge on the education of young people? Smith (2002) investigated the relationship between identity, difference and contemporary globalization in the micro-political context of one UK secondary school. In his study, Smith (ibid.: 117) was interested in how the school prepared young people to 'participate and engage in these new, or newly recognized, encounters'. His study focused on how the school communicated ideas about contemporary globalization and identity, particularly in relation to distance and difference within the context of learning about LDCs. This context was chosen for three reasons: first, because of the way in which constructions of 'other places' – their exotic or demonic descriptions – communicate ideas about people and places; secondly, because the changing nature of the relation-ship between the AINs and LDCs is a significant element in the cultural, economic and political processes of contemporary global-ization; and, thirdly, because a focus on LDCs also raised issues of race and ethnicity and the construction of notions of difference. Thus a focus on LDCs can be seen to be an opportunity to explore the ways in which the processes of contemporary globalization work themselves out in practice in educational settings.

The school – called Meadows School – was an 11–18 school with 970 pupils and 55 staff. Meadows is located in a village in England, 10 miles from the nearest town. According to the Head of Religious Education, Meadows is in the 'white highlands' (ibid.: 118). The monocultural nature of the school was influential in a decision to make explicit reference to the global contexts of learning at Meadows. At Meadows staff from the music, art, drama, French and science departments felt that issues relating to LDCs played some part in their subject areas, linked to the school aims, and in the English National Curriculum 'development' is an aspect of the geography curriculum.

Smith (ibid.: 123) quotes various teachers, including the head-teacher, who stress that education should be global in scope, locating 'young people within a community beyond that of the locality' which helps to 'break down the barriers between cultures'. This engagement with diversity and difference is not only delivered through the school curriculum at Meadows but the school's aims also identify the need to challenge the stereotypes on which a lack of understanding of other cultures and other cultural histories are often based.

What Smith finds, however, is that despite these strong commit-ments at Meadows there are contradictions in the ways in which the school communicates ideas about distance and difference to the young people who attend the school. For example, Smith points to one interview in which a teacher refers to the school's *links* with Hong Kong and Japan (both AINs) and to the school's *sponsorship* of a Ugandan schoolboy (where Uganda represents LDCs) (ibid.: 124). He also quotes from his fieldnotes which refer to an observation of a geography lesson: 'Miss Baker tells them to turn to p. 31 and the picture of the Maasai on that page. Miss Baker [says] "You can see that these people are 'primitive' by the lack of clothing these people are wearing"' (ibid.: 125). Miss Baker uses some interesting language here which conjures up images of difference – 'these people', 'primitive', 'lack of clothing' – all terms which otherize the Maasai and strengthen a sense of difference. Also when asked about how much the young people learn about Uganda (where the sponsored school boy lives) one teacher tells Smith that it is 'not too much . . . [because the pupils are] not interested in that: [they would] switch off' (ibid.). The school defines Uganda by the lack of things that we, in the west, take for granted. What Smith finds at Meadows is a contradiction between the rhetoric of critically challenging stereotypical notions of distance and difference and the reality of classroom practices which help to reinforce those stereotypes.

What this small case study shows is that the cultural, economic and political processes which are illustrative of the process of contemporary globalization impact on educational institutions and educational policy in complex, contested and contradictory ways. On the one hand the neo-liberal economic drivers of contemporary globalization have, as we explored earlier in this chapter, introduced issues into the school curriculum in relation to economic development and the relationships between AINs and LDCs. On the other hand, the uncritical ways in which these relationships are communicated as 'facts' undermine the challenge to difference, distance and stereotyping which the spread of cultural awareness, as a consequence of the rapid expansion of communications systems which has accompanied the processes of contemporary globalization, might have allowed.

Schools are engaged in social, economic and political processes. These involve the skilling of young people to become active citizens of the communities in which they are growing up. Those communities, whilst they are localized and immediate, are a part of wider, more globalized communities. What Smith (2002) shows, in his study of Meadows School, is how complex these relationships are. The school, as a community, as an educational institution, is strongly influenced by the processes of contemporary globalization – in terms of, for example, curriculum control, curriculum content, assessment of those processes and so on. But the school, through these self-same processes actively constructs *and transmits to young people* an image of the world and its communities which is often (unwittingly) biased, stereotypical and reinforcing of difference.

Conclusions: globalization – a new dawn or the new imperialism?

For some the individual, cultural, economic and regulatory changes which are both the cause of and the consequences of contemporary globalization herald the only possibility of a better world. But does this Utopian vision stand up to scrutiny or is it just rhetoric? Contemporary globalization can mean many (contradictory) things. There are clear benefits for some. These include economic expansion and the spread of markets into LDCs bring consumer benefits. Equally, as some of the examples above illustrate, for some people there can be negative consequences of this economic expansion. Furthermore, as a historical project it is necessarily incomplete. What is clear is that the spread of the benefits of contemporary globalization is far from even – with the western nations often gaining more from the processes than the LDCs and with different social and economic groups gaining disproportionately. Equally, bearing the weight of the costs has also been uneven: 'Globalization is not a singular condition, a linear process or a final end-point of social change' (Held et al., 1997: 258). It is not an economic nor a social end-state towards which all economies are converging (Gray, 1999).

Just as much as there is support for globalization there is scepticism about the corporate Utopia of contemporary globalization. The globalization resistance 'movement' offers a sharp example of the forces drawn up against globalization. Globalization resistance is a loose amalgam of protesters against, among other issues, starvation, poverty, environmental degradation, capitalism, debt repayment, transnational corporations, the free market and economic protectionism (see Bircham and Charlton, 2002). Gray has argued that globalized capitalism can be seen as disorganized capitalism. Whilst there is a pattern to the social, cultural, economic and political processes of contemporary globalized capitalism it is not the same to say that the two are causally linked. Gray argues that much of what national governments do as a 'necessary response' to globalization is in fact putting up a smoke-screen to change policy and pass the blame. What passes for organized development on a global scale can be seen as a localized taking of an opportunity. Equally, Klein's (2000) critique of the 'logoization' of contemporary culture, which has branded social relations in a space defined by Virgin, Microsoft, Nike and Starbucks, amongst others, argues that the social costs of this process should not be seen as a new dawn. In contrast to these negative interpretations of the impact of globalization Gray concludes that there may well be positive consequences. In an analysis of 11 September (when terrorist forces struck at the heart of the symbols of American economic and military power – perhaps symbolic of the heart of contemporary globalization) what Gray (2002: 19) refers to as 'soldiers in a new kind of war' were operating. The 'global alliance' against the 'forces of evil' that sprang up as a consequence of these attacks could, he argues, lead to a safer world through a more diverse world. What 11 September showed was that we now operate within a new geopolitical order, which to some extent has disturbed the comfortable, western view of a global geopolitical order wherein the USA is supreme commander of global capitalism.

So where does this leave us? Clearly changes have taken place in many education systems throughout the world which have been a response to the new geopolitical order of contemporary globalization. These changes also contribute to the trajectory of the project of globalization. But these complex arrangements have opened up spaces as well as closing them down. Globalization is both everywhere and limited. States may appear weak in its wake, but they remain the focal point of much of our everyday lives. Furthermore, the very conditions that give rise to the critique of globalization give rise to the conditions of the possibility of that critique. Globalization is a social construct, it is necessarily, then, *our* construct. Educational policies and practices open up the possibility for responding to the construct of contemporary globalization constructively. These responses will need to be predicated on a pluralistic, contested, manifold, provisional form of knowledge where no one form of knowledge production dominates and where individuals and groups see their connectivity to others rather than their distance from them. Is this how we would characterize contemporary, formal education?

Student task

Choose an example of a curriculum (from any phase in the formal sector of education – primary, secondary, FE or HE) and assess the extent to which the curriculum exhibits a response to the issues identified as the processes of contemporary globalization outlined in this chapter.

Suggested further reading

I would choose to recommend six books for you to follow up the ideas in this chapter at some length:

1 Burbules N. and Torres C.A. (eds) (2000) *Globalization and Education: Critical Perspectives*. New York and London: Routledge. This edited collection gives a wide-ranging account of the relationships between contemporary globalization and education. Along the way it takes in the issues of education policy, neo-conservatism, managerialism, gender, pedagogies, international education, citizenship, multiculturalism, culture, social movements and the Internet. At times the arguments are difficult, but stick with it – it is a rewarding read.
2 Gray, J. (1999) *False Dawn: The Delusions of Global Capitalism*. London: Granta Books. In this book you will find a very readable account of the unstable nature of globalized capitalism and strong arguments against the organized nature of the impact of contemporary globalization.
3 Klein, N. (2000) *No Logo*. London: Flamingo. This volume provides a readable, detailed and fascinating analysis of late capitalism. It is a strong attack on globalized economics, from the sweatshops and 'export processing zones' of the Far East to Gap, Nike and the superstore, super-commercialization of the west.
4 Mebrahtu, T., Crossley, M. and Johnson D. (eds) (2000) *Globalization, Educational Transformation and Societies in Transition*. Oxford: Symposium Books. This book will give you many country-based case studies of the processes of contemporary globalization working themselves through into educational systems and practices.
5 O'Sullivan, E. (1999) *Transformative Learning: Educational Vision for the 21st Century*. Toronto, London and New York: University of Toronto Press/Zed Books. This is perhaps the best. Although I have not drawn on it directly in my chapter, if you want an excellent account of the contested, multiple perspectival nature of the terrain occupied by social and environmental justice, then look no further than this. This is a book I go back to again and again and it contains, for me, one of the most elegant accounts of the inter-relationship between peace, justice, the environment and education that I have read.

6 Scott, A. (ed.) (1997) *The Limits of Globalization: Cases and Arguments*. This volume provides a much wider perspective than Burbules and Torres (2000) by focusing on issues of global politics, economics, transport, ethnicity and popular culture – including Elvis in Zanzibar. It is much more of a background text than Burbules and Torres, but it is useful in helping you understand where education fits in in all this.

Notes

1 The events of 11 September 2001 when the World Trade Center in New York and the Pentagon in Washington, DC, were attacked by suicide bombers using aircraft as missiles – known generally as 9/11 – have become an emblem for some of the processes which underpin the process of contemporary globalization. For a good description of what happened on 9/11 and what might have lead up to it, see Baxter and Downing (2001).
2 TEMPUS is a mobility programme funded by the European Union. For details, see Absolom (1993) and Wilson (1993).
3 Interestingly the US government has recently announced a US$5 billion development assistance programme – but there are strings – the criteria for receiving this assistance include a commitment at policy level to 'good governance', better health care, improved education and more enterprise (Farish, 2002).
4 This diversity of identity being played out on/in the Internet is richly illustrated by the growing number of examples reported in the mass media relating to the displaying of false gender identities or age identities (usually by men in order to lure women and girls into dangerous sexual liaisons).
5 Although it is clear that a phrase like 'women's movement' is a highly contested generalization. There are many communities within this community and many varieties of feminism to be found therein.
6 This same memorandum is quoted in Lipman (2002). It should be noted, however, that many transnational corporations now recognize their responsibility to trade ethically. As I have suggested elsewhere (Robinson, J, 2002), a recognition of social and environmental justice issues may well be the new triple bottom line for businesses.

References

Absolom, R. (1993) The TEMPUS scheme: mobilizing higher education for change in central and eastern Europe. *Innovations in Education and Training International* (formerly *Educational and Training Technology International*) 30(2): 122–8.
Angus, M. (1995) Devolution of school governance in an Australian state school system: third time lucky. In D.S.G. Carter and M.H. O'Neill (eds) *Case Studies in Educational Change: An International Perspective*. London: Falmer Press.

Appadurai, A. (1990) Disjuncture and difference in the global cultural economy. *Public Culture* 2(2): 37–50.

Archer, M. (1990) Foreword. In M. Albrow and E. King (eds) *Globalization, Knowledge and Modernity*. London: Sage.

Bath, C.R., Tanski, J.M. and Villareal, R.E. (1998) The failure to provide basic services to the *Colonias* of El Paso County: a case of environmental racism?, In D.E. Camacho (ed.) *Environmental Injustices, Political Struggles: Race, Class, and the Environment*. Durham, NC, and London: Duke University Press.

Baxter, J. and Downing, M. (eds) (2001) *The Day that Shook the World: Understanding September 11th*. London: BBC News.

Ben-Peretz, M. (1995) Educational reform in Israel: an example of synergy in education. In D.S.G. Carter and M.H. O'Neill (eds) *Case Studies in Educational Change: An International Perspective*. London: Falmer Press.

Berger, J. (1995) Democracy for sale. *The Observer* 17 December: 4.

Berry, K.A. (1998) Race for water? Native Americans, Eurocentrism, and western water policy. In D.E. Camacho (ed.) *Environmental Injustices, Political Struggles: Race, Class, and the Environment*. Durham, NC, and London: Duke University Press.

Bircham, E. and Charlton, J. (eds) (2002) *Anti-Capitalism*. London: Bookmarks.

Blackmore, J. (2000) Globalization: a useful concept for feminists rethinking theory and strategies in education? In N.C. Burbules and C.A. Torres (eds) *Globalization and Education: Critical Perspectives*. New York and London Routledge.

Burbules, N.C. (2000) Does the Internet constitute a global educational community? In N.C. Burbules and C.A. Torres (eds) *Globalization and Education: Critical Perspectives*. New York and London: Routledge.

Burbules, N.C. and Torres, C.A. (2000) Globalization and education: an introduction. In N.C. Burbules and C.A. Torres (eds) *Globalization and Education: Critical Perspectives*. New York and London: Routledge.

Burton, D. (1997) The myth of 'expertness': an analysis of the cultural and pedagogical obstacles to the restructuring of eastern European curricula through TEMPUS projects. *Journal of In-service Education*, 23(2): 219–29.

Burton, D. and Robinson, J. (1999) Cultural interference: clashes of ideology and pedagogy in internationalising education. *International Education*, 28(2) 5–30.

Camacho, D.E. (1998) The environmental justice movement: a political framework. In D.E. Camacho (ed.) *Environmental Injustices, Political Struggles: Race, Class, and the Environment*. Durham, NC, and London: Duke University Press.

Castells, M. (1989) *The Informational City*. Oxford: Blackwell.

Clarke, J.N. and Gerlack, A.K. (1998) Environmental racism in southern Arizona? The reality beneath the rhetoric. In D.E. Camacho (ed.) *Environmental Injustices, Political Struggles: Race, Class, and the Environment*. Durham, NC, and London: Duke University Press.

Ellsworth, E. (1997) *Teaching Positions: Difference, Pedagogy, and the Power of Address*. New York: Teachers College Press.

Farish, W. (2002) Globalisation – the American perspective. Paper presented at the Institute of Director's 2002 annual convention: 'Globalization: the real nature and impact', London, April.

Fine, P. (2002)Time to parler Anglais? *The Times Higher Education Supplement*, 22 March: 12.

Ginsburg, M.B. (1991) Preface. In M.B. Ginsburg (ed.) *Understanding Educational Reform in a Global Context: Economy, Ideology and the State*. New York and London: Garland.

Goleman, D. (1998) *Working with Emotional Intelligence*. London: Bloomsbury.

Gray, J. (1999) *False Dawn: The Delusions of Global Capitalism*. London: Granta Books.

Gray, J. (2002) The end of globalization. *Resurgence* May/June: 19–20.

Harvey, D. (1989) *The Conditions of Postmodernity*. Oxford: Blackwell.

Harvey, D. (2000) *Spaces of Hope*. Berkeley and Los Angeles, CA: University of California Press.

Heidegger, M. (1971) *On the Way to Language*. London: Harper & Row.

Held, D., Goldblatt, D., McGrew, A. and Perraton, J. (1997) The globalization of economic activity. *New Political Economy* 2(2): 257–77.

Kaser, M. and Phillips, D. (1992) Introduction. *Oxford Studies in Comparative Education* 2(1) 7–14.

Klein, N. (2000) *No Logo*. London: Flamingo.

Korten, D.C. (1995) *When Corporations Rule the World*. West Hartford, CT: Berrett-Koehler.

Kummer, K. (1995) *International Management of Hazardous Waste*. Oxford: Clarendon Press.

Lash, S. and Urry, J. (1987) *The End of Organised Capitalism*. Cambridge: Polity Press.

Lefebvre, H. (1991) *The Production of Space* (trans. D. Nicholson-Smith). Oxford and Malden, MA: Blackwell.

Lipman, Z. (2002) Globalisation, environmental justice and hazardous waste trade. Paper presented at the 'Environmental justice and global citizenship' conference, Copenhagen, February.

Lynch, J. (1996) Learning and teaching: the international transfer of dysfunctional paradigms. Paper presented at the 'International issues in teaching and learning' conference, Bristol, January.

Mahony, P. and Hextall, I. (1997) Teaching in the managerial state. Paper presented at the AARE conference, University of Queensland, November.

Mebrahtu, T., Crossley, M. and Johnson, D. (eds) (2000) *Globalisation, Educational Transformation and Societies in Transition*. Oxford: Symposium Books.

Mitter, W. (1992) Education in eastern Europe and the former Soviet Union in a period of revolutionary change: an approach to comparative analysis. *Oxford Studies in Comparative Education*, 2(1) 15–28.

Neubert, S. (1995) Texas education reform: Why? Why not? Who? What? And so what? In D.S.G. Carter and M.H. O'Neill (eds) *Case Studies in Educational Change: An International Perspective*. London: Falmer Press.

Offe, C. (1985) *Disorganized Capitalism*. London: Hutchinson.

Oliver, D. and Heater, D. (1994) *The Foundations of Citizenship*. Hemel Hempstead: Harvester Wheatsheaf.

Rheingold, H. (1994) *The Virtual Community*. London: Secker & Warburg.

Ritzer, G. (1993) *The McDonaldization of Society*. London: Pine Forge Press.

Robinson, J. (2001) Education for social and environmental justice: a review essay. *Environmental Education Research*, 7(2) 189–93.

Robinson, J. (2002) The real nature and impact of globalisation. *British Journal of Administrative Management* 31(May/June): 24–5.

Robinson, M. (2002) The environment and human rights: an interview with Mary Robinson. Paper presented at the Institute of Director's 2002 annual convention, 'Globalisation: the real nature and impact', London: April.

Sandweiss, S. (1998) The social construction of environmental justice. In D.E. Camacho (ed.) *Environmental Injustices, Political Struggles: Race, Class, and the Environment*. Durham, NC, and London: Duke University Press.

Shiva, V. (2000) The world on the edge. In W. Hutton and A. Giddens (eds) *On the Edge: Living with Global Capitalism*. London: Jonathan Cape.

Smith, M. (2002) Globalisation and local experience: encounters with difference in a UK school. *The Sociological Review*, 50(1): 117–35.

Soja, E.W. (1996) *Thirdspace: Journeys to Los Angeles and Other Real and Imagined Places*. Oxford and Malden, MA: Blackwell.

Soja, E.W. (2000) *Postmetropolis: Critical Studies of Cities and Regions*. Oxford and Malden, MA: Blackwell.

Steffy, B.E. and English, F.W. (1995) Radical legislated school reform in the United States: an examination of Chicago and Kentucky. In D.S.G. Carter and M.H. O'Neill (eds) *Case Studies in Educational Change: An International Perspective*. London: Falmer Press.

Wallerstein, I. (1990) Cukture and the Ideological Battleground of Modern World.

White, H.L. (1998) Race, class, and environmental hazards. In D.E.Camacho (ed.) *Environmental Injustices, Political Struggles: Race, Class, and the Environment*. Durham, NC, and London: Duke University Press.

Wilson, L. (1993) TEMPUS as an instrument of reform. *European Journal of Education*, 28(4): 429–36.

Wylie, C. (1995) The shift to school-based management in New Zealand – the school view. In D.S.G. Carter and M.H. O'Neill (eds) *Case Studies in Educational Change: An International Perspective*. London: Falmer Press.

Zohar, D. and Marshall, I. (2000) *Spiritual Intelligence: The Ultimate Intelligence*. London: Bloomsbury.

Index